DATE			

D1172086

© THE BAKER & TAYLOR CO

*Rural Development
in China*

A WORLD BANK PUBLICATION

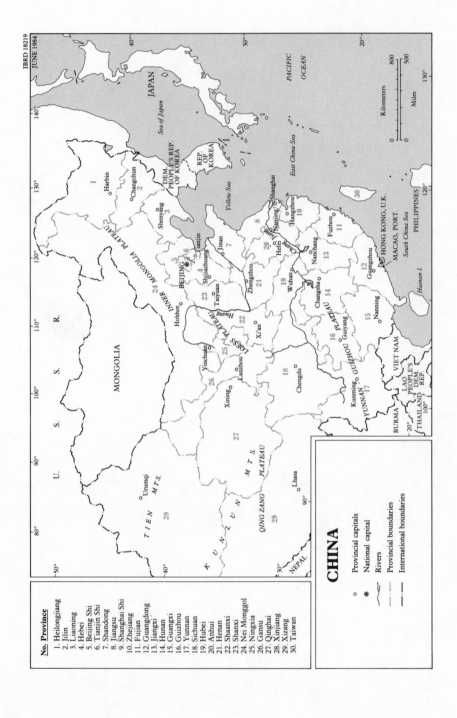

No. Province
1. Heilongjiang
2. Jilin
3. Liaoning
4. Hebei
5. Beijing Shi
6. Tianjin Shi
7. Shandong
8. Jiangsu
9. Shanghai Shi
10. Zhejiang
11. Fujian
12. Guangdong
13. Jiangxi
14. Hunan
15. Guangxi
16. Guizhou
17. Yunnan
18. Sichuan
19. Hubei
20. Anhui
21. Henan
22. Shaanxi
23. Shanxi
24. Nei Monggol
25. Ningxia
26. Gansu
27. Qinghai
28. Xinjiang
29. Xizang
30. Taiwan

CHINA

○   Provincial capitals
⊛   National capital
〜   Rivers
— · —   Provincial boundaries
– – –   International boundaries

IBRD 18219

JUNE 1984

Rural Development in China

Dwight Perkins and Shahid Yusuf

PUBLISHED FOR THE WORLD BANK

The Johns Hopkins University Press

BALTIMORE AND LONDON

The Johns Hopkins University Press
Baltimore, Maryland 21218, U.S.A.

Editor   Virginia de Haven Hitchcock
Maps   World Bank Cartography Division
Figure   Catherine Ann Kocak
Binding design   Joyce C. Eisen

Library of Congress Cataloging in Publication Data

Perkins, Dwight Heald.
  Rural development in China.

  "Published for the World Bank."
  Bibliography: p.
  Includes index.
    1. Agriculture and state—China. 2. Rural development—
Government policy—China. 3. China—Economic policy—
1976–   . 4. China—Social policy. I. Yusuf, Shahid,
1949–   . II. Title.
HD2098.P47   1984   338.951   83-49366
ISBN 0-8018-3261-6

BST

Contents

FIGURE

TABLES

MAPS

Preface

~~~~~~

WHEN CHINA BEGAN to discuss the possibility of joining the World Bank almost six years ago, the Bank knew little of the economy and institutions of the People's Republic. Interest quickened as the Bank prepared to welcome the world's most populous nation into its midst, and thus we were asked to survey and synthesize the available information on rural development in China so that it would be accessible to the widest possible audience within the Bank.

Even as the first draft was taking shape, however, the Chinese government began to release detailed statistical information on agriculture. In one stroke it made obsolete the informed speculation on which had rested much of the existing analysis of how the rural sector had evolved, what its strengths were, and how severe its remaining problems were. We were encouraged to go beyond encapsulating past work and to make a fresh assessment of China's rural development strategy.

Much has been written on the various facets of Chinese rural development, and, no doubt, one can expect a steady stream of publications to augment this already handsome stock in the years ahead. But the individual seeking a brief self-contained introduction, which threads together the diverse topics embraced by the field of rural development and which effectively uses newly released data to refine and extend the accumulated knowledge, is likely to suffer some frustration. The volume of literature on the subject is, at first brush, overwhelming, but for one seeking an informed and comprehensive introduction and without the appetite to wade through a score of specialized treatises, the offerings are quite meagre. It is our hope that we have taken a modest step toward filling this gap and, at the same time, have written a book that even those familiar with the Chinese economy may find of use.

This study has evolved over several years, and we are grateful to all those who encouraged and guided us through the successive phases. Hollis Chenery has our special thanks. While at the World Bank, he perceived the need for such a study, pointed us in the right direction, and encouraged us to attempt something appreciably more ambitious than a survey of the literature.

We are also indebted to Shahid Javed Burki for his unstinting support and advice through the duration of the project. Four anonymous referees provided us with detailed and incisive comments on an earlier draft, and several Bank staff had useful suggestions on individual chapters. To all of them we owe a debt of gratitude.

Rural Development
in China

Chapter 1

~~~~~~

Introduction

RURAL DEVELOPMENT POLICY in China directly shapes the lives of 800 million people, roughly one-third of the world's farm population. That fact alone would make China's experience of importance to the rest of the world. But interest in China's rural policies is not simply a product of the nation's size. China's leaders have implemented nationwide many programs that others have thought about but seldom undertaken, except half-heartedly or on a trial basis. China's "surplus" labor power has been mobilized for rural construction projects at a historically unprecedented level. The problem of excessive migration from the countryside to the cities, a common phenomenon in developing countries, has been dealt with by a nearly complete prohibition of such movement. Efforts to improve nutrition and health at an early stage of development—the essence of the "basic needs" strategy—were markedly successful as early as the 1950s. And there is much else.

If one society were much like another, these programs could be described, their successes and failures measured, and recommendations made more or less automatically about what ought to be tried elsewhere. But China is not like all other societies. There are even significant differences within that subgroup of East Asian nations that share a common Confucian heritage. For reasons that will become apparent in later chapters, any understanding of how China has accomplished what it has in the rural areas must come to grips with the nation's historical heritage and how that heritage has been built on, and modified by, the Chinese Communist Party.

Characteristics of China's Rural Development Policies

What have been the central features of China's rural development policies since 1949? There have been, of course, many changes in policy during the past three decades, and some of these changes represented a complete reversal of what had been tried before. But there have also been themes common to both the periods when Mao's "radicalism" and Deng's "pragmatism" held sway.

Foremost among these common themes has been the government's capacity to implement village-level programs on a nationwide basis through bureaucratic and Party channels. Most nations can affect the lives of villagers by manipulating the prices of agricultural products or by introducing occasional visits by a farm extension worker. Few could order village leaders to mobilize half the rural labor force to build irrigation systems and roads for weeks and months on end, with little or no direct remuneration for those mobilized. And what other nation of poor peasant farmers could carry out a program to encourage rural families to have only one child and to place severe sanctions on those who have more than two?

Whether so much central power to carry out programs at the village level has, on balance, benefited rural development in China is a question to which we will return. If China's Party and bureaucracy had not been able to reach down into the countryside, the excesses of the Great Leap Forward in 1958–59 would have caused much less damage. Similarly, excessive zeal in carrying out the policy of single-child families could undermine family planning successes already achieved through more moderate measures.

Whether beneficial or not, China's formidable capacity for implementation cannot be questioned. But where did this capacity come from? A Confucian heritage of obedience to those senior to you in the hierarchy had something to do with it, but the Guomindang before 1949 had the same Confucian heritage, but little influence in the villages. What did the Communist Party do that changed this, and why did it do it? The primary motive was political—to consolidate power—but did the requirements of politics benefit the economy, or was there a constant tension between political and economic goals? These issues are discussed in Chapter 5.

A second consistent characteristic of China's rural development policies has been a commitment to giving the rural poor a large share of the benefits of whatever programs were implemented. This commitment may have weakened over time in part because both the landlord and rich peasant classes have long since been eliminated. But no Party leadership could or can today afford to ignore the interests of the great majority of the rural population. The reason is simple. The Chinese Communist Party was built on the grievances of the poor peasant majority. And the People's Liberation Army, still a major route into the Party as well as a power in its own right, draws most of its recruits from the rural areas. When Chinese speculate about whether political stability and Deng Xiaoping's policies will continue into the late 1980s and 1990s, their faith in continued stability often rests on a belief that current policies have done well by the peasants. To what extent this belief is supported by actual performance is discussed at length in later chapters. The point here is that people in leadership positions in China—people who mainly reside in urban areas—see their future and the future of the policies they believe in as being intimately tied to the prosperity of the countryside.

The significance of this commitment to serve the rural poor has been fundamental to a wide range of policies. China's emphasis on preventive medicine and on health efforts that reach into the remote regions of the country, as contrasted to the urban-based curative emphasis in so many developing countries, can be understood only in terms of this commitment. Land reform was carried out in a way that not only eliminated landlords, but ensured that the poorest people in the village received most of the benefits.

China's commitment to the rural poor, however, has not been unqualified. As subsequent chapters will illustrate, the urban bias so common to the developing world does exist. The origin of this bias was the desire of the leadership to turn China into a modern industrial state with a modern military force able to defend the nation against all foreign powers. That desire led to the adoption of a Stalinist development strategy in the 1950s, with its emphasis on machinery and steel. Despite increases in investment in agriculture in the 1960s and much rhetoric about taking "agriculture as the foundation," the emphasis on machinery and steel continued when Mao Zedong had the greatest influence on economic policy (1958–59 and 1966–76).

The stress on machinery and steel was based on the belief that it would lead to rapid growth in national income and national power. There was little, if any, conscious desire to pursue policies that would mainly benefit an urban technocratic elite. To the contrary, investment in housing and other urban infrastructure was held to a minimum. To keep the existing infrastructure from being overwhelmed, however, the government placed severe limits on migration from rural to urban areas. Paradoxically, a measure to limit investment in urban areas produced certain characteristics often associated with urban bias. Industry became increasingly more capital-intensive, and the gap between urban and rural incomes widened, as covered in Chapter 6.

Purpose and Organization of the Book

The discussion to this point may give the impression that this book is about politics and broad policy goals rather than economics. That is far from the case. The chapters that follow deal primarily with more or less conventional attempts to measure what happened to agricultural production and the distribution of income, health, and education in the countryside. The approach is both historical and quantitative. It is historical both in the sense that we look at the pre-1949 base on which policies of the Chinese government were built and in the sense that we trace the shifts and turns in policy since 1949. The study is quantitative in that our concern is to measure the effect of various programs by using statistics and appropriate statistical techniques when the necessary data are available. Published agricultural production and input data are, on the whole, available, but education and health statistics for the rural areas are sparse.

In many cases the shifts and turns in Chinese agricultural policy can be explained without resort to political considerations. One key issue facing Chinese agriculture, for example, has been whether output could be raised by massive investment in essentially traditional inputs, or whether increases depended mainly on the large-scale application of modern inputs such as chemical fertilizer. But purely economic and technical considerations cannot explain how China was able to implement schemes that mobilized large amounts of labor, or why Mao insisted on paying more attention to rural than to urban health. The success or failure of these policies can be measured by conventional economic methods, but the underlying rationale for them starts with politics and values.

The analysis in this book begins with a chapter outlining the role of agriculture in China's overall development strategy. The essential point is that China's agricultural and industrial development strategies have been carried out to an unusual degree in isolation one from the other. As a result, China still has many of the characteristics of a dual economy, despite three decades of rapid industrial growth. Agriculture has benefited from the existence of a modern industrial sector—to provide chemical fertilizer, for example—but compared with other rapidly growing economies, rural development in China has been a self-contained effort.

Chapters 3 and 4 deal with the rate of growth of agricultural output both nationally and regionally and with the inputs that made that growth possible. One important question is what factors account for the wide variation in growth rates between the fast-growing coastal and slow-growing interior provinces. Another, already mentioned above, is whether the main source of growth has been the application of ever increasing amounts of chemical fertilizer (and related inputs) or the mobilization of rural labor.

Underlying all of these issues is the question of the prospects for the growth of Chinese agriculture in the future. Will China be able to feed a rising population with rising incomes from its own resources, or will it have to turn increasingly to food imports?

Chapter 5 discusses how China was organized to achieve these increases in farm output and income. There are both the specific issues of how cooperatives and communes were structured and the more general question of where the capacity of the Chinese Communist Party to restructure rural society came from. Included is a discussion of the radical reforms of the early 1980s under the "responsibility system."

The final three substantive chapters are concerned with who has benefited from China's rural development policies, and how they have benefited. Chapter 6 explores the extent to which income in the rural areas has been redistributed in favor of the poor. Recently published data give the clearest picture yet of where pockets of poverty still persist and the beginnings of an answer to why such pockets have proved so difficult to eliminate.

Good health is usually related to, but not synonymous with, higher income. Perhaps the single most remarkable achievement of Chinese rural efforts has been the sharp reduction in death rates and resulting marked increase in life expectancy in the Chinese countryside. Comparable results are found only in countries with per capita incomes several times higher than those prevailing in rural China. Although the broad outlines of China's achievements in rural health are well known, the analysis of how these results were achieved, as Chapter 7 makes clear, has only just begun.

Finally, Chapter 8 discusses the role of education in Chinese rural development. Education serves many purposes: as an input into production, as a means of establishing political control, as a vehicle for escape from the drudgery of farm life, and as a form of consumption with benefits unrelated to its effect on productivity. All of these aspects are considered, but available knowledge of China's education system has a strong urban bias, and only a crude outline of what has been happening in the rural areas is possible.

This study is not the definitive work on China's rural development experience. It is more a summary of what outsiders have learned about that experience during the past three decades, including some new work based on heretofore unavailable data. We make no attempt to draw concrete lessons for other countries. That task is left up to others who know those countries and who can draw their own conclusions once they are more familiar with all that China has accomplished.

Chapter 2

~~~~~~

China's Dual Economy

MANY DEVELOPING COUNTRIES have dual economies. In the early stages
of modern economic growth the industrial and mining sectors of these
countries were usually small and confined to a few cities on the
periphery of a rural hinterland or were located in remote, mineral-rich
areas. In the colonial period these industries were often run by foreigners, who sometimes imported their own skilled labor. Colonial
governments often attempted to build a cocoon around these modern
enclaves and to run the rural areas separately. In extreme cases efforts
were made to preserve traditional ways of life except where labor was
required for modern enterprises.

Modern development in China in the first decades of the twentieth
century never reached the extremes of enclave-style dualism. Modern
cities did grow up along China's coast before 1949, and foreigners
concentrated there. Foreigners also helped administer these cities, and
in fact they ran the foreign concessions, but they never achieved the
kind of dominant role they played in their colonies. The populations of
China's coastal cities were overwhelmingly Chinese, commerce was
dominated by Chinese merchants, and even the modern factory sector
was owned half by Chinese and half by others, mainly Japanese.

The influence of these islands of modern growth on the rural hinterland was not limited by a deliberate effort to build barriers between the
modern and traditional economies, but by the small size of these cities in
relation to the vast population of the rural interior. As late as 1953, only
8 percent of China's population lived in cities with more than 100,000

people, and many of these cities were still administrative rather than industrial and commercial centers.[1] Throughout the period from roughly 1912 until the outbreak of full-scale war with Japan in 1937, industry had grown at an average rate of 8 percent a year, but it was from such a small base that modern manufacturing still accounted for only 7 percent of gross domestic product (GDP) in 1933 and 17 percent in 1952.[2] Industrialization did lead farmers to market grain for the modern sector, and cropping patterns changed to meet the requirements of the new enterprises for cotton and other cash crops. Still, most farm families were not much affected by what was occurring in Shanghai, Tientsin, and elsewhere.

Industrialization after 1949, however, was neither modest in scale nor confined to a few coastal cities. Between 1952, when recovery from wartime destruction was largely complete, and 1980, Chinese industry grew at an average rate of 11 percent a year, increasing nineteenfold during more than a quarter century.

As a result of industrialization, agriculture's share of net material product (national income in Chinese terminology) in 1952 fell from 58 percent to 39 percent in 1979 in current prices (see Table 2-1). In fixed prices the fall is more rapid because agricultural prices rose relative to those of industry. In 1978 prices agriculture accounted for 36 percent of net material product in 1978, down from 68 percent in 1952.[3] At the same time, national product grew at an average rate of nearly 6 percent a year during the twenty-six years.[4] Either way, per capita Chinese income rose substantially, from 2 to 2.8-fold between 1952 and 1978.

One would think that growth and structural change of this magnitude would begin to have a profound effect on China's rural population. Yet the aggregate statistics show only modest changes. The urban population in the late 1970s, for example, was only 12 to 13 percent of the total population, or slightly below the level of the 1950s (see Table 2-2). Agricultural value added from 1952 to 1979 grew an average of 5.1 percent a year in current prices, but only 2.3 percent in constant prices.[5] Per capita output thus hardly rose during the quarter century (less than 10 percent), although incomes did better because of rising purchase prices for farm products.

How could so much growth and structural change have occurred without having a more profound effect on the rural areas? In essence, since the early 1950s China has followed a Stalinist policy of investing in machines and steel to make more machines and steel, but it departed from Soviet policy in one important respect. Instead of allowing the rural population to migrate to the cities to be fed by grain requisitioned

Table 2-1. *Share of Agriculture in Net Material Product*
(current prices)

Year	National income (millions of yuan)	Agricultural value added (millions of yuan)	Share of agriculture (percent)
1949	35,820	24,500	68.4
1952	58,925	34,000	57.7
1957	90,810	42,500	46.8
1962	92,500	44,400	48.0
1965	138,870	64,100	46.2
1970	192,490	79,500	41.3
1975	250,510	98,700	39.4
1978	301,100	106,500	35.4
1979	335,000	131,800	39.3
1980	366,700	146,600	40.0
1982	424,700	189,300	44.6

Note: Net material product in Chinese is referred to as national income. It excludes many services included in national income as defined by non-Marxist economists.

Sources: The agricultural income figures in current prices and as a share of national income are from Ministry of Agriculture, *Zhongguo nongye nianjian, 1980*, p. 373. The national income figures for 1949–75 were derived from the agricultural income and percentage share figures. The 1978–80 national income figures are from State Statistical Bureau releases and State Statistical Bureau, *Statistical Yearbook of China, 1981* and *1983* (Hong Kong: Economic Information Agency, 1982), p. 20 and p. 22, respectively.

at low prices from the peasantry, China attempted to prohibit migration and to hold down compulsory grain deliveries. Unlike the Soviet Union, with its per capita grain output of 415 kilograms in 1948–52 and hence large "surplus" above subsistence even in the immediate postwar years, Chinese grain output in the 1950s was less than 300 kilograms per person, or only a little above subsistence needs.[6] China could not afford a policy of large, forced grain deliveries, which would lead to a Stalin-like stagnation in agricultural production. In fact, as the figures in Table 2-3 indicate, grain sales (with foreign trade in grain netted out) did not rise at all after the mid-1950s despite a large increase in grain output between 1957 and 1979.

Thus Chinese planners in a real sense attempted to isolate the rural from the urban sector and in so doing created, or at least reinforced, a dualism in China's economy and society that they probably did not intend. There were still some linkages between the urban and rural sectors, but they were much weaker than what would have been ex-

Table 2-2. *Population in Urban and Rural Areas*

Year	Total (millions of persons)	Urban		Rural	
		Millions of persons	Percent	Millions of persons	Percent
1950	(550.80)	61.69	11.2	(489.11)	(88.8)
1952	574.82	71.63	12.5	503.19	87.5
1957	646.53	99.49	15.4	547.04	84.6
1960	(660.25)	130.73	19.8	(529.52)	(80.2)
1965	725.38	101.70	14.0	623.68	86.0
1970	(825.00)	102.30	12.4	(722.70)	(87.6)
1975	919.70	111.71	12.1	807.99	87.9
1979	970.92	128.62	13.2	842.30	86.8
1981	996.22	138.70	13.9	857.52	86.1
1982	1,003.94	144.68	14.4	859.26	85.6

Note: Data in parentheses were derived from urban population figures and the percentage share of urban in the total.

Sources: *Zhongguo jingji nianjian, 1981*, p. VI-3; *Zhongguo jingji nianjian,1982*, p. VIII-3; and Zhang Zehou and Chen Yuguang, "On the Relationship between the Population Structure and National Economic Development in China," *Social Sciences in China*, vol. 2, no. 4 (December 1981), p. 73. The 1982 figures are midyear figures from the 1982 census. Population Census Office, *Zhongguo disanci renkou puchade zhuyao shuzu* (Beijing: China Statistics Publishers, 1982), pp. 14–15. The urban figures exclude the population of towns (*zhen*) but include some agricultural workers.

Table 2-3. *Sales of Grain*
(thousands of metric tons)

Year	Retail sales of grain (1)	Exports (+) or imports (−) of grain (2)	Sales (including exports) of domestic grain (1) + (2)
1952	29,610	1,529	31,139
1957	37,235	1,926	39,161
1965	36,820	− 3,989	32,831
1975	41,965	− 929	41,036
1979	49,030	− 10,705	38,325
1981	61,070	− 12,839	48,231
1982	67,305	n.a.	n.a.

n.a. Not available.

Sources: State Statistical Bureau, *Statistical Yearbook of China, 1981*, pp. 338, 372, 388, 394, and 398; and State Statistical Bureau, *Zhongguo tongji zhaiyao, 1983* (Beijing: China Statistical Publishers, 1983), p. 70.

pected, given the size of China's development effort during the past three decades.

Evidence from the Government Budget

An analysis of the government budget provides one kind of evidence of the limited scope of rural-urban linkages. As in other economic systems modeled on that of the Soviet Union, China's government budget includes not only expenditures on government administration and the military, but virtually all expenditures for fixed capital investment as well. The only fixed capital investment item of quantitative significance that is not included is investment by rural communes in themselves. Thus the government budget is one of the best single indicators of the degree to which the urban sector was being financed by rural surpluses or vice versa.

Data on government revenues and expenditures are presented in Table 2-4. Measured in terms of socialist concepts, nearly one-third of national income was channeled through the government budget. Using Western concepts of gross national product (GNP), the budget would still approach 30 percent of the total. Who benefited from these expenditures, and where did the money come from?

Table 2-4. *Government Revenues and Expenditures*

| | | Revenues | |
| | *Expenditures, billions of* | *Amount (billions* | *Percentage of* |
Year	*current yuan*	*of current yuan)*	*national income*
1952	17.60	18.37	31.2
1957	30.42	31.02	34.2
1965	46.63	47.33	34.1
1970	64.94	66.29	34.4
1975	82.09	81.56	32.6
1978	111.10	112.11	37.2
1979	127.39	110.33	32.7
1980	121.27	108.52	29.9
1982	115.33	112.40	26.5

Sources: State Statistical Bureau, *Statistical Yearbook of China, 1981*, p. 403; and, for 1982, Wang Bingqian, "Report on the Final State Accounts for 1982," June 7, 1983.

The Expenditure Side

On the expenditure side, the main beneficiaries were not the rural areas. Although small amounts of money for education and health probably reached the rural areas, most government consumption expenditures went to the military or to administration and similar items that had little direct effect on rural production or consumption.[7]

It is possible to be more precise with those expenditure items going exclusively to the agricultural sector and with the capital construction portion of the government budget. The data in Tables 2-5 through 2-7 show that agriculture, with more than 80 percent of the people, received only a small proportion of a very large government budget. The shares of the total budget for direct support of communes and other agricultural activities did not increase at all. Direct investment in agriculture did rise from the very low levels of the 1950s, and, if one includes investment in heavy industries producing farm inputs, the increase in agriculture's share is even larger, from around 10 percent of total investment in the mid-1950s to about 15 percent throughout much of the 1960s and 1970s. In absolute terms the increase was greater still because total expenditures also increased substantially during this same period, and price increases were minimal. Still, heavy industry received the lion's share of funding, including significant portions of investment in nonproductive items (such as worker housing) and "others" (such as infrastructure, among other things).

Table 2-5. *Share of Agriculture in Capital Construction Investment*

	Sector of investment (percentage of total)			
Year	*Agriculture*	*Heavy industry*	*Light industry*	*Other*
1952	13.3	34.3	9.1	43.3
1957	8.6	51.6	5.9	33.9
1962	21.3	55.0	4.0	19.7
1965	14.6	50.8	4.2	30.4
1975	9.8	51.8	8.9	29.5
1979	11.6	50.3	6.1	32.0
1981	6.8	40.3	10.0	42.9

Sources: Zhongguo jingji nianjian, 1981, p. VI-20; Ministry of Agriculture, *Zhongguo nongye nianjian, 1980*, p. 333; and State Statistical Bureau, *Statistical Yearbook of China, 1981*, pp. 301–02.

Table 2-6. *State Expenditures and Credits to the Agricultural Sector*
(millions of current yuan)

Year	State invest-ment in agriculture	State support for rural communes	Other current agricultural expenditures	Bank credit to agriculture[a]
1952	583	n.a.	1,694	140
1957	1,187	n.a.	2,099	n.a.
1962	1,439	440	2,045	n.a.
1965	2,497	60	4,257	n.a.
1970	n.a.	200	3,719	n.a.
1975	3,840	920	6,293	n.a.
1978	4,266	1,620	6,075	1,730
1979	5,792	9,010[b]		n.a.
1980	n.a.	8,210[b]		n.a.

n.a. Not available.

a. Figures are for the net increase in credit over the previous year.

b. Figures for each category separately are not available for 1979 and 1980.

Sources: Zhongguo jingji nianjian, 1981, p. VI-20; Ministry of Agriculture, *Zhongguo nongye nianjian, 1980,* pp. 333–35; Wang Bingqian, "Report on the Final State Accounts for 1979, the Draft State Budget for 1980, and the Financial Estimates for 1981," August 30, 1980; and Wang Bingqian, "Report on the Final State Accounts for 1980 and Implementation of the Financial Estimates for 1981," December 1, 1981.

Table 2-7. *Share of Farm Machinery, Chemical Fertilizer, and Pesticides in Heavy Industry Investment*
(annual average rate in millions of yuan)

Period	Investment in heavy industry (1)	Investment in farm machinery, etc. (2)	Ratio (2)/(1) (percent) (3)
1953–57	5,120	152	3.0
1958–62	13,325	765	5.7
1963–65	4,025	394	9.8
1966–70	10,495	955	9.1
1971–75	18,412	1,868	10.1
1976–78	21,928	2,439	11.1
1979	25,040[a]	1,645	6.6

a. Derived from figures in columns (2) and (3).

Sources: Derived from Yang Jianbai and Li Xuezeng, "The Relations between Agriculture, Light Industry, and Heavy Industry in China," *Social Sciences in China,* no. 2 (June 1980), p. 200; and Ministry of Agriculture, *Zhongguo nongye nianjian, 1980,* p. 335.

Table 2-8. *Share of Accumulation in National Income according to Chinese Definitions*

Period	Percent	Year	Percent
1953–57	24.2	1976	30.9
1958–62	30.8	1977	32.3
1963–65	22.7	1978	36.5
1966–70	26.3	1979	34.6
1971–75	33.0	1980	31.6
		1981	28.5
		1982	29.0

Sources: Dong Furen, "Relationship between Accumulation and Consumption," in Xu Dixin and others, *China's Search for Economic Growth: The Chinese Economy since 1949* (Beijing: New World Press, 1981), p. 88; State Statistical Bureau, *Statistical Yearbook of China, 1981*, p. 21; and State Statistical Bureau, *Zhongguo tongji zhaiyao, 1983*, p. 5.

The result of these investment priorities was that fixed assets per industrial worker rose from 3,000 yuan per worker for 5.26 million industrial workers in 1952 to nearly 9,000 yuan per worker for 50.05 million industrial workers in the late 1970s.[8] In contrast, a rural work force of 294 million in the late 1970s had only 310 yuan of fixed assets per person (excluding land). It is hardly surprising, therefore, that industrial value added per worker rose from 1,650 yuan in 1952 (in 1978 prices) to 2,809 yuan in 1978, while agricultural value added per farm worker for the same period rose by less than 10 percent to only 364 yuan in 1978 (in 1978 prices). The urban-rural ratio in fixed assets per worker of nearly 30:1 does exaggerate the real difference since land and all capital improvements of land are excluded, but there is little question that industrial workers had far more capital to work with than did their rural counterparts.

Thus China up until the late 1970s was a nation accumulating capital at a very high rate (Table 2-8) and directing most of it to increasingly capital-intensive industrial enterprises, mainly in the producer goods sector in urban areas. Only a small proportion of the fruits of this investment in urban enterprises found its way back to the countryside in the form of agricultural inputs or increased sales of industrial consumer goods.

The Revenue Side

The picture on the expenditure side, therefore, is reasonably clear. But what was happening on the revenue side during this period? Was agriculture being milked to supply capital for this industrialization effort, or did heavy industry provide for its own needs?

A commonly heard phrase is that industrialization is impossible in less developed nations unless the bulk of the capital inputs that industry requires is provided from agriculture. Although this statement has a certain validity for a nation in which virtually all national product is generated by agriculture and related services or by rural handicrafts, it is not valid for a nation that has had a decade or two of reasonably rapid modern industrial development. If industry can plow a high percentage of the annual increments in output back into investment, it is soon able to provide for all of its own investment needs. In essence, this is what has happened in China. The one major qualification is that China, like most developing countries, must import certain investment goods that it cannot produce at a reasonable cost, and for that purpose foreign exchange is required. China's foreign exchange earnings, through the 1970s at least, depended on agricultural exports and what the Chinese refer to as processed agricultural exports (for example, cotton textiles), although the share of these items declined sharply in the late 1970s and early 1980s.

Leaving foreign exchange aside for the moment, the issue is what portion of government revenues comes directly or indirectly from the rural areas. Rural communes bear the burden of only two kinds of taxes large enough to matter in this analysis. First is the agricultural tax, which is paid directly by the communes and is, in effect, a tax on land, although formally it is calculated as a percentage of "normal" yield. The normal yield used to make the calculation, however, has remained fixed for long periods. In the early 1950s the agricultural tax amounted to 12 percent of the gross value of crop output or 3 billion yuan a year in absolute terms. This tax has been increased by only very modest amounts during the past two decades, and, as a percentage of the value of crop output, it fell to 6 percent in 1970 and then to 5 percent in 1978. In absolute terms, in 1979 the tax was equivalent to about 11 million tons of grain or around 3 billion yuan.[9]

Of far greater importance after the early 1950s were the taxes paid on consumer goods produced in the cities and then sold at retail in the rural areas. One such tax was a fixed percentage markup above cost of production of each consumer good, with a different percentage rate for each commodity. The other tax was on the profits of industrial producers, wholesalers, and retailers.[10] Enterprises were allowed to retain only a tiny fraction (5 to 10 percent) of their total profits, with the rest turned over to the state.

Formally these taxes on industrial and commercial profits were paid by producers and wholesalers. In the 1950s their combined markup above cost averaged 47 percent for all industrial consumer goods. For the purposes of the analysis, it is assumed that the relevant elasticities were such that this entire burden was passed on to the consumer. This assumption contains some error, but not enough to undermine the rough order of magnitudes of the following calculations.

Data on retail sales nationwide and to the rural sector are presented in Table 2–9. If the 47 percent markup is applied to retail sales in rural areas in 1957, taxes on industrial consumer goods sold in rural areas are estimated to have been 5 billion yuan. An estimate for 1979 requires additional assumptions and is subject to a wider margin for possible error. Many items sold at retail in rural areas in 1979 probably either escaped taxes (free market sales if they were included in the total) or had lower markups above cost than 47 percent. The prices of producer

Table 2-9. *Retail Sales in Rural and Urban Areas*
(millions of current yuan)

Year	Total	In rural areas		In urban areas, consumer goods
		Consumer goods	Producer goods	
1949	14,050	7,790	670	5,590
1950	17,060	n.a.	n.a.	n.a.
1952	27,680	13,710	1,410	12,560
1957	47,420	20,320	3,260	23,840
1962	60,400	22,520	6,030	31,850
1965	65,730	25,120	8,020	32,590
1970	84,100	32,880	12,920	38,300
1975	124,610	43,950	22,470	58,190
1978	152,750	52,670	29,370	71,710
1979	175,250	63,080	32,400	79,770
1980	214,000	84,370	34,600	95,030
1982	257,000	109,150	38,850	109,000

n.a. Not available.

Sources: Ministry of Agriculture, *Zhongguo nongye nianjian, 1980*, p. 330; State Statistical Bureau, *Statistical Yearbook of China, 1981*, p. 333; State Statistical Bureau, "Communique on Fulfillment of China's 1982 National Economic Plan," April 29, 1983; and State Statistical Bureau, *Zhongguo tongji zhaiyao, 1983*, p. 69.

goods sold to agriculture, in particular, actually declined. One plausible approach, although not the only one, is to assume that the 47 percent markup applies to two-thirds of all rural retail sales, with no markup on the remaining one-third. This assumption leads to an estimate of 1979 taxes of 20 billion yuan. Slightly higher (or lower) estimates would not significantly alter the conclusions that follow. Adding on the agricultural tax to these taxes on retail sales, total taxes paid by farmers rose from 8 billion yuan in 1957 to 25 billion yuan in 1979, or 26 percent of total state revenues in 1957. This figure fell to about 20 percent in 1979.

To obtain a figure for the net flow of state funds out of (or into) agriculture, an estimate of state expenditure in the rural areas is needed. In addition to the investment in capital construction mentioned above, the main categories of state expenditures in rural areas included such things as expenditures on meteorology to support farm production, rural relief, and rural educational and medical services. In the mid-1950s, the combined total of these expenditures was about 3 billion to 4 billion yuan (Tables 2–6 and 2–7). The comparable figure in 1979 was under 17 billion yuan, a bit more if the rural share of expenditures on culture, education, health, and science is included. Combining revenue and expenditure estimates, the net outflow of funds from the rural sector to the state were from 4 billion to 5 billion yuan in the mid-1950s and under 8 billion yuan by the late 1970s. In other words, in the 1950s agriculture contributed roughly 16 percent of the funds for state investment in industry, national defense, and general government administration, whereas by the late 1970s the rural areas contributed less than 6 percent of the funds for these sectors.[11]

An analysis of the net financial contribution of the agricultural sector would not be complete without at least mentioning the fact that grain and certain other commodities are delivered to the state at below market prices. Faced with rapidly rising urban demand for grain in 1952–53, the Chinese government imposed compulsory delivery quotas on the farmers and held grain prices at the level prevailing before the quotas were introduced. The essence of what occurred is illustrated in Figure 1. Demand for grain before the first five-year plan and rapid industrialization can be represented by the demand curve D_1. The supply curve S_p represents the supply of marketed grain, not total output. With the beginning of the first five-year plan demand shifted out to D_2, but prices were held at P_1 and urban demand, as a result, rose to $P_1 b_1$. Since demand of this size could not be met with voluntary deliveries, compulsory quotas were introduced. The difference between payments actually made to farmers and payments that would have been necessary to

generate such large deliveries on a free market is represented by the
rectangle $P_1 b_1 b_2 P_2$.

A systematic quantitative estimate of $P_1 b_1 b_2 P_2$ is not possible given
data limitations, but a general order of magnitude can be obtained. In
the first year that quotas were introduced, grain purchases increased
from 30.5 million to 41.5 million tons, or by 36 percent.[12] Since supply
was probably quite inelastic, it would have taken a very large price
increase to elicit a voluntary increase in supply of this size. Immediately

Figure 1. *Quotas and the Grain Market*

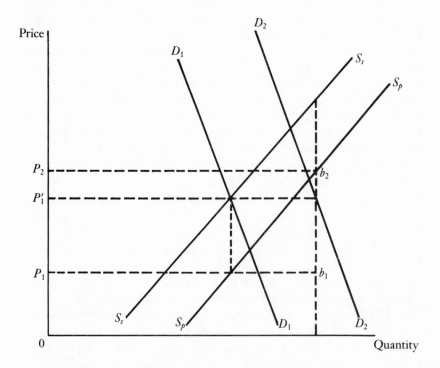

D_1, Urban demand before first five-year plan

D_2, Urban demand after beginning of first five-year plan

S_p, Farmer supply of marketed grain

S_r, Urban supply for grain that includes a fixed percentage markup covering trading costs and
sales taxes

P_1, Price received by farmer in period 1

P_1', Price paid by purchaser in period 1

P_2, Price received by farmer if a free farm purchasing market had prevailed after the beginning
of the first five-year plan

before the quotas were introduced, prices increased 20 to 30 percent in many areas. If such price increases accurately reflected underlying long-term supply conditions, the value of $P_1 b_1 b_2 P_2$ might be 2 billion to 3 billion yuan, or nearly as much as the agricultural tax at that time.[13] Ironically, most of the benefits of this quota policy went to urban consumers in the form of an enlarged urban consumer surplus. Tax revenues of the state also rose, but by only a modest amount. Farmers, therefore, were contributing not to national capital formation, but to a higher standard of living for urban residents—a not unusual occurrence in today's developing countries.

Beginning in the early 1960s, the state began to modify its grain marketing policies in two important ways. On the one hand, grain purchase prices were raised without matching increases in urban sales prices, leading the subsidy to urban consumers to rise markedly and become a major drain on governmental resources, particularly by the early 1980s. On the other hand, the state began to import 5 million to 6 million tons of grain each year and to send some urban residents back to the countryside, thereby causing the demand curve to shift inward or at least not to shift further out. The net result was a probable reduction in the tax element in grain marketings relative to what it would have been without these changes in policy and possibly in absolute terms as well.

Thus, inclusion of the tax element in grain purchase policies increased the contribution of the agricultural sector to the nonagricultural sector by a substantial amount in the 1950s but by a much lesser amount in the 1960s and 1970s. The principal conclusion, that by the 1970s rural areas contributed only small amounts of net revenue to the urban areas, is not altered.

Agriculture and Foreign Trade

If one thinks in terms of the two-gap model, where capital and foreign exchange are treated as separate factors of production, agriculture, as indicated above, made little contribution to the level of nonagricultural investment or capital formation after the 1950s, but it continued to make a major contribution to filling the foreign exchange gap.

Aggregate data on Chinese agricultural exports are presented in Table 2-10. Except for the years following the bad harvests of 1959–61, agricultural exports held at a level of around 35 to 40 percent of total Chinese exports. If the agricultural portions of what the Chinese call processed agricultural products (items such as cotton textiles, where 60

Table 2-10. *Composition of Chinese Exports*

| | Total value of exports | | Share in exports (percent) | | |
Year	Millions of U.S. dollars	Millions of reminbi	Industrial and mining products	Agricultural products	Processed agricultural products[a]
1952	820	2,710	17.9	59.3	22.8
1957	1,600	5,450	28.4	40.1	31.5
1962	1,490	4,710	34.7	19.4	45.9
1965	2,230	6,310	30.9	33.1	36.0
1970	2,260	5,680	25.6	36.7	37.7
1975	7,260	14,300	39.3	29.6	31.1
1978	9,750	16,770	37.4	27.6	35.0
1980	18,270	27,240	51.8	18.7	29.5
1982	21,820	42,000	55 + [b]	45 − [b]	

a. Processed agricultural products include such items as cotton textiles and canned foods.
b. Mineral fuels and lubricants and a few other nonagricultural products are included in the 1982 figures for agriculture. Their quantities are small.
Sources: *Zhongguo jingji nianjian, 1981*, pp. VI-22, 30; Ministry of Agriculture, *Zhongguo nongye nianjian, 1980*, pp. 331–32; State Statistical Bureau, *Statistical Yearbook of China, 1981*, pp. 357–58; State Statistical Bureau, "Communique on Fulfillment of China's 1982 National Economic Plan," April 29, 1983; and State Statistical Bureau, *Zhongguo tongji zhaiyao, 1983*, p. 74.

percent or more of the value added comes from agriculture) are considered, then agriculture contributed closer to 60 or 70 percent to total exports.

Although a case can be made today that China's comparative advantage lies with manufactures, not land-intensive farm products, in the 1950s and 1960s the People's Republic had few alternative sources of foreign exchange. Some of this foreign exchange was used to import products destined for the rural areas, notably chemical fertilizer, but most was used to import products for the industrialization program. Thus agriculture contributed heavily to the development of the nonagricultural sector. The size of this contribution could be measured by simulating what would have happened without this source of foreign exchange earnings, but such an exercise would be a diversion from the main purposes of this study. Furthermore, although there is little question about the importance of agriculture's foreign exchange contribution in the past, that contribution was decreasing by the latter half of the 1970s as China developed alternative sources of foreign exchange.

By 1980, agricultural and processed agricultural exports accounted for just under 50 percent of the total, and the larger part was processed agricultural exports, which included a substantial and probably rising value added contribution by industry. The contribution of agriculture to exports in 1982 fell even further.

Industry's Nonbudgetary Contributions to Agriculture

There are theoretically three distinct nonbudgetary contributions that the urban sector can make to rural development. First, industry and research institutes provide modern agriculture with crucial inputs and with new techniques to make more productive use of those inputs. Second, the urban sector draws off population from the rural areas, thereby relieving pressure on rural consumption standards, at least in circumstances where that population is surplus (its marginal product is below its average consumption level). Of course, the transfer of rural labor to the cities also can be seen as a rural input into urban activities, and the contribution can be quite large when the rural areas send their most educated workers to the cities. Finally, urban areas are an important source of demand for agricultural products and a source of supply of urban consumer, as well as producer, products.

In China the contributions of industry, and the urban sector in general, to agriculture outside of the budgetary sphere were greater than those within, but were still modest when compared with such rapid industrializers as Japan or the Republic of Korea.

The contribution of chemical fertilizer, new plant varieties developed in research institutes, and other modern inputs to China's agricultural development are discussed more fully in Chapter 4. Even where the factories producing these inputs were located in rural areas, urban-based industries provided those factories with technical assistance and key inputs, such as steel. Since in the absence of these modern inputs agricultural development would have been much slower at best, by any measure the contribution of industry and of research institutes to agriculture was large.

Because of policies pursued by the Chinese government, however, the urban areas did nothing whatsoever to relieve rural population pressure. In fact, by insisting that urban graduates of middle schools go to live for long periods in the countryside, the government actually increased rural population pressure. Between 1957 and 1979, while population as a whole increased an average of 1.9 percent a year, the urban population grew an average of only 1.2 percent a year (Table 2-2). The main reason for the slow growth in urban population, despite the rapid development of industry, was the virtual ban by the government of migration from rural to urban areas. Rural residents first had to get permission from their commune to leave. To obtain an industrial job they needed the approval of the urban labor bureau, and to find a place to live they needed permission from local public security officials. In general, permission at one or all of these levels was not given. Hence new urban jobs had to be filled from the ranks of existing urban residents or by rural people who could commute to urban jobs without changing their residence. The implications of these restrictions for the distribution of income are the subject of Chapter 6. These restrictions severed a rural-urban connection found in most nations experiencing rapid industrialization. In China, rural-urban migration neither relieved rural population pressure nor provided a key input for urban development. By the early 1980s these policies had been modified to the extent of allowing many sent-down urban youth to return to the cities, but other restrictions on rural-to-urban migration remained in force.

Rising urban demand for farm products contributes to agricultural development in several related ways. If, for example, agricultural output per capita rises rapidly without large increases in urban population or urban per capita incomes, the terms of trade facing the agricultural sector are likely to fall sharply because of the price inelasticity of demand for most farm products. Alternatively, if the share of the urban population in the total is increasing and urban per capita incomes are on the rise as well, demand for food can be sustained without a decline in farm prices.

In nations where a large portion of grain requirements can be imported, a rapidly rising urban demand for food can enable farmers to switch to vegetables and other cash crops where the return per unit of land is much higher than for grain. In Korea, for example, farmers have achieved large increases in income by shifting a higher percentage of their resources into these cash crops, while rising grain requirements have been increasingly met with imports. In the absence of grain imports, of course, the amount of resources that can be shifted out of grain is more limited because cash crops are not substitutes for grain. Grain is the main source of calories in the diets of all nations, whether it is consumed directly or fed to hogs and cattle and then consumed as meat. Because China's capacity to import a large share of its grain requirements was much more limited than that of Japan or Korea, the possibility for farmers to shift resources to cash crops was also more limited. Introduction of the "responsibility system" in the early 1980s did lead to a rapid acceleration in the production of nongrain crops and to an increase in imports, but China has a long way to go before it is in a position similar to that of Japan or Korea.

Although Chinese farmers could not follow those of Japan or Korea by shifting away from grain toward a major emphasis on cash crops, rural cash incomes per capita did rise in real terms. In constant prices, state purchases of agricultural products grew at almost exactly the same rate as the increase in the gross value of agricultural output (3.2 percent a year). But in current prices agricultural value added grew at an annual rate of 5.2 percent between 1957 and 1979, and state purchases of farm products averaged 5.6 percent a year (Table 2-11). The difference, of course, resulted from a substantial rise in the state purchase prices for farm products. There were large increases in the 1950s, in the early 1960s during the 1959–61 crisis years, and in the late 1970s, with more modest increases in the early 1970s.

Table 2-11. *Purchases and Purchase Prices of Agricultural Products*
(millions of yuan)

Year	Purchases of agricultural products (1)	Farm product purchase price index (1952 = 100) (2)	State purchases of agricultural products (1952 constant prices) (1) ÷ (2)
1952	14,080	100.0	14,080
1957	21,750	120.2	18,095
1962	21,100	164.6	12,820
1965	30,710	154.5	19,880
1970	34,780	160.4	21,680
1975	47,860	171.6	27,890
1978	55,790	178.8	31,200
1979	71,360	218.3	32,690
1980	84,220	233.9	36,010
1981	95,500	247.7	38,550

Sources: The data for 1952–80 are from State Statistical Bureau, *Statistical Yearbook of China, 1981*, pp. 345, 411–12. The data for 1982 are derived from "Communique on Fulfillment of China's 1982 National Economic Plan," April 29, 1983. Agricultural purchase data from other sources usually refer only to purchases by state commercial departments. The above figures include some purchases by individuals, but do not include private trading within the agricultural community.

Rising farm purchase prices were not for the most part the result of general inflationary pressures. Retail prices paid by farmers grew at much more modest rates (Table 2-12), and thus the terms of trade turned sharply in favor of the rural areas during the three decades. Despite the policy of restricting urban growth and grain imports, the state had to pay higher and higher prices to keep the marketed share of agricultural produce from falling. Conceivably the same end could have been achieved by increasing the compulsory delivery quotas, but the cost might have been decreased incentives and slower growth in output. Another alternative would have been to accelerate the growth of farm output, but this would have been difficult for reasons that will be discussed at length in the next two chapters.

China's inability to rely increasingly on grain imports thus made it difficult for farmers to raise their incomes by shifting into cash crops, but the same limitation meant that the state had to pay higher and higher prices to meet domestic food requirements. Farmers benefited in real terms by being able to increase their purchases from the urban sector at a rate considerably higher than that at which farm output was increasing (Table 2-13). This rising supply of urban-produced consumer and producer goods and the reverse flows of farm products to the urban areas were the main rural-urban links from the 1950s through the 1970s.

Table 2-12. *Retail Price Indexes*
(1952 = 100)

Year	Urban retail prices of workers and employees[a]	Rural retail prices, state only	Prices of industrial products in rural areas, producer goods only
1950	86.6	90.6	91.2
1952	100.0	100.0	100.0
1957	109.6	107.7	102.2
1965	120.3	118.2	107.9
1975	120.8	113.3	99.9
1979	127.6	115.4	100.2
1980	137.2	120.5	101.2
1981	140.7	121.1	n.a.

n.a. Not available.

a. There is an index for state-fixed urban prices that rises at a somewhat lower rate, but this index for all workers and employees appears to be more inclusive.

Sources: *Zhongguo jingji nianjian, 1981*, pp. VI-23, 29, 31; and *Zhongguo jingji nianjian, 1982*, p. VIII-26.

Table 2-13. *Real Growth Rates of Retail Sales*
(percent a year)

Category	1952–57	1957–65	1965–75	1975–79	1952–79	1980–81
Urban retail sales	11.6	2.8	5.9	6.7	5.9	10.1
Rural retail sales						
Consumer goods	6.6	1.5	6.2	9.0	5.1	18.7
Producer goods	17.7	11.2	11.7	9.5	12.3	2.2

Sources: These annual rates were calculated by dividing current price retail sales data by the appropriate price index in Table 2-12 and then converting the resulting figures to annual percentage rates. Retail sales data are in State Statistical Bureau, *Statistical Yearbook of China, 1981*, p. 333; and *Zhungguo jingji nianjian, 1981* and *1982*.

Because of the shifting terms of trade, the flow from urban to rural areas was rising considerably faster than that in the reverse direction.

Conclusion

Normally when a nation has experienced a quarter century of industrial growth averaging 10 percent and more a year, the dual nature of the economy that is characteristic of the early stages of growth begins to break down. Connections between the rural and urban sectors become increasingly intimate, and eventually the urban sector absorbs much of the rural population and transforms agriculture into, in effect, just one more industrial sector, albeit a large and essential one. The full process of absorption takes longer than thirty years, even in rapid industrializers, and the increasing capital intensity of the best available industrial techniques also slows this transformation.

Connections between the rural and urban areas in China have become more intense during the past quarter century in only one respect, however. Industry, some of it based in urban areas, has provided a steadily rising share of inputs into agricultural production and industrial consumer goods for rural consumption. Otherwise, rural-urban economic relations have not intensified much since the early 1950s, and in one important respect they have declined. Agriculture no longer provides a significant share of the capital for industry, and even agriculture's role as a major provider of foreign exchange is declining.

In many countries the weak rural-urban connection or dual nature of the economy mainly reflects the fact that the nation is still in the very early stages of industrial development. In China, where roughly half of the GNP is generated by industry, the dual nature of the economy is in important ways the result of a deliberate policy to limit urbanization.

During their first thirty years of rule, therefore, policymakers in the People's Republic of China have eschewed the most common method of historically eliminating rural poverty, that of removing the rural population to urban areas. Instead, these policymakers have attempted to solve at least the worst features of rural poverty by action directed at the countryside itself. These efforts are the subject of the chapters that follow, and the effects of the efforts to restrict urbanization will be a recurring theme of this study.

Notes to Chapter 2

1. From Dwight H. Perkins, *Agricultural Development in China, 1368–1968* (Chicago: Aldine, 1969), appendix E.

2. These percentages are derived from John K. Chang, *Industrial Development in Pre-Communist China* (Chicago: Aldine, 1969), pp. 78–79. The estimates of GDP on which these percentages are based are in 1957 prices and are taken from Dwight H. Perkins, "Growth and Changing Structure of China's Economy," in Dwight H. Perkins, ed., *China's Modern Economy in Historical Perspective* (Stanford, Calif.: Stanford University Press, 1975), p. 117.

3. These percentages are rough and were made by Dwight H. Perkins, "An American View of the Prospects for the Chinese Economy" (in Chinese), compiled by *jingji yanjiu, guowai jing jixuezhe lun Zhongguo ji fazhanguo zhong guojia jingji* (Beijing: Finance and Economics Press, 1981), p. 4.

4. The precise growth rate of national income varies, depending on which year's constant prices are used. The later the year used, the lower the growth rate. The 6 percent figure is based on a Chinese index in "comparable" but unspecified prices in State Statistical Bureau, *Statistical Yearbook of China, 1981* (Hong Kong: Economic Information Agency, 1982), p. 20. In 1978 prices (see source in footnote 3), the growth rate would be just under 5 percent a year.

5. The growth rate of current prices was derived from Table 2-1. The Chinese have not yet published constant price estimates of agricultural value added. The figure here is based on data in the source cited in footnote 3.

6. Soviet figures are derived from Food and Agricultural Organization, *FAO Production Yearbook, 1970* (Rome), pp. 15 and 86.

7. This is not the appropriate place for a full incidence analysis of Chinese expenditures and revenues in a general equilibrium context, but if such an analysis were made, it would probably not fundamentally alter the conclusions in this discussion.

8. These and other estimates in this paragraph are derived from data in Table 2-1 and Yang Jianbai and Li Xuezeng, "The Relations between Agriculture, Light Industry, and Heavy Industry in China," *Social Sciences in China*, no. 2 (June 1980), pp. 182–212. According to Yang and Li, fixed assets per worker were 11,000 yuan in heavy industry and 5,000 yuan in light industry, and in 1972 the ratio of heavy to light industrial workers was 1.0:0.6. The ratio was assumed to be the same in the late 1970s and was used to derive the overall industry average of 9,000 yuan per worker.

9. See Nicholas R. Lardy, *Agriculture in China's Modern Economic Development* (Cambridge: Cambridge University Press, 1983), p. 104.

10. For a study of China's taxes and the tax burden in the 1950s, see George Ecklund, *Taxation in Communist China* (Chicago: Aldine, 1966).

11. The figure of 16 percent was obtained by subtracting 3.5 billion yuan in state rural expenditures from total state expenditures of 31 billion yuan in 1957 and then dividing that figure (27.5 billion yuan) into a net outflow estimate of 4.5 billion yuan.

12. Official data on grain purchases can be found in Dwight H. Perkins, *Market Control and Planning in Communist China* (Cambridge, Mass.: Harvard University Press, 1966), p. 248.

13. If the base purchase price of grain in the 1950s was 140 yuan per ton, an increase of more than 40 percent would make the price 200 yuan per ton. The 60 yuan difference multiplied by 41.5 million tons gives a figure of 2.5 billion yuan. These figures are for illustrative purposes only.

Chapter 3

~~~~~~

Agricultural Production

THE PERFORMANCE OF AGRICULTURAL PRODUCTION is not the only test of the effectiveness of China's "self-contained" rural development effort, but it is an important one. The basic question is whether Chinese rural development policies have achieved rapid and sustained increases in output. This seemingly simple question, however, does not have such a simple answer. The problems are, first, to describe Chinese agricultural growth during the past three decades and, second, to determine what the word "rapid" means in the Chinese context.

In the past a major objective of research on Chinese agriculture was to estimate the total output of grain in a given year. Controversy surrounded the issue of whether to accept estimates published or leaked to visitors by Chinese officials or to derive independent estimates.

Although there are still problems with Chinese agricultural data, liberalized policies on data publication have put to rest the controversies over fundamentals. The issues that remain include the reliability of the Chinese crop-reporting system, what is included and excluded from the gross value of agricultural output, the appropriate deductions necessary to obtain value added from gross value data, and other similar questions. During the Cultural Revolution, for example, agricultural statistics depended on the reliability of the data collection systems of the communes and brigades, and only recently have provincial state statistical bureaus reinstituted methods to cross-check these figures.[1] Thus there is some question whether the large jumps in grain output from 283 million tons in 1977 to 305 million tons in 1978 and to 332 million tons in

1979 were entirely real or whether there was significant underreporting in the earlier year. Serious scholars, however, no longer attempt to substitute their own estimates for those officially released by the government.

The main purpose in this chapter is to present the data on agricultural production, yields, and growth rates and to make comparisons between regions within China and between China and other countries. The tables and other data presented here provide one important basis for the analysis of the sources of growth that follow in Chapter 4.

Growth Rates of Agricultural Output

Data on Chinese agricultural production are presented in Tables 3-1 to 3-5.[2] Since grain accounts for most of the calories in the Chinese diet, data on grain are considered first. The most reliable figures for the earlier years are for 1955–57. When estimates for 1978–80 are compared with those for the earlier period, it is apparent that grain output grew only slightly faster than the increase in population, a rate of 2.25 percent a year. As Chinese planners themselves have pointed out, per capita grain consumption in the mid-1970s was the same as in the mid-1950s, and 2 percent a year is not a particularly impressive rate by international standards. Nor is a 2 percent rate adequate to meet China's needs. The population growth rate appears to have declined to less than 1.4 percent by the late 1970s, but, given the low levels of income prevailing in China, rising incomes under the incentive programs introduced at the same time meant rising per capita demand for grain.

But has the supply of grain grown at only 2 percent a year? The growth rate is quite sensitive to which years are chosen as the base.[3] The years 1955–57 came just before the disasters of the Great Leap Forward, which led to a sharp decline in grain output in 1959–61. Recovery to the earlier levels was not achieved until 1965. If 1964–66 is used as a base, then the growth rate rises to 3.4 percent, a more impressive rate compared with other countries. But much of this growth occurred in the mid-1960s and after 1977, with something of a slow-down in between. The big jump in 1978 and particularly 1979 also coincides with the sharp rise in farm purchase prices (discussed in Chapter 2) and the reinstitution of cross-checks and other methods designed to discern the accuracy of commune reports. Thus simultaneously both the incentive to underreport and the ability to do so was reduced. But was output underreported only during the Cultural Revolution (1966–76), or dur-

ing the early 1960s as well? Outsiders, and possibly the Chinese themselves, do not know.

The gross value of agricultural output grew at a rate of 3.2 percent a
year between the mid-1950s and the mid-1970s, but the gross value
figures include such items as subsidiary processing, whose share in the
total rose during that time. If only the value of crop output is considered, the rate drops to 2.2 percent. If the rising share of purchased

Table 3-1. *Gross Value of Agricultural Output*

Year	1952 prices and coverage	1952 prices (1957 coverage)	1957 prices and coverage	1970 prices (same as 1957 coverage)	1980 prices
1949	32,590	24,479	29,892	42,810	—
1952	48,390	40,800	44,383	63,580	—
1955	55,540	46,647	—	—	—
1957	60,350	49,366	53,700	79,315	—
1962	—	—	43,000	63,510	—
1965	—	—	59,000	87,140	—
1970	—	—	71,600	105,750	—
1971	—	—	73,800	109,000	—
1975	—	—	—	128,500	—
1979	—	—	—	158,430	—
1980	—	—	—	162,700	—
1981	—	—	—	171,970	231,200
1982	—	—	—	190,890	256,630

Sources: For 1952 price data with 1952 coverage that includes farmer self-processing of food,
State Statistical Bureau, *Ten Great Years* (1960), p. 118.

For 1952 price data with coverage that excludes farmer self-processing of food and other
farm manufacturing activities, official estimates are derived following the method of Shigeru
Ishikawa, *National Income and Capital Formation in Mainland China* (Tokyo: Institute of Asian
Economic Affairs, 1965), pp. 50 and 56.

For 1957 price data, the 1957 figure is from State Statistical Bureau, *Ten Great Years*, p. 118;
the 1949 and 1952 figures were derived by using an index derived from the 1952 price data; and
the 1962, 1965, 1970, and 1971 figures are from Ministry of Agriculture, *Zhongguo nongye
nianjian, 1980*, p. 325.

For 1970 and 1980 price data, the 1977, 1978, 1979, and 1980 figures are from the
"Communique of the State Statistical Bureau on the Fulfillment of the 1978 National Eco-
nomic Plan," June 27, 1979, and similar communiques on the 1979 and 1980 plans; and the
other figures are from Ministry of Agriculture, *Zhongguo nongye nianjian, 1980*, p. 292; and
State Statistical Bureau, *Statistical Yearbook of China, 1981* (Hong Kong: Economic Information
Agency, 1982), p. 17.

The 1982 figures were derived by using the reported 11 percent increase in real output. The
figure in 1982 prices was 278.5 billion yuan.

Table 3-2. *Agricultural Value Added*
(billions of yuan)

Year	Gross value	Deductions for cost	Value added
		1952 prices and coverage	
1952	48.39	12.20	36.19
1955	55.54	13.88	41.66
1957	60.35	14.28	46.07
		1970 prices and coverage	
1965	87.67	39.30	48.37
1976	133.98	60.75	73.23
1978	145.90	66.15	79.75
1980	162.70	73.77	88.93

Note: 1978 and 1980 value added to gross value of output ratio was assumed to be the same as in 1976. This assumption may slightly overstate value added in 1978 and 1980. More accurate estimates must await publication by China of its own estimates of value added in constant prices.

Sources: The 1952–57 data are from Ishikawa, *National Income and Capital Formation in Mainland China*, p. 56.

The 1975, 1976, and 1980 gross value of agricultural output figures are from Table 3-1.

The cost deduction is based on a figure of cost per mu (one mu equals one-fifteenth of a hectare) for grain multiplied by the total arable land (100 million hectares). The cost figures are from a nationwide survey of 2,162 production teams reported in *Guangming ribao* (December 7, 1978).

Table 3-3. *Agricultural Growth Rates*
(percent per year)

Period	Gross value of agricultural output	Agricultural value added
1952–57	4.5	4.9
1957–65	1.2	n.a.
1965–75	4.0	3.8
1975–80	4.8	5.0
1957–80	3.2	n.a.
1981–82	8.3	n.a.

n.a. Not available.

Sources: The gross value of output growth rates were derived from 1970 price figures in Table 3-1. The value added figures are for 1965–76 and 1976–80. Linking the 1950s value added figures for those with the 1960s and 1970s must await data on value added in 1957 in 1970 prices.

Table 3-4. *Grain Output*

Year	Millions of metric tons	Year	Millions of metric tons
1952	164	1967	218
1953	167	1968	209
1954	170	1969	211
1955	184	1970	240
1956	193	1971	250
1957	195	1972	240
1958	200	1973	265
1959	170	1974	275
1960	143.5	1975	284.5
1961	147.5	1976	286
1962	160	1977	283
1963	170	1978	305
1964	187.5	1979	332
1965	194.5	1980	320.6
1966	214	1981	325
		1982	353

Note: Included in grain are potatoes (at one-fourth or one-fifth weight, depending on the year) and soybeans, although for some years only soybeans used directly for human consumption are included. All grain is unhusked.

Sources: Ministry of Agriculture, *Zhongguo nongye nianjian, 1980*, p. 34; and State Statistical Bureau, *Statistical Yearbook of China, 1981*, p. 145, and "Communique on the Fulfillment of China's 1982 National Economic Plan," April 29, 1983.

inputs in gross value is subtracted to arrive at agricultural value added, the growth rates are similar to or a little less than the gross value figures because of a rising share of deductible inputs.

But the question remains whether these rates represent rapid or modest growth. If the standard of comparison is China's own historical experience, current rates of growth are high. Chinese agricultural production did not stagnate before 1949. Between the end of the fourteenth century and the middle of the twentieth century, historical records indicate that China's population grew from 65–80 million people to more than 500 million. These records also indicate that agricultural output kept pace with population partly because new lands were opened up to cultivation and land depopulated by Mongol devastation (in the twelfth and thirteenth centuries) was resettled, and partly because grain yields per hectare increased.[4]

Historically, however, annual growth rates never exceeded 1 percent and averaged less than 0.5 percent. Furthermore, by the twentieth century, and particularly by the 1950s, one of the main traditional ways of increasing output—expanding the area under cultivation—was no longer feasible except in limited areas of the far northeast, the last frontier area. The northeast had been opened up to Chinese migrants in the late nineteenth century, and by the 1950s the only virgin land left in any quantity was in Heilongjiang Province. Thus increased output had to come entirely from increased yields per hectare. In addition, because the population growth rate had more than doubled, grain yields had to increase more than 2 percent a year, five to ten times the rate achieved previously. In historical perspective, therefore, the agricultural growth since 1949 has been impressive.

In contemporary international perspective, however, China's agricultural performance is not particularly noteworthy. As many analysts have pointed out, Chinese agricultural growth rates are not much, if any, higher than those of India. For China, the real question is not whether growth is faster or slower than that of India, but whether Chinese farm output grew as much as its potential allowed, or whether it fell short because of mistakes in policy and performance.

Table 3-5. *Growth Rates of Agricultural Products*
(percent)

Product	1952–57	1957–65	1965–75	1975–80	1957–80	1981–82
Grain	3.5	0.0	3.9	2.8	2.1	4.9
Cotton	4.7	3.1	1.3	2.6	2.2	15.3
Oil-bearing seeds	0.0	−1.8	2.2	11.2	2.7	24.0
Sugarcane	7.6	3.2	4.5	6.5	3.5	27.2
Jute, ambary, hemp	−0.3	−0.9	9.6	9.4	5.8	−1.7
Silk cocoons	−1.9	−0.8	6.3	10.9	4.6	−1.9
Tea	6.3	−1.3	7.7	7.6	4.5	14.3
Hogs	10.2	1.7	6.7	1.7	3.3	−0.8
Sheep, goats	9.8	4.4	1.6	6.1	2.8	−1.5
Aquatic products	13.3	−0.5	4.0	0.4	1.6	7.0
Gross value of agricultural output	4.5	1.2	4.0	4.8	3.2	8.3

Sources: All growth rates are derived from data published by the State Statistical Bureau or from the Ministry of Agriculture, *Zhongguo nongye nianjian, 1980*, pp. 34–36, 309, 311, 316; State Statistical Bureau, *Statistical Yearbook of China, 1981*, pp. 145–47, and "Communique on the Fulfillment of China's 1982 National Economic Plan," April 29, 1983.

Grain versus Cash Crops

A strong case can be made that increasing agricultural output in China is a particularly difficult task and therefore that China's overall growth rate has been quite respectable under the circumstances. There are several ways of making this case. To begin with, several economies have achieved rapid rates of growth in the agricultural sector by concentrating on cash crops with a high value of output per hectare. Farmers in the Republic of Korea, for example, have achieved much of their high growth by concentrating on vegetables for the cities and on a few other cash crops. Rice has also done well, but the other grain crops have lagged far behind, and the gap between consumption and domestic supply has been made up by ever rising levels of grain imports. Much the same phenomenon can be observed in Japan.

Despite the government slogan about taking grain as the key link, Chinese farmers have also put greater emphasis on cash crops. The evidence of this shift is the higher rate of growth for most cash crops compared with that for grain between 1957 and 1980 (Table 3-5). There has also been a modest increase in acreage under cash crops (Table 3-6). These shifts have been particularly pronounced in 1981–82 after the agricultural responsibility system was introduced.

The tendency to favor cash crops, however, has not been uniform. After the Great Leap Forward, farmers shifted away from cash crops, presumably in an effort to meet their food requirements in the face of near famine conditions. Cash crops bounced back in 1965–75 and grew even more rapidly after 1975. The performance in 1965–75 is a bit surprising because the period is now criticized in the Chinese press for its overemphasis on grain.[5] It may be that Chinese farmers paid some

Table 3-6. *Share of Various Crops in Sown Acreage*
(percent)

Crop	1952	1957	1962	1965	1970	1975	1979	1981
Grain	87.8	85.0	86.7	83.5	83.1	80.9	80.3	79.2
Cash crops	8.8	9.2	6.3	8.5	8.2	9.0	10.0	12.1
Green manure	1.6	2.2	2.5	3.8	5.8	6.6	5.7	4.6
Other	1.8	3.6	4.5	4.2	2.9	4.5	4.0	4.1

Sources: Ministry of Agriculture, *Zhongguo nongye nianjian, 1980*, p. 349; and State Statistical Bureau, *Statistical Yearbook of China, 1981*, p. 144.

attention to incomes and profit from the more lucrative cash crops even when the political leadership disapproved.

Since 1977, however, the approved agricultural development strategy has emphasized cash crops and higher incomes. But does it follow that China can adopt the pattern set by Korea and Japan? A few simple calculations will show why growth based on crops other than grain is not a feasible strategy for China. To begin with, China's population during the next twenty years is likely to grow by at least 1 percent a year and will probably grow at a slightly higher rate. On top of this, if current development plans are successful, personal incomes are likely to grow at anywhere from 2 to 5 percent a year in real terms. Since Chinese incomes per capita are low, much of the increased income will be spent on food, either grain or items such as meat, which require grain as an input. Precise estimates of the income elasticity of demand for grain in China (direct and indirect) are not available, but a reasonable range for the next decade would be 0.4 to 0.5.[6] Thus, the demand for grain in China is likely to rise at a rate of at least 2.0 percent a year, more likely at an annual figure between 3 and 4 percent a year.

Even when China concentrated on increasing grain output, its grain imports in the latter half of the 1970s were running at 10 million tons a year, and in 1980 they had climbed to nearly 14 million tons. If, because of a greater shift to cash crops than has occurred to date, grain output grows at only 1 percent a year during the next two decades, the gap between demand and supply would be 2 to 3 percent a year. By the end of two decades China would either be importing nearly 200 million tons a year or would have had to reimpose tight (in contrast to the current very loose) grain rationing. The figure of 200 million tons may seem preposterous, but in 1979 Korea imported 145 kilograms of grain per capita. The same per capita figure applied to China would mean imports of 145 million tons or more. Clearly, China is not going to import so much grain.[7] World grain prices would skyrocket, and, in any case, China cannot afford the foreign exchange to import such large quantities even at current prices. This situation is not likely to change during the next decade or so. Tighter rationing is also not really a solution because rationing would undermine incentives and exacerbate already poor labor discipline.

China's Grain Yields Compared

It is clear that most of China's grain requirements for the foreseeable future must be met by domestic production. Further, to avoid shortages, domestic production of grain is likely to have to grow by at least 3 percent a year, the same rate as during 1965–80, but a higher rate than during 1957–80. Since most of this increase in output will have to come from increasing yields (for reasons that will be discussed below), one way to decide whether achieving a growth rate of 3 percent or higher is likely to be easy or difficult is to compare Chinese grain yields with those of other nations to determine whether what China must accomplish is ordinary (in a world context) or extraordinary.

The Chinese grow rice in areas where water is consistently plentiful, and rice yields are nearly as high as those of some of the most advanced rice producers (see Table 3-7). There are, to be sure, problems of comparability with these figures. Much of Japan and Korea produce only one crop of rice a year, or, where double cropping is possible, the second crop is usually wheat or barley. Parts of China, however, triple crop, with two crops of rice and one of wheat. Yields per sown hectare

Table 3-7. *International Comparisons of Grain Yields*
(kilograms per sown hectare)

Country or region	Rice (paddy)	Wheat	Corn
China (1979)	4,245	2,137.5	2,985
Highest-yielding provinces	5,257.5	3,570	4,515
	4,815	2,572.5	3,817.5
	4,777.5	2,490	3,420
Lowest-yielding provinces	3,645	1,567.5	2,565
	3,630	1,140	2,512.5
	3,562.5	1,057.5	2,122.5
Asia (1980)	2,800	1,631	2,242
India	2,049	1,437	1,103
Indonesia	3,187	n.a.	1,241
Korea	4,918	3,286	4,600
Japan	5,128	3,052	3,000
United States (1980)	4,935	2,249	5,711
Africa (1980)	1,714	1,024	1,222
World (1980)	2,750	1,873	2,995

Note: The Chinese rice figures are the average yields for paddy in the richest and poorest provinces excluding those with less than 1 million hectares in rice. The comparable cutoff for wheat and corn was 500,000 hectares.

n.a. Not available.

Sources: Ministry of Agriculture, *Zhongguo nongye nianjian, 1980*, pp. 103–06. The world figures are from FAO, *FAO Production Yearbook, 1980* (Rome, 1981), pp. 96–99, 102–03. The international data are for 1980 and the Chinese data for 1979.

Table 3-8. *Rice Acreage, Output, and Yield*

Item	1949	1952	1957	1965	1975	1979	1981
Production (million tons of paddy)	48.65	68.43	86.78	87.72	125.56	143.75	143.96
Sown acreage in rice (millions of hectares)	25.71	28.38	32.24	29.82	35.73	33.87	33.29
Arable acreage in rice (millions of hectares)	23.24	n.a.	25.34	n.a.	21.20[a]	n.a.	n.a.
Double cropping index for rice	111	n.a.	127	n.a.	170[a]	n.a.	n.a.
Yield per sown hectare (tons)	1.89	2.42	2.69	2.94	3.47[a]	4.25	4.32
Yield per arable hectare (tons)	2.09	n.a.	3.43	n.a.	5.9[a]	n.a.	n.a.

n.a. Not available.

a. Data are for 1976.

Sources: State Statistical Bureau, *Ten Great Years*, pp. 119–129; State Statistical Bureau, *Statistical Yearbook of China, 1981*, pp. 141, 145, 156; *Peking Review* (October 28, 1977), pp. 29–30; and *Zhongguo nongye nianjian, 1980*, pp. 34–35. The 1957 double cropping data were derived from provincial data [for sources, see Dwight H. Perkins, *Agricultural Development in China, 1368–1968* (Chicago: Aldine, 1969), p. 44]. Most of the figures for 1975 were derived from percentage increases over 1949 or through other data manipulations, and some of the figures are for 1976.

on this triple-cropped land are not particularly impressive, but total output per year or the yields per arable hectare in several large provinces are actually above those of Korea and are similar to those of Japan's heavily subsidized rice farmers (see Table 3-8). Since Chinese rice yields are already so high, it will probably be more difficult to increase yields further than it would be in a country with lower yields, such as India. It is not that China is close to some biological limit—far from it. It is simply that China already uses many of the known methods of increasing rice yields, and further increases will involve the use of untried or currently unknown techniques, such as the experiments with hybrid rice.

Yields of crops other than rice may not be quite so impressive, but still stand up quite well to international comparison (Table 3-7). As is the case for rice, there are great differences in yields of particular crops between regions.

Despite the fact that Chinese grain yields are fairly high by international standards, increases in yields per hectare account for all of the increased output so far. In fact, as the data in Table 3-9 indicate, sown acreage in grain actually declined by more than 10 percent from 1955–

Table 3-9. *Sown Acreage in Grain Crops*
(thousands of hectares)

Crop	1955–57	1979	Ratio 1979/1955–57
Rice	31,575	33,873	1.07
Wheat	27,184	29,357	1.08
Corn	15,748	20,133	1.28
Potatoes	10,514	10,952	1.04
Coarse grains	36,170	17,701	0.49
Soybeans	12,079	7,247	0.60
All grains	133,270	119,263	0.89

Sources: N. R. Chen, *Chinese Economic Statistics* (Chicago: Aldine, 1967), pp. 286–87; and Ministry of Agriculture, *Zhongguo nongye nianjian, 1980*, pp. 101–07.

57 to 1979, and there have been further declines since, as farmers have switched to cash crops.

Yields for grain increased for two reasons. Improved varieties and more inputs (discussed in the next chapter) increased the average yield of all major grain crops (Table 3-10). Wheat and corn yields increased most rapidly, as plant scientists worked to close the gap between China and the more advanced countries. The other source of overall yield increase was the switch to higher yielding grains, notably rice, wheat, and corn. Between 1955–57 and 1979, 98 percent of the total increase in output was accounted for by these three crops (Table 3-11). Coarse grain yields rose almost as fast as the overall average increase, but

Table 3-10. *Grain Yields and Growth Rates*

Crop	1955–57 (kilograms per hectare)	1979 (kilograms per hectare)	Annual growth rate (percent)
Rice	2,614	4,245	2.1
Wheat	875.5	2,137.5	4.0
Corn	1,376	2,985	3.4
Potatoes[a]	1,588	2,595	2.2
Coarse grains[b]	886	1,594	2.6
Soybeans	812	1,027.5	1.0
All grains	1,492	2,782.5	2.7

a. Potatoes have been converted to one-fifth their actual gross weight (the 1957 figures were converted from the original data at one-quarter gross weight).

b. Coarse grains include millet, sorghum, and other unspecified grains, but not corn.

Sources: Chen, *Chinese Economic Statistics*, pp. 318–19; and Ministry of Agriculture, *Zhongguo nongye nianjian, 1980*, pp. 101–07.

Table 3-11. *Composition of Increases in Grain Output*
(thousands of metric tons)

Crop	1955–57	1979	Growth (1979 over 1955–57) Amount	Share (percent)
Rice	82,417	143,750	61,333	43.4
Wheat	23,800	62,280	38,480	27.2
Corn	21,609	60,035	38,426	27.2
Potatoes	20,883	28,410	7,527	5.3
Coarse grains	32,057	28,210	− 3,847	− 2.7
Soybeans	9,800	7,460	− 2,340	− 1.7
Other[a]	n.a.	1,970	n.a.	1.4
All grains	190,733	332,115	141,382	100.0

n.a. Not available.

a. This is an unexplained residual in the 1979 data.

Sources: Chen, *Chinese Economic Statistics*, pp. 338–39; and Ministry of Agriculture, *Zhongguo nongye nianjian, 1980*, pp. 101–07.

farmers cut acreage in these crops by half. Soybeans, treated here as a grain following Chinese reporting practices, experienced only modest yield increases and suffered a sharp decline in sown acreage.

One of the fundamental questions for the future is whether China can continue to sustain this rate of increase in grain yields. Further shifts away from coarse grains seem sure to slow down if for no other reason than that there is not much land left that can be shifted. Soybeans should not fall further unless China intends to rely increasingly on imports for this important component in the typical Chinese diet. Potatoes will not pick up the slack because Chinese eat potatoes only as a last resort. Thus future growth will depend even more than in the past on what happens to rice, wheat, and corn yields. Since the yields of these three crops are already high by international standards, China will have to be among the world leaders in research on new plant varieties if grain output is to continue to grow at rates comparable with those achieved in the past.

One way to increase future yields may be to spread the most modern techniques to the more backward regions within China. Yields vary enormously between provinces. Yield per arable hectare in the highest-yielding province (Zhejiang) for all grains taken together was eight times the level of the lowest-yielding province (Inner Mongolia) in 1979 (see Appendix A, Table A-5).

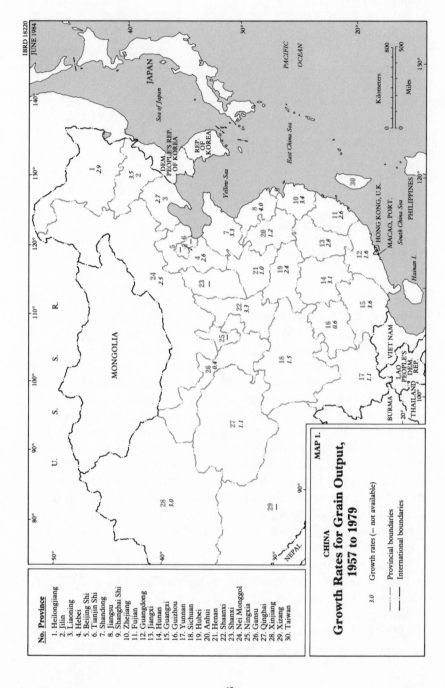

No. Province

1. Heilongjiang
2. Jilin
3. Liaoning
4. Hebei
5. Beijing Shi
6. Tianjin Shi
7. Shandong
8. Jiangsu
9. Shanghai Shi
10. Zhejiang
11. Fujian
12. Guangdong
13. Jiangxi
14. Hunan
15. Guangxi
16. Guizhou
17. Yunnan
18. Sichuan
19. Hubei
20. Anhui
21. Henan
22. Shaanxi
23. Shanxi
24. Nei Monggol
25. Ningxia
26. Gansu
27. Qinghai
28. Xinjiang
29. Xizang
30. Taiwan

CHINA

MAP 1.

Growth Rates for Grain Output, 1957 to 1979

3.0   Growth rates (— not available)

······   Provincial boundaries

———   International boundaries

IBRD 18220
JUNE 1984

Regional growth rates for grain output indicate, however, that it will not be easy to increase yields in the low-yielding provinces to anything like the levels achieved in the southern and eastern coastal provinces where, among other things, water is plentiful. In fact, as the data in Map 1 indicate, the provinces with rapidly increasing yields during 1957–79, in many cases, already had been producing high yields in the 1950s. Most of the provinces with rapidly increasing grain yields either were located on the Chinese coast, experienced substantial immigration into regions with low ratios of man to land (Xinjiang, Inner Mongolia, Jilin, and Heilongjiang), or were rich rice regions (Hubei, Hunan, Jiangxi). The regions of slow growth were mainly the west and the chronically poor interior and dry provinces of Anhui and Henan on the North China Plain. In other words, there was a positive correlation between the grain growth rates for 1957–79 and the level of yields in 1957.[8] The standard deviation for grain yields among provinces actually increased between 1957 and 1979, although the deviation divided by the mean yield showed some decline.[9]

If slow growth in China's northwestern and southwestern provinces was largely the result of a more traditional outlook among peasant farmers, the growth rate of yields might be expected to accelerate as this outlook eroded. Although a case can be made that China's western interior is in fact more backward in these respects than the coast, it is doubtful that inherited values are at the heart of the yield problem in the region. The northwest is too far from the coast to benefit from annual monsoon rains, and the area's rivers carry relatively little water. Much of the southwest has adequate rainfall and large rivers, but the region is mountainous. Thus low yields and low output in China more often reflect particularly intractable natural conditions rather than a lack of imagination or skill on the part of local farmers.

Notes to Chapter 3

1. Information supplied to the American Economics Delegation in October 1979. A brief description of the Chinese statistical system is also contained in State Statistical Bureau, *The Present Conditions of the Statistical Work in China* (Beijing, 1981). See also Francis C. Tuan and Frederick W. Crook, *Planning and Statistical Systems in Chinese Agriculture* (Washington, D.C.: U.S. Department of Agriculture, 1983).

2. A careful attempt to compile and analyze the sometimes conflicting figures for particular crops and inputs before the publication of more complete data in the 1980s was made by Bruce Stone, "A Review of Chinese Agricultural Statistics, 1949–1978," in Anthony M. Tang and Bruce Stone, *Food Production in the People's Republic of China* (Washington, D.C.: International Food Policy Research Institute, 1980).

3. For a recent look at the nature of cycles in Chinese agriculture, see Anthony M. Tang, "Trend, Policy Cycle, and Weather Disturbance in Chinese Agriculture, 1952–1978," *American Journal of Agricultural Economics*, vol. 62, no. 2 (1980), pp. 334–48.

4. This historical discussion is based on Dwight H. Perkins, *Agricultural Development in China, 1368–1968* (Chicago: Aldine, 1969). Chinese advances over the ages in pelletizing seeds, improving and mechanizing sowing practices, and developing fertilizers are described in F. Bray, "Agriculture," in J. Needham, *Science and Civilization in China*, vol. 6, *Biology and Biological Technology*, part 2 (Cambridge: Cambridge University Press, 1984), pp. 241–98.

5. This literature and some of the implications of a neglect of regional comparative advantage are discussed in Nicholas Lardy, "Comparative Advantage, Internal Trade, and Distribution of Income in Chinese Agriculture," Yale University, 1982, processed.

6. If Chinese income doubles during the next two decades, current income elasticities of demand for grain (including grain to feed animals and for alcohol) will fall from current levels, probably around 0.5–0.6, to about 0.3–0.4. These figures are not formal estimates, but were derived from international experience based on a discussion with C. Peter Timmer.

7. For a more substantial discussion of China's grain trade policies and prospects, see A. Doak Barnett, *China's Economy in Global Perspective* (Washington, D.C.: Brookings Institution, 1981), chap. 3.

8. If the 1957–79 growth rate for grain is taken as the dependent variable (y) and 1957 provincial average yield as the dependent variable (x), the regression for the twenty-two provinces for which data are available is ($y = 1.957 + 0.155x$) ($r = 0.236$). Data are from Appendix A, Tables A-1 and A-5.

9. The standard deviation (σ_x) for 1957 yields was 1.589 and for 1979 was 2.351; divided by the mean, the figures are 0.74 for 1957 and 0.55 for 1979.

Chapter 4

~~~~~~

Sources of Agricultural Growth

AGRICULTURAL GROWTH RATES have kept ahead of population growth rates during the past decade and a half in China. Despite this performance, however, per capita Chinese agricultural product is still only marginally above the subsistence levels of some of the world's poorer nations. In 1952, for example, Chinese per capita crop output was only 25 to 29 percent above that of India, and a comparison for the 1970s would yield similar results.[1] China, therefore, has never had the luxury that some countries have had of being able to ignore agricultural production problems to concentrate resources on developing industry. Agricultural policies in the Soviet Union in the 1930s and 1940s, for example, were geared not to increasing farm output, but to extracting a larger agricultural surplus for industry. For China, the issue has never been *whether* to put a major effort into raising agricultural product, but *how* to go about doing it.

There are two levels at which the question of how to raise agricultural output can be addressed. At one level are the direct inputs into production, such as land, labor, and various forms of capital. Plants will not grow unless they have land to grow on and water and chemical nutrients to feed them. At a second level is the issue of how to organize society to effectively mobilize and efficiently use these inputs. Is farm labor, for example, best mobilized under a system of individual family farms, or can more be achieved by the collective efforts of dozens or hundreds of families working together within a cooperative? Policies at the two levels are, of course, related. Chemical fertilizer can be applied to crops only within the framework of a rural organization of some kind, and no amount of imagination applied to reorganizing rural society will affect output unless the use of such inputs as chemical fertilizer is increased. Still, the issues that dominate discussion at the first level are fundamentally different from those at the second level and are best treated separately.

Controversy has pervaded Chinese discussion of agricultural strategy at both levels. This chapter focuses on the first-level issues of which direct inputs have had the greatest effect on output. The second-level questions of how best to organize rural society to achieve production and other goals are the subject of the following chapter.

The Analytical Framework

Analysis of the sources of agricultural growth at the first level has two purposes. One purpose is simply to identify which inputs contributed how much to increases in production. The second purpose is to estimate whether the productivity of those inputs has risen, fallen, or remained constant.

There are two standard ways of estimating the contribution of individual factor inputs and total factor productivity in agriculture. One method is to use econometric techniques to formally estimate an agricultural production function. The other is to add up individual input series using value weights based on the prices of the various inputs and then to divide that aggregate input index into an output index to obtain an index of total factor productivity. If the prices of individual inputs equal their marginal product, as would be the case under perfect market conditions, then the two methods should give similar results.

The few attempts made to estimate Chinese agricultural production functions econometrically have not been very successful. The only large cross-sectional sample of data on farms available to scholars outside of China was collected by J. L. Buck and his collaborators in the 1930s. For the period after 1949 there are the national time series estimates of inputs and outputs and a cross section of provincial data for a few years in the 1950s. Econometric estimates using these data have not yielded plausible production functions.

The economist interested in factor productivity in Chinese agriculture, therefore, is left with what is in essence an accounting exercise. This exercise can be divided into three parts:

1. What is the increase in output that is being analyzed? Estimating Chinese agricultural output was the subject of Chapter 3.
2. What are the inputs that have contributed to that growth, and how much has each input grown during the period being analyzed? This step involves deriving an annual series for each input. Much of this chapter is devoted to presenting estimates for key inputs.
3. What weights should be used to add up these inputs into one aggregate input index?

The issue here is whether it is possible to derive plausible estimates of the marginal product of each input for the period being considered. Market prices are an appropriate estimate of marginal product if the inputs are sold in perfect markets to farmers who wish to maximize their profits. Such an assumption is clearly invalid for labor inputs and much of fixed capital as well. For purchased inputs, such as chemical fertilizer and certain kinds of machinery, the perfect market assumptions are less dubious, but still give at best a vague approximation of decisionmaking processes in Chinese communes.

The following analysis, therefore, begins with the general production function

$$Q = F(L, L_d, K, C, t)$$

where Q = agricultural output, L = labor, L_d = land, K = capital, C = current inputs, and t = time.

Differentiating with respect to time the equation becomes,

$$\frac{dQ}{dt} = \frac{\partial F}{\partial t} + \left(\frac{\partial F}{\partial L} \cdot \frac{dL}{dt} \right) + \left(\frac{\partial F}{\partial L_d} \cdot \frac{dL_d}{dt} \right)$$

$$+ \left(\frac{\partial F}{\partial K} \cdot \frac{dK}{dt} \right) + \left(\frac{\partial F}{\partial C} \cdot \frac{dC}{dt} \right).$$

The question then becomes whether plausible estimates can be made for each of the variables in this equation except for $\partial F/\partial t$, which is derived as a residual. A more elaborate version of this equation would further subdivide these inputs into modern inputs (chemical fertilizer and power machinery) and traditional inputs (organic fertilizer and labor with shovels and hoes). In China, debate over the contribution of different inputs occurred on two levels. On one level was the issue of how production could be augmented by the massive application of traditional inputs. Controversy on the second level accepted the need for modern inputs, but debated whether to emphasize the biological package (chemicals combined with improved plant varieties) or the mechanical package (labor-saving machinery of various kinds).

Historical Perspective on the Traditional Inputs

A brief historical account of China's agriculture helps to explain the contribution of land to increases in agricultural output or, more accurately, the contribution of land plus water, since land is of little use for crops without water. This historical perspective also helps to explain why traditional inputs alone were not likely to solve China's agricultural production problem.[2]

Expansion of Cultivated Land

China was not always a nation of 800 million farmers and their families. In the fourteenth century the population of China was about 65 million to 80 million, of whom perhaps 55 million to 70 million lived on farms. Most of these people lived in the southern half of the country because successive Mongol invasions had largely depopulated the north. From 1400 until the 1850s China enjoyed long periods of comparative peace, interrupted occasionally by local rebellions and, significantly, by the fall of the Ming dynasty and the rise of the Qing in the 1640s. During periods of peace birth rates were well above death rates, and population grew slowly but inexorably until it passed 400 million around 1800. The Taiping Rebellion and the Japanese invasion of 1937 combined to reverse or slow population growth, and by 1949 China's population had risen only another 35 percent to 540 million.

As population grew, people migrated back to the devastated lands of the north. There were few barriers to migration. By 1700 Chinese territory encompassed most of the land within China's present borders, plus some areas now lost. Ethnic minorities hostile to the dominant Han Chinese were driven into the mountains or absorbed. Few wealthy landowners attempted to keep large tracts of land in pasture as has been done in Latin America. Only in the northeast was Han Chinese migration prohibited by the ruling Manchus, who wished to keep their ancient hunting preserves intact. But even the restriction on migration into the northeast broke down in the latter part of the nineteenth century and was then abolished altogether. By 1953 there were 42 million people in the former Manchu homeland.

Thus, the Chinese spent six centuries searching for new land to develop, and by 1950 there was not much unoccupied land left. In the northernmost reaches of the northeast, however, there were still forests to be cut down and land to be pioneered. There were also enormous tracts of land in the northwest, but most were desert, exploitable only after expensive investments to bring water from nearby and not-so-nearby mountains. Nor could Chinese farmers push crops farther up the sides of hills and mountains. That effort had been pursued for centuries as well, to a point where sensible conservation policies required a partial retreat back down the mountainside so trees could be replanted and erosion reduced.

The Problem of Water Supply

The lack of new lands to be opened up to crops was only part of the problem. Most of China's arable land had been farmed for centuries, with improved methods gradually being introduced to extract higher yields from this most limited resource. In much of the southern half of China, for example, small reservoirs had been built on hills, with irrigation channels running down to neighboring fields. By using such methods, Chinese farmers succeeded in irrigating half to two-thirds of the cultivated acreage in the regions of the Yangtze River on south by the early 1900s. Centuries ago rice yields in these areas were already far above levels found in much of Southeast Asia and India today.

There thus was nothing new about the idea of mobilizing surplus rural labor to construct public works. What was different about the plans of the People's Republic was the scale of the effort. Billions and even tens of billions of man-days per year were to be devoted to rural construction.

For this effort to be successful there first had to be a pool of underemployed labor, and, at least in the off-season, large numbers of farm workers had to be unemployed or occupied in very low-productivity activities. Second, the Chinese leadership had to devise a way to mobilize this labor. Finally, there had to be productive activities for this labor force to do.

China is in the temperate zone, and, at least in the north, the winters are cold and dry. In the 1930s able-bodied male farm workers were idle an average of only 1.6 months a year, with 80 percent of this time between November and February.[3] Even in the winter months in the north farmers were engaged in some productive activities, ranging from repair of equipment to household handicrafts. Nevertheless, farmers were idle in these months perhaps as much as one-third of their working

days. In the early 1950s, therefore, there were several billion man-days
of idle labor available to be mobilized if a means to do so could be
devised.[4]

The methods used to mobilize this labor were the agricultural producers' cooperative and, after 1958, the rural people's commune. The
reasons cooperatives and communes were seen to be particularly useful
for mobilizing rural surplus labor are the subject of the next chapter on
organizational reform. For now, it is enough to know that collectivization successfully increased the amount of available labor. Billions of
man-days went into rural construction efforts, and there were many
experiments with deeper plowing, closer planting, and other new techniques. The effect of all this effort on agricultural output, however, was
the reverse of what had been expected. In 1960, grain output fell by
more than 25 percent and did not fully recover to the levels of 1957–58
until five years later. Although reliable data are not available, evidence
suggests that nongrain farm output fell by even more.

Labor mobilization for rural public works did not, by itself, lead
China into a period of sustained agricultural development because it was
based on an inadequate understanding of China's agricultural problem.
Farmers must have land, and the land must have water. Rural public
works are one important way to bring new land under cultivation by
building irrigation systems to provide that land with water. This is an
obvious point and one that was well understood by both Chinese
farmers and officials at least as early as the Song dynasty (960–1275
A.D.). The result, at least in southern China, was a gradual expansion of
the irrigated acreage by construction of local systems to control water to
the fields. But most of the land that could be put in crops had long since
been developed. What then was left to do for the labor mobilized by
cooperatives and communes?

The answer in the southern half of China was to improve most of the
water management systems and to extend new systems into the few
remaining regions in which this was possible. In the north there were
also a few areas where labor mobilization alone was sufficient to transform a local area. Along the Taihang Mountains, in such areas as
Xiyang and Lin counties, where such national models as the Dazhai
Brigade were located, truly remarkable achievements were recorded. In
Lin County a canal several tens of kilometers long was dug out of the
sides of a cliff to bring an ample supply of water to formerly parched
land. Little capital equipment was used other than picks, shovels, and a
little dynamite.

The problem was that for most of the northern regions of China the water shortage could not be alleviated significantly by such measures. China's monsoon climate causes southern coastal regions to receive semitropical levels of rainfall, but the north receives much smaller amounts, and in some years the monsoon rains do not come at all. In some of the populated regions of the north, farmers attempt to raise crops where average annual rainfall is less than 250 millimeters, and elsewhere they make do on less than 500 millimeters. Nor are the rivers in north China of much help. The annual discharge of the Yellow River, by far the longest river in the north, is less than one-twentieth the discharge of the Yangtze.[5] Furthermore, the Yellow River is one of the most silt-laden in the world. As a result, little water from the river is available for irrigation, because the silt must first be removed or it will clog the irrigation channels. Silt cannot be removed by local action on the lower reaches of the river. Therefore, reforestation, grassland development, and the construction of numerous dams on the less populated upper reaches is required, an effort that is in its early stages and will take more inputs than labor alone to be successful.[6]

Even if the rural public works of the Great Leap Forward (1958–59) had been carried out after careful planning on the basis of systematic designs, it is unlikely that such methods would have had a significant positive effect on agriculture in northern China. In fact, many projects were carried out on the basis of poorly conceived designs and frequently did as much harm as good.[7] As data in Table 4-1 indicate, by the time recovery from the crisis of 1959–61 was more or less complete, there was actually less total arable land and irrigated portions of that land than before the Great Leap in 1957. The expansion in irrigated acreage after 1965 occurred not as a result of rural public works projects, but primarily because of a program of tube well development on the North China Plain. Not only did China have one of the smallest amounts of land per capita in the world (see Table 4-2), but the amount of land under cultivation was actually declining, and the amount of irrigated land was increasing less than 1 percent a year.

Increases in Modern Inputs

Although efforts to mobilize surplus labor for rural public works have continued, during the past two decades Chinese agriculture has been characterized by large increases in the use of modern inputs. Much of the increase in production can be explained by these inputs.

The following section is largely a description of how inputs have

Table 4-1. *Acreage Data*
(millions of hectares)

Year	Cultivated acreage[a]	Irrigated acreage Total	Power irrigated
1949	97.9	16.0	n.a.
1952	107.9	20.0	0.3
1957	111.8	27.3	1.2
1962	n.a.	30.5	6.1
1965	103.6	33.1	8.1
1970	n.a.	36.0	n.a.
1975	99.7	43.3	n.a.
1979	99.5	45.0	25.3
1981	n.a.	44.6	25.2

n.a. Not available.
a. Chinese cultivated acreage is widely believed to be underreported.
Sources: Cultivated acreage data are from *Zhongguo jingji nianjian, 1981*, p. vi-9, which states that the figures are biased downward. Irrigated acreage figures are for "effectively irrigated area" and are from Ministry of Agriculture, *Zhongguo nongye nianjian, 1980*, p. 345, except for 1949, which is from State Statistical Bureau, *Ten Great Years* (1960), p. 130. Power irrigation figures are from State Statistical Bureau, *Statistical Yearbook of China, 1981* (Hong Kong: Economic Information Agency, 1982), p. 185.

Table 4-2. *International Comparisons of Arable Land per Capita*
(hectares per person)

Region or country	Arable land per capita	Arable land per capita of farm population
China	0.10	0.12
World	0.38	0.82
Asia (excluding China)	0.24	0.44
Korea, Republic of	0.07	0.15
India	0.27	0.44
Japan	0.05	0.27
United States	0.97	27.50

Sources: Except for China, the arable land figures are for 1974. The population data are for 1975, and the agricultural population figures are for 1970 (FAO, *FAO Production Yearbook, 1975*, various pages). The Chinese figures are based on arable land of 99.5 million hectares, a total population of 971 million, and agricultural population of 842 million (the 1979 figures).

increased since the early 1960s and a qualitative analysis of the kinds of technical barriers already overcome or still to be surmounted. The section is followed by a quantitative analysis within the consistent framework introduced at the beginning of this chapter.

The Biological Package

The argument that increases in modern inputs have accounted for much of the increase in Chinese agricultural output rests first of all on the rapid rise in the use of chemical fertilizers since the crisis years of 1959–61. Fertilizer, of course, does not do its work alone, but as part of a package that includes improved plant varieties, timely supplies of water, pesticides, and other changes in farming practices.

Data on Chinese chemical fertilizer production and imports are presented in Table 4-3. During the entire nineteen years from 1962 to 1980, production of chemical fertilizer increased an average of about 19 percent a year. Imports grew at an average rate of 25 percent until 1970, but slowed to less than 2 percent after that. There is a problem with these figures, however. Until 1977 Chinese chemical fertilizer was reported in terms of gross weight instead of tons of nutrient. Because much of China's chemical fertilizer is manufactured in small-scale plants whose output is low in nutrient content, the gross weight figures give a somewhat exaggerated picture of the actual amount of nutrients available to Chinese farmers. Most of the output of small-scale nitrogenous fertilizer enterprises, for example, is ammonium bicarbonate, with a nitrogen content of only 17.5 percent. In contrast, urea, the main product of the recently imported large-scale plants, is 46 percent nitrogen. Because the share of fertilizer from small-scale plants rose steadily throughout the late 1960s and 1970s, the rate of increase in available nutrient was less than that of gross output. As the large plants came on line the reverse was the case, but China's State Statistical Bureau began reporting output in terms of nutrient only after 1977.

Chemical fertilizer, of course, is not the only source of plant nutrients. One of the gains from labor mobilization under the communes has been a large increase in the availability of organic fertilizers. Surveys providing reliable estimates of organic fertilizer use are not available, but visitor reports support the view that large amounts are collected and applied to the fields. Hogs and draft animals would account for a large part of organic supplies, but the communes make prodigious use of grasses, river mud, and any number of similar sources.[8] Since the number of hogs increased from 84 million head in 1957 to 305 million

Table 4-3. *Chemical Fertilizer Production and Imports*
(millions of metric tons)

	Production		Imports		
Year	Standardized gross weight	Nutrient	Standardized gross weight	Nutrient	Consumption, nutrient
1949	0.03	0.006	0.12[a]	(0.02)	0.026
1952	0.19	0.04	0.21	(0.04)	0.08
1957	0.74	0.15	1.22	(0.27)	0.37
1962	2.31	0.46	1.24	(0.24)	0.63
1965	8.77	1.73	2.73	(0.64)	1.94
1970	12.31	2.44	6.42	(1.48)	(3.92)
1975	28.50	5.25	4.94	(1.15)	(6.40)
1979	52.16	10.65	8.39	1.72	10.86
1980	n.a.	12.32	10.02	(2.00)	12.69
1982	n.a.	12.78	11.11	(2.22)	15.13

Note: Figures in parentheses on nutrient imports and total consumption were derived by taking 20 percent of the gross weight of imports or supply.

a. Figure is for 1950.

Sources: Production data: Ministry of Agriculture, *Zhongguo nongye nianjian, 1980*, p. 338, except for 1980, which is from State Statistical Bureau, "Report on the Results of the 1980 National Economic Plan," April 29, 1981, and 1982, which is from State Statistical Bureau, "Communique on Fulfillment of China's 1982 National Economic Plan," April 29, 1983.

Imports: State Statistical Bureau, *Statistical Yearbook of China, 1981* and *1983*, p. 386 and p. 436, respectively.

Consumption: The 1952–65 and 1979–82 figures are from State Statistical Bureau, *Statistical Yearbook of China, 1981*, p. 185; and State Statistical Bureau, "Communique on Fulfillment of China's 1982 National Economic Plan," April 29, 1983. The 1949 and 1970–75 figures were derived by adding imports to production.

head in 1980, by 1980 manure from hogs may have provided an additional 2 million tons of nitrogen to China's soil.[9] Much of this presumably was used on private plots since most hogs were privately raised.

If chemical fertilizer production plus imports provided 128 kilograms of nutrient per hectare of arable land as of 1980, it is likely that organic sources raised this total to nearly 200 kilograms.[10] Thus, compared with other countries, China already has one of the world's highest rates of fertilizer use per hectare (Table 4-4).

For chemical fertilizer to have a large effect on yields, it must be used on plant varieties that respond to fertilizer. Research to develop new varieties appropriate for China began in the 1920s.[11] In addition, research in Japan and on Japanese-controlled Taiwan was of direct relevance to at least the rice-growing areas of China. China's own research effort was expanded greatly after 1949, building on this early base. By the early 1960s China already had dwarf high-yielding varieties of rice, well before the International Rice Research Institute in the Philippines was even established.

These high-yielding varieties of rice were quickly accepted by Chinese farmers. The commune system, for all its managerial problems, has proved to be an effective system for spreading new techniques. In individual peasant agriculture a major barrier to the adoption of new methods is the gap between the extension worker who knows the new technology and individual farmers who must decide whether to use it. If the extension worker knows his business, and if he has gained the farmers' trust through regular contact, the gap is closed and new techniques spread rapidly. If the extension worker is poorly trained and sees the extension service as a vehicle for escaping to a white-collar job in an urban bureaucracy, however, the gap becomes a yawning gulf.

The commune system helps to bridge this gulf in several ways. Most important, the brigades and communes have one or more of their members trained in the new techniques. The extension worker, instead of being a stranger who must build trust, is one of the village's own and a key figure in deciding which plant varieties to use. Further, because another barrier to the adoption of new methods is the risk of failure, the

Table 4-4. *International Comparisons of Agricultural Inputs*

Region or country	Chemical fertilizer consumption (NPK per hectare in kilograms)[a]	Arable land per hand tractor (hectares)
China	127.8	59.5
World	65.9	n.a.
Asia	37.2	n.a.
Japan	380.1	1.66
Korea, Republic of	304.0	40.31
India	25.9	n.a.

n.a. Not available.

NPK refers to nitrogen, phosphate, and potassium.

Sources: Chemical fertilizer: the Chinese figure is for 1980 and is in the State Statistical Bureau release of April 29, 1981. The other data are for 1977–78 and are from United Nations, *Statistical Yearbook 1978* (New York, 1978), pp. 643–51.

Hand or garden tractors: FAO, *FAO Production Yearbook, 1975*, p. 292. In China in 1979 there were 1.671 million hand tractors (Ministry of Agriculture, *Zhongguo nongye nianjian, 1980*, p. 341) for use on 99.5 million hectares of arable land.

commune can reduce this risk by sharing it among all members. Each team or brigade can have its own experimental plot. One possible problem with the household-based responsibility system introduced in the early 1980s is that it could weaken the incentives for individuals to become extension workers. On the other hand, the strengthening of the profit motive may accelerate the search for improved varieties even with a weakened extension system.

Where appropriate high-yielding varieties existed—as with rice—the pace of adoption was rapid. Even in the early 1960s, however, there were problems with the research end of the system. Research efforts concentrated on rice and a few other important grain crops, but miscellaneous grains, such as sorghum and millet, received less attention, and vegetables received hardly any research time at all.

The Cultural Revolution after 1966 had the laudable objective of breaking down the isolation of agricultural research scientists from an awareness of the real needs of the countryside. No longer could these scientists hide away in their laboratories. They were required to spend a large portion of their time in the fields, and their laboratories and agricultural schools were to be relocated in the countryside. Like so much else that happened during the Cultural Revolution, a reasonable objective was implemented in such an extreme way that its only real effect was to destroy China's agricultural research effort. Even by the mid-1970s Chinese agricultural research had yet to recover from the attacks of the late 1960s. Research centers existed, but visiting foreign delegations found little in the way of basic research likely to lead to a new generation of high-yielding varieties.[12] Only after 1976 was a real effort made to put scientists back in their labs and fields and to provide them with research support. In the meantime a decade had passed when no new scientists had been trained, and the skills of existing scientists had rusted. Much of China's senior agricultural research establishment still depended on scientists trained in the West before 1949.

By the late 1970s, therefore, China had made substantial, but uneven, progress in applying the biological package to the goal of raising crop yields. The progress was considered substantial because, as Chapter 3 indicated, yields of rice in the most advanced regions of the country matched those of such international leaders as Japan; it was considered uneven because yields of some other grain and nongrain crops were not particularly high by world standards. Although there are many explanations for these low yields, including the lack of water in the north, there is little doubt that the lack of appropriate high-yielding plant varieties is an important contributing factor.

In looking to the future, this past performance has both its positive and negative sides. On the negative side, China has been living off of scientific progress that is now roughly two decades old. There may be considerable unrealized potential in these plant varieties developed long ago, but there are grounds for skepticism about this. On the positive side, the lack of progress in the development of improved varieties of several crops probably means that a systematic scientific effort will lead to significant breakthroughs in the future. It will take time to rebuild China's research apparatus, and, once rebuilt, scientific breakthroughs will take time; but once achieved, the commune system as it existed before 1980 was well-suited for assuring their speedy adoption. It remains to be seen whether the extension process will work equally well under the household-based responsibility system established in the early 1980s.

The Mechanical Package

Countries with large amounts of rural labor and comparatively little land usually do not expend large resources on agricultural mechanization. Such mechanization, however, has been on the minds of China's leaders since the mid-1950s, when it was used as one of the economic justifications for pushing ahead with collectivization. Individual peasant families, it was then argued, had neither the funds to pay for machinery nor large enough plots to use machinery efficiently. By the 1970s mechanization had once again become a centerpiece of the discussions over agricultural policy.

China's push for farm mechanization in the 1970s did not result from any growing shortage of labor for farm work. As the estimates in Table 4-5 make clear, China's agricultural labor force grew substantially during the past quarter century, roughly 2.0 percent a year or about the same rate as population growth. Furthermore, there is little doubt that as this labor force rose the marginal product of labor in China's countryside fell. The data presented in Table 4-6 clearly indicate how the average net value of a day's work declined after 1965. These figures actually understate the decline, since they are in current prices, and the purchase of farm products rose substantially after 1957. Appendix B uses these figures and others to derive a plausible estimate of the marginal product of China's rural labor force. Suffice it to say that the marginal product, although not zero, was low and falling. Talk of a rural labor shortage, common during the late 1960s and early 1970s, did not reflect a growing gap between labor supply and demand, but indicated only that rural construction projects characterized by low productivity could always use more workers, crops could be weeded one more time, and more water could be carried to the fields.

Despite this large and growing supply of labor in the countryside, farm mechanization got under way in earnest in the 1960s and accelerated in the 1970s. The data on rural electric power consumption in Table 4-7 are as good an indicator as any, since most such power is used

Table 4-5. *Rural Labor Force*
(millions of persons)

Year	Total labor force (1)	Agricultural labor force (2)	(2) ÷ (1) (percent) (3)
1952	207.39	173.17	83.5
1957	237.68	193.10	81.2
1962	259.17	212.78	82.1
1965	286.74	233.98	81.6
1970	344.23	278.14	80.8
1975	381.61	294.60	77.2
1979	405.86	294.25	72.5
1981	432.80	303.10	70.0

Sources: Zhongguo nongye nianjian, 1980, p. 4. The 1981 agricultural figure is from State Statistical Bureau, *Statistical Yearbook of China, 1981*, p. 106 and includes only rural workers who work in agriculture, forestry, water conservancy, and meteorology.

Table 4-6. *Collective Income per Capita, per Day, and per Mu*
(yuan)

Year	Gross output per mu	Cost per mu	Value of a collective labor day	Distributed income Per mu	Per capita
1957	26	10.3	0.68	14	49
1965	n.a.	26.2	0.70	n.a.	n.a.
1976	76	40.5	0.56	32	65

Note: 15 mu = 1 hectare.
n.a. Not available.

Sources: 1957: Based on a nationwide survey of 228 cooperatives [*Tongji yanjiu*, no. 8 (1958), pp. 8–9]. The cost figures include agricultural taxes.

1965 and 1976: Cost and labor day value figures are from a survey of 2,162 teams [*Guangming ribao*, (December 7, 1978)]. The gross output and distributed income figures are from the State Statistical Bureau release of June 27, 1979, plus assumptions about the size of the rural population (690 million) and collectively run cultivated acreage (94 million hectares).

Table 4-7. *Rural Electric Power Consumption*

Year	Total (billions of kilowatt-hours)	Per hectare (kilowatt-hours)	From small hydro-electric stations (billions of kilowatt-hours)
1952	0.05	0.45	n.a.
1957	0.134	1.20	n.a.
1962	n.a.	15.75	n.a.
1965	3.7	36.00	n.a.
1970	n.a.	94.50	n.a.
1975	18.4	184.50	n.a.
1978	25.3	255.00	10.0
1979	28.3	283.50	n.a.
1980	32.1	322.60	n.a.
1982	39.7	399.00	n.a.

n.a. Not available.

Sources: The 1952 and 1978 figures are from State Statistical Bureau, *Beijing Review* (July 27, 1979), p. 29. The 1979 and all of the per hectare figures were derived from Ministry of Agriculture, *Zhongguo nongye nianjian, 1980*, p. 343. The 1957–75 total electric power figures were obtained by multiplying the per hectare figures times the total number of hectares in Table 4-1. The 1980 figure (total) is from State Statistical Bureau, "Report on the Results of the 1980 National Economic Plan," April 29, 1981; and the 1982 figure is from "Communique on Fulfillment of China's 1982 National Economic Plan," April 29, 1983.

to run machines rather than to light homes. Rural power consumption in the 1950s was negligible, but by 1978 rural areas consumed more electricity than did the entire nation in 1957. Most of the more developed regions were tied in to large regional grids, but, thanks to the proliferation of small hydroelectric stations, even many remote areas had some electricity.

Data on farm machinery, such as those in Table 4-8, tell much the same story. Except for a few thousand tractors on state farms in the northeast, there was little mechanization in the 1950s. In the early 1960s, however, the pace of mechanization began to accelerate. The first step was to distribute large numbers of pumps to areas with adequate supplies of water. At the same time some of the more onerous and labor-intensive tasks, such as the threshing and milling of grain, began to be mechanized. By the 1970s, as tractors became more common in the countryside, China's rural planners began to speak of mechanizing plowing and other land-preparation activities. There was even talk of completely mechanizing farm activities within a few years.

Table 4-8. *Agricultural Mechanization*

Year	Total horsepower of farm machinery (million horsepower)	Power irrigation and drainage equipment (million horsepower)	Walking tractors (thousands)		Large and medium tractors (thousands)	
			Production	Stock	Production	Stock[a]
1952	0.25	0.13	n.a.	n.a.	n.a.	1.3
1957	1.65	0.56	n.a.	n.a.	n.a.	14.7
1965	14.94	9.07	3.6	4.0	n.a.	72.6
1970	n.a.	20.00	51.4	n.a.	7.1	203.0
1975	n.a.	40.00	209.4	n.a.	78.4	n.a.
1978	159.75	65.58	324.2	1,373	113.5	557.0
1979	181.91	71.22	317.5	1,671	126.0	667.0
1980	200.49	74.65	218.0	1,874	98.0	745.0
1982	226.00	76.70	298.0	2,290	40.0	812.0

n.a. Not available.

a. These are defined as having a capacity of 20 horsepower or more.

Sources: These data are mainly from *Statistical Yearbook of China, 1981*, pp. 173, 231. 1970: The 1971 stock was 3.7 times that of 1962 (*Beijing Review*, April 13, 1973, p. 10). 1982: "Communique on Fulfillment of China's 1982 National Economic Plan," April 29, 1983.

An air of unreality, however, surrounded many of the announced mechanization targets. Planners spoke of tractors being used primarily for cultivation, but even the casual visitor could see that most tractors were being used on the roads as substitutes for trucks to get farm products to and from the market.

Mechanization of agriculture continued into the 1980s, but for the first time with explicit recognition that some forms of mechanization put large numbers of people out of work long before industry was ready to absorb them. The role of farm mechanization, therefore, is to substitute for labor where labor is in short supply, as in newly developed regions of the northeast and northwest, or during peak periods of demand, such as when farmers are harvesting one crop and preparing the fields for and transplanting a second crop. Where inexpensive and comparatively simple technology is readily available, as for threshing, mechanization of peak period activities is nearly complete. For activities such as transplanting rice, where machines that are both effective and inexpensive are not readily available, mechanization is still in its early stages. Despite many years of design effort and experimentation, in the late 1970s only 1 percent of China's rice was being transplanted by machine.[13]

Another role of mechanization has been to substitute machine power where people and animals simply cannot do the job effectively—in effect, where no rural wage, however low, would make the choice of human labor desirable. Power pumps can move much more water at far lower cost than animals or humans, however large the nation's labor surplus. Mechanization also can substitute for tasks that are particularly onerous, such as hand-milling grain, which is done mainly by women. Even if the only alternative is increased leisure, farm families still wish to eliminate these unpleasant activities.

Finally, there are social gains from familiarizing the countryside with machines. During periods such as the Cultural Revolution, and in quieter times as well, there has been great emphasis on narrowing the differences between city and countryside.[14] The purposes have been both economic, to accelerate the spread of new techniques, and social or political, to break down class barriers between an urban elite and the mass of peasants.

It is comparatively easy to state the objectives of mechanization, in China, but it is nearly impossible to measure the gains, even the purely economic gains, in any precise way. By the late 1970s, China's communes were spending around 1 billion yuan on electric power[15] and well over a billion yuan on the purchase of farm machinery.[16] Given that demand for power—and probably for machinery as well—was substantially greater than available supplies, it is reasonable to assume that the increase in output resulting from these inputs was substantially larger than their cost, but it is impossible to tell by how much.[17]

The Role of Rural Small-scale Industries

One of the unique features of China's efforts to increase agricultural production has been the degree to which required inputs have been supplied by small-scale enterprises located in the countryside near those who use their products (Tables 4-9 and 4-10). The rationale for relying on rural small-scale industry in the Chinese countryside has been presented at length in other books and articles, and only a brief summary of the evolution of the program and its underlying rationale is given here.[18]

In essence, the choice between small rural-based and large urban-based enterprises is a tradeoff between the advantages of location, on the one hand, and economies of scale, on the other. China, like most developing countries, has a weak and expensive rural transport net-

Table 4-9. *Small-scale Enterprises Run by Communes and Brigades*

Year	Gross value of output		Number of enterprises (thousands)	Employment (millions of persons)	Accumulation and taxes (millions of yuan)
	Millions of yuan	Percentage of commune total			
1974	13,367	14.7	n.a.	n.a.	n.a.
1976	27,230	23.3	800+	n.a.	n.a.
1977	39,120	30.5	1,390	17	n.a.
1978	43,140	29.7	n.a.	n.a.	8,800
1979	49,110	29.9	1,480	29.09	10,450
1981	67,040	33.9	1,338	29.70	14,700
1985 plan	n.a.	50	n.a.	n.a.	n.a.

n.a. Not available.

Sources: Ministry of Agriculture, *Zhongguo nongye nianjian, 1980*, pp. 365–66; and State Statistical Bureau, *Statistical Yearbook of China, 1981*, pp. 192–98.

Table 4-10. *Share of Small Plants in Total Output*
(percent)

Year	Nitrogenous fertilizer	Cement
1961	2	n.a.
1965	12	n.a.
1968	33	n.a.
1970	43	40
1973	54	50
1975	n.a.	57

Note: Small plants include county-level state-owned enterprises.

n.a. Not available.

Sources: These are all official Chinese estimates as reported in Jon Sigurdson, *Rural Industrialization in China* (Cambridge, Mass.: Council on East Asian Studies, 1977), pp. 136–37, 153; Central Intelligence Agency, *People's Republic of China: Chemical Fertilizer Supplies, 1949–74* (Washington, D.C.: August 1975), pp. 14–18.

work. When bulky items of low value per ton must be moved long distances to reach a rural location, transport costs tend to drive up the price of the item to the point at which the cost is higher than any likely return achievable from its use. Underdeveloped rural marketing systems have much the same effect. If cement or fertilizer is distributed through the inefficient systems common to developing countries, the cost at the destination is that much higher. China, to be sure, has an elaborate network of rural supply and marketing cooperatives, but these are tied in to a highly centralized national system of planned or rational allocation of key commodities. Bureaucratic barriers of many different kinds, as a result, stand between the individual production team and any allocation from the state distribution system. Any proper calculation of the social cost of key inputs to the Chinese farmer would produce a figure far higher than the actual cost of production when the item left the factory.

The core of China's program for developing rural small-scale industry included cement, chemical fertilizer, and farm machinery plants.[19] The underlying rationale is most easily illustrated with cement. China is blessed with many small outcroppings of limestone and coal that are not usable by large-scale plants because of the high cost of moving such bulky items from so many locations to one distant center. Transporting the cement back to these distant areas adds further to the expense. The obvious solution is to build small plants near the local outcroppings and to sell the output within a five- or ten-mile radius of each plant. There are established techniques for producing cement in plants with several tens of thousands of tons capacity per year, and the equipment for these plants is simple and can be readily produced in China. In fact, much can be and is produced in small local plants. The quality of the cement produced is low, but is adequate for lining canals and other rural construction activities. The main social cost of this cement is the opportunity cost of the local labor used to quarry local limestone, mine local coal, and staff the cement plant, and in rural China that opportunity cost is not high.

The rationale for small chemical fertilizer plants is much the same, but less compelling. Transport costs are lowered by a rural location, as with cement, but the quality of locally produced chemical fertilizer is low (ammonium bicarbonate, the main small-scale product, is low in nutrient content and highly volatile). Furthermore, equipment for such plants is not as readily available from local machinery plants, and some of the machines used to produce that equipment are imported. Finally, not all local coal is an appropriate feedstock for the plants.

With farm machinery, the rationale for local small enterprises is not so much the high transport costs as the inadequacies in the distribution system. If machinery is to be used regularly, repair facilities have to be nearby. As local repair facilities gradually become more effective, they begin to manufacture first parts and then whole pieces of equipment. It was not uncommon for small rural machinery plants that originally had bought a lathe or two to have their own foundry by the mid-1970s and to be busy producing lathes to expand their capacity to manufacture locally needed farm machines.

The impetus behind the rapid development of rural small industry in the decade that ended with the death of Mao in 1976 had several sources. Strong ideological support from high levels of the Party was only part of the story. High-level support meant that allocations of steel were set aside for rural use rather than being gobbled up by large and politically powerful urban enterprises. Technical personnel were also sent to the country when needed, and large urban plants had to allocate resources to train rural personnel. There is little doubt, however, that much of the impetus for the program came from below and was not just imposed from the top. Local enterprises enabled local cadres to provide for many of their own needs rather than fight their way up through the bureaucracy to obtain a needed piece of equipment, if they were fortunate enough to obtain the necessary approvals. Because of the high transport costs, many local enterprises made profits that could be retained for local use. Even when the formal accounts showed a loss, which recently released data indicate was frequently the case, the real social benefits to the local area were often above social costs. State-set wages were paid to workers who would otherwise have been doing low-productivity work, and cement was provided at a state-fixed price that was often well below what communes would have paid on an open market, if such had existed.

Since 1978 the rural small-scale industry program has come under attack from many of China's senior planners on the grounds that these plants waste scarce materials and often run chronic deficits. These attacks, however, were not a broadside against all rural industries, but mainly a critique of those which violated key elements of the economic rationale for such enterprises. Some small enterprises were located in areas without key raw materials, thus necessitating high transport costs. Others produced fertilizer or machinery of such low quality and at such a high cost that larger more distant firms could easily do better despite high transport costs. As a result, many small machinery enterprises are being converted back into repair shops or into subcontractors specializing in the production of a limited number of standardized parts for urban factories. Small enterprises that rely on distant raw materials are being closed altogether. The smallest plants are also being closed in favor of those at the larger end of the small-scale spectrum. By 1981 the number of small enterprises run by communes and brigades had fallen by 10 percent since 1979, while total output had actually increased by 37 percent (Table 4-9).

As in so many other areas, China has acquired a wealth of experience with small-scale industries that are designed to provide agriculture with key inputs as well as to process food and do subcontracting for urban industries. At one time or another many different scales of operation and degrees of specialization have been tried. Many of the choices made proved to be inefficient, but many others now provide a solid base on which the program can continue. In fact, there are planners in China today who consider these industries the basis for a decentralized form of urbanization. Instead of two dozen large cities with 10 million or 20 million people each, these planners see the possibility of as many as 10,000 smaller towns often with no more than 20 thousand or 30 thousand people each.[20]

Estimating Factor Productivity

There has been a large and rapid increase during the past two to three decades in the use of both modern and traditional inputs. Only land has declined, although measured in terms of quality, land also has increased, albeit not dramatically. It would be of considerable interest to be able not only to describe the increase in inputs, but, by using the methodology introduced at the beginning of this chapter, also to specify the precise contribution of each factor input and of increases in the productivity of those inputs. Although this is not possible because of the limitations of the currently available data, crude calculations based on the figures in this chapter can indicate the orders of magnitude involved.

In essence, the nature of the exercise is to derive indexes of output and of the key inputs. To weight the different inputs, plausible estimates of the marginal product of each type of input must be derived. There are several ways, however, of simplifying the calculation.

To begin with, as shown in Table 4-1, official data indicate that the amount of cultivated land declined by more than 11 percent, although when underreporting is considered, the decline may have been smaller. At the same time investment in irrigation drainage construction, tube wells, and power pumps has augmented the value of that land: that is, it has increased the land's marginal product in terms of the accounting framework used here.

Land improvements of this kind, of course, were central to the Maoist vision of how to raise agricultural output. Those who believe that the activities of the mobilized commune had a large positive effect on agricultural output, therefore, are basically arguing that the quality of the land improved greatly. Skeptics of this approach are likely to measure increases in the quality of land, such as expansion of irrigated acreage and other similarly concrete changes. If, for example, conversion of unirrigated land into irrigated land is assumed to double its value, then the land value of China nationwide still decreased (but by under 1 percent) between 1957 and 1979.

If this latter line of reasoning is in general correct, there is no need to estimate the marginal product of land ($\partial F/\partial L_d$) because the other term in the equation, dL_d/dt is so near zero. If the former line of reasoning is closer to the truth, then an estimate of marginal product is necessary. These issues are discussed later in the chapter.

A second simplification is to think of all current inputs in the biological package as a single complementary package of improved seeds, chemical and organic fertilizers, and insecticides. There is reason to believe that use of organic fertilizers increased as a result of labor being mobilized to collect such fertilizers, but the only good data available are for chemical fertilizers (Table 4-3). Various estimates are also available for the yield response to varying amounts of chemical fertilizer. For this discussion, yield responses of seven and ten kilograms of grain per kilogram of chemical nutrient are assumed. This translates in value terms into 1.52 to 2.16 yuan of output per kilogram of nutrient. These figures are assumed to be the marginal product of the entire biological package, not just of the fertilizer. An increase of 10 million tons in chemical nutrient, therefore, translates into an increase in crop output of 18 billion to 26 billion yuan.

The next step is to derive an input series for labor and for the mechanical package as a whole. Because population has grown at an average rate of 2 percent per year for thirty years and only a tiny fraction of that labor force has been allowed to migrate to the cities, the rural population has grown substantially. Furthermore, participation rates in agriculture, particularly those of women, have increased.

The rural labor force estimates are from Table 4-5.[21] It is also possible to derive rough estimates of the number of days spent in collective agriculture per capita or per worker. Dividing an estimate of the distributed income per day of a large sample into average per capita distributed income produces an estimate of 72 labor days per capita in 1957 and 117 days per capita in 1976. If family size and workers per family remained unchanged during this period, these figures would translate into 161 days per worker in 1957 (based on a sample of 228 cooperatives) and 262 days in 1976. Depending on precisely how the calculation is made, the number of labor days used in rural collective activities came to about 31 billion man-days in 1957 and 77 billion man-days in 1979 (assuming that the number of days worked per laborer was the same in 1979 as in

1976).[22] Because the main effect of certain kinds of mechanization (such as tractors, power threshers, and milling machines) is to save labor or to increase the productivity of labor, part of the rapid development of mechanization in the late 1970s can be thought of as increasing China's rural labor power to an even greater level than is indicated by the above estimates of labor per day.

Estimations of the marginal product of labor or of the mechanical package as a whole are rather problematic. One estimate of labor's marginal product appears in Appendix B and can be thought of as representing the upper end of a plausible range.

Finally, there is the question of which output series to use. In most discussions of agricultural productivity in China output figures used are either the "gross value of agricultural output" or "grain output." Both concepts suffer from the fact that it is difficult to come up with appropriate input series for either concept of output. For the grain series, the problem is that available input data do not include estimates of the proportion of each input that is applied to grain. The gross value of agricultural output series, however, includes items for which there may not be input data. As indicated in Chapter 3, crops account for only a part, and a declining part, of gross agricultural output. Much of the input data used here, for example, refers to inputs to collectively owned land used to raise crops. Little is known about inputs to private plots or to subsidiary farm activities, including much of the livestock raising. Thus, much of the data on increases in inputs is more relevant to the 50.7 billion yuan rise in crop output during 1957–77 than it is to the 79.1 billion yuan rise in the gross value of agricultural output.

These remarks can be used to convert the equation at the beginning of this chapter into the simplified form:

$$\frac{dQ}{dt} = \frac{\partial F}{\partial t} + \left(\frac{\partial F}{\partial C} \cdot \frac{dC}{dt} \right) + \left(\frac{\partial F}{\partial L} \cdot \frac{dL}{dt} \right) + \left(\frac{\partial F}{\partial L_d} \cdot \frac{dL_d}{dt} \right).$$

The above assumptions about the range of quantitative estimates can be converted into tabular form, as in Table 4-11. The value of this method is that it puts the various assumptions into a consistent framework.

Clearly, quite different results can be produced depending on how the increases in output and the contribution of various inputs to that increase are measured. This procedure, however, does make it possible to rule out certain explanations of the sources of agricultural growth in China. In particular, it is not possible to argue both that labor mobilization for rural construction had a significant effect on crop output and that simultaneously agricultural productivity rose (agricultural inputs were used with increasing efficiency). If the marginal product of rural labor was high, productivity gains per unit of input were most likely negative. Only if it is argued that the mass mobilization of rural labor for collective activities had only a modest effect on output, can a plausible case be made that factor productivity in Chinese farming was rising.

Table 4-11. *Estimates of the Productivity Residual, 1957 to 1979*
(billions of 1970 yuan)

Input contribution	Low assumptions	High assumptions
1. Biological package $\dfrac{\partial F}{\partial C} \cdot \dfrac{dC}{dt}$	18	26
2. Labor and labor-augmenting machinery $\dfrac{\partial F}{\partial L} \cdot \dfrac{dL}{dt}$	18	31
3. Land and land-augmenting capital and machinery $\dfrac{\partial F}{\partial L_d} \cdot \dfrac{dL_d}{dt}$	0	+
4. Total contribution of inputs $[(1) + (2) + (3)]$	36	57 +
5. Increase in crop output $\dfrac{dQ}{dt}$ (1970 prices)	50.7	50.7
6. Residual $\dfrac{\partial F}{\partial t}$ $[(5) - (4)]$	14.7	less than -6.3

Notes: 1. The "low" figure is calculated by multiplying the average price of grain (0.2164 yuan per kilogram × the yield response per kilogram of fertilizer nutrient (7:1) × the increase in the supply of fertilizer, 1957–79 (11.98 million tons). The "high" figure is the same except that the yield response is assumed to be 10:1.

2. The agricultural labor force figures in Table 4-5 are multiplied by 161 labor days per year in 1957 and 262 labor days per year in 1979 (assumed to be the same as 1976) to obtain the total number of labor days worked. The "high" calculation assumes a daily marginal product per worker of 0.56 yuan (see Appendix B for derivation), and the "low" figure assumes a marginal rate of 0.4 yuan. (Lower marginal product estimates would, of course, raise the residual.) The higher calculation also assumes that machinery augmented the increase in rural labor by a factor of 1.2.

3. Land of a given quality is assumed to have not grown at all in the low estimate (improved irrigation and other improvements just offsetting the decline of acreage). If land was increasingly underreported over time, or if it is assumed that land was improved markedly, then the contribution of land to output was positive, but it is not possible to come up with a meaningful figure.

4. Crop output in 1979 (in 1970 prices) was 105.965 billion yuan (Ministry of Agriculture, *Zhongguo nongye nianjian, 1980*, p. 130) and in 1957 (in 1957 prices) it was 43.282 billion yuan [Shigeru Ishikawa, *National Income and Capital Formation in Mainland China* (Tokyo: Institute of Asian Economic Affairs, 1965), p. 50]. The latter figure was multiplied by the 1979/1957 agricultural purchase price index (1.276) to obtain 1957 crop output in 1970 prices.

Conclusion

Mao Zedong believed that the mobilization of China's rural labor force could transform Chinese agriculture without resort to massive injections of modern inputs. Since there is no question that China's rural labor force was in fact mobilized on an internationally unprecedented scale, the issue to be debated is whether this mobilization had the anticipated effect on farm output. In terms of the calculations in Table 4-11, Mao Zedong's view implies a large positive figure in row 3 for the contribution of land improvements, or a large figure in row 2 because of high labor input, or both together. The desirability of mechanization supported by Mao and his associates would further raise the labor contribution in row 2.

If this view of the sources of growth in Chinese crop output is correct, then it follows that production increases were achieved at the cost of increasing mismanagement, declining personal incentives, and other sources of reduced efficiency in the raising of crops. How else can one explain the negative contribution of the factor productivity residual (row 6) to growth? In effect, this line of reasoning suggests that both Mao and his severest critics were partly right. Mao's methods did greatly increase the inputs available to Chinese agriculture, but the organization required for this achievement (such as communes, mass campaigns, and so forth) played such havoc with management and incentives that many of the benefits of increased inputs, both modern and traditional, were lost.

There is a quite different view of the sources of growth in Chinese agriculture that starts from the proposition that the beliefs of Mao and his colleagues in the potential benefits of the mass mobilization of labor were never well founded. Although there were areas of China where the massive application of labor power could lead to marked improvements in the quality and quantity of land, more multiple cropping, and other gains, on a national scale these gains were quite modest. Mobilized labor could expand the irrigated acreage in much of south China, but, as indicated earlier, this had been discovered in the Song dynasty, not after 1949. Only in more recently settled areas of the southwest was it possible to expand the irrigated acreage in this manner on any scale. In the north the contributions of labor mobilization were even more marginal, except along the edges of the Taihang Mountains and a few other areas quite limited in size.

If this second view of the limited gains from labor mobilization is roughly correct, then it no longer follows that overall factor productivity gains were negative, or that the communes had a strong deleterious effect on rural incentives and the quality of farm management. If the marginal productivity of labor was extremely low to start with and land quality improved only modestly, then there were increases in total factor productivity between 1957 and 1979. The size of these productivity gains is very sensitive to the estimate of the marginal productivity of labor used in the calculations in row 2. The "low" estimate in Table 4-11 is only one of several possibilities. Whether the true figure is higher or lower must await further research.[23]

The policy implications of the two opposing points of view presented here are quite different. In the first view, the main issue is one of improving organization to enhance personal incentives and raise the level of management. This view is widely held in China, especially among many who are critics of Maoist economic policies. In the second view, the principal issue is one of increasing inputs, particularly modern inputs such as chemicals and large-scale irrigation systems, and of promoting research to further raise the productivity of those inputs.

The policy recommendations of these two views are not mutually exclusive. Better incentives will enhance the value of better research and vice versa. The issue is which of these two views will have the greater effect on productivity. For what it is worth, the authors lean toward the view that, over the long run, major increases in farm output will come from more and better inputs. As experience with the responsibility system in the early 1980s has demonstrated, however, there also are considerable gains in the shorter term from reorganization and improved incentives. The reorganizations involved, of course, are the antithesis of what Mao had in mind.

Notes to Chapter 4

1. The figures vary depending on whether Chinese or Indian prices are used to value the output of the two countries. Alexander Eckstein, *The National Income of Communist China* (Glencoe, Ill.: Free Press, 1961), p. 67.

2. For a more detailed and systematic discussion of the issues discussed in this section, refer to Dwight H. Perkins, *Agricultural Development in China 1368–1968* (Chicago: Aldine, 1969).

3. Data are from the survey of John Lossing Buck, *Land Utilization in China* (Nanking: University of Nanking, 1937), pp. 295–96.

4. If the average farm worker had from 1.2 to 1.3 idle months between November and February, or twenty-five to thirty working days, and the rural labor force in the 1950s was around 250 million people, then the total available number of labor days would be more than 6 billion per year.

5. See James E. Nickum, *Hydraulic Engineering and Water Resources in the People's Republic of China* (Stanford, Calif.: Stanford University Press, 1977), p. 10.

6. For a discussion of some of the earlier schemes to control the Yellow River, see Alva Lewis Erisman, "Potential Costs of and Benefits from Diverting River Flow for Irrigation in the North China Plain," Ph.D. dissertation, University of Maryland, 1967.

7. Many works discuss the problems created by the Great Leap Forward. See, for example, Leslie Tse-chiu Kuo, *The Technical Transformation of Agriculture in Communist China* (New York: Praeger, 1972).

8. Handbooks are published in China describing in detail the kinds of organic materials that can be used, how to use them, their chemical content, and so forth. See, for example, *Feiliao zhichi* (Shanghai: Shanghai People's Press, 1974).

9. Walker roughly estimates that 87 million to 92 million hogs would produce the equivalent of 2.586 million tons of ammonium sulfate, which has a nitrogen content of 20 to 21 percent. Kenneth Walker, *Planning in Chinese Agriculture* (Chicago: Aldine, 1965), p. 56.

10. Chinese sources provide detailed chemical analysis of the various kinds of organic fertilizer, and communes report the tons of organic material used, but data on the chemical content of the mix of organic materials actually used are not generally reported.

11. See the discussion in Benedict Stavis, *Making Green Revolution* (Ithaca, N.Y.: Cornell University Press, 1974), pp. 83–87.

12. See, for example, the report of the American Plant Studies Delegation, *Plant Studies in the People's Republic of China* (Washington, D.C.: National Academy of Sciences, 1975).

13. *Guangming ribao* (December 7, 1978).

14. These social and political aspects receive considerable attention in Benedict Stavis, *The Politics of Agricultural Mechanization in China* (Ithaca, N.Y.: Cornell University Press, 1978).

15. In 1978 the rural areas consumed 25 billion kilowatt-hours of electricity, and the price of electricity varies depending on use from 0.03 yuan per kilowatt-hour in one region (a subsidized rate for agricultural use) to 0.06 or 0.08 yuan per kilowatt-hour in certain industrial uses. The figure of 1 billion yuan in the text thus is a crude estimate and assumes that most electric power used for agriculture is at the lower end of the rate scale. No attempt has been made to estimate the true social cost of electricity.

16. In the mid-1970s hand tractors were priced at 2,000 yuan each and more, so that the 300,000-plus hand tractors produced each year in the late 1970s would have cost well over 600 million yuan; and this was only one of many kinds of machinery being produced.

17. The problem is compounded by the fact that team and commune decisionmakers were profit maximizers only some of the time. Thus, even if the market-clearing price and the size of the consumer surplus were known, there would be a problem of relating the resulting figure to the actual social gains to Chinese society.

18. For a more thorough discussion, see the works of Carl Riskin as well as Jon Sigurdson, *Rural Industrialization in China* (Cambridge, Mass.: Harvard Council on East Asian Studies, 1977); and the report of the American Rural Small-scale Industry Delegation, *Rural Small-scale Industry in the People's Republic of China* (Berkeley: University of California Press, 1977). For a study of developments in the late 1970s, see Christine Wong, "Two Steps Forward, One Step Back? Recent Policy Changes in Rural Industrialization," paper presented to a Social Science Research Council workshop, in February 1980, processed.

19. The Chinese speak of the "five small industries" and include local electric power stations and small steel plants in the five.

20. See "Two Views on China's Urbanization," *Beijing Review* (March 17, 1980), p. 7; and Zhang Zehou and Chen Yuguang, "On the Relationship between the Population Structure and National Economic Development in China," *Social Sciences in China*, vol. 2, no. 4 (December 1981), pp. 55–83.

21. An earlier estimate of the size of the labor force based on less complete data is in Thomas

G. Rawski, *Economic Growth and Employment in China* (New York: Oxford University Press, 1979).

22. Tang, in his calculation of factor productivity in agriculture, assumes that rural labor grew at roughly the same pace as population. This method does not allow for the substantial increase in the number of days each worker spent in collective work. Anthony M. Tang, "Food and Agriculture in China: Trends and Projections," in Anthony M. Tang and Bruce Stone, *Food Production in the People's Republic of China* (Washington, D.C.: International Food Policy Research Institute, 1980).

23. For a stronger argument for the presence of productivity gains that uses a similar methodology, see Thomas Wiens, "Declining Factor Productivity? A Counterview" (1979), processed.

Chapter 5

~~~~~~

Organizational and Institutional Changes

WHAT SETS CHINA APART from many other developing countries is not that it has increased the use of chemical fertilizer, but how much it has relied on organizational reform to achieve rural development. Over the years, government policies have shifted periodically, depending on whether the prevailing ideological sentiments favored economic growth or egalitarian concerns. China's rural institutions were reformed initially for several reasons, an increase in agricultural production being only one, although an important one. Of even greater importance was the desire of the Party to consolidate its political control of the countryside. When the reforms initially failed to increase production as much as had been expected, the Chinese leadership used its control over rural resources, which it had gained through the new structures, to pursue a politically beneficial program to alleviate rural poverty.

Institutional change is discussed on two levels in this chapter. On the first level, the primary question deals with the nature and purpose of the reforms. The biggest issue, of course, was whether to collectivize at all, but there were numerous subsidiary issues, such as defining the role of the market within a system of collectivized agriculture.

Even a brief recital of the kinds of reforms undertaken in China after 1949 indicates that the ability of the Party to bring about fundamental changes in rural society was truly formidable. The second level of this discussion of organizational change, therefore, attempts to discover the source of such an unusual capability to implement reforms. Was it primarily rooted in a unique Chinese tradition, or was it the product of the special nature of the Chinese revolution?

This chapter provides the link between the earlier discussion of agricultural production and the chapters that follow on income distribution and basic needs. The issues raised are also fundamental to any attempt to determine whether China's experience is applicable to other developing nations. Could a nation with different traditions or one lacking an organization like that of the Chinese Communist Party transform rural society to such an extent? A concrete answer to this question would require a detailed analysis of the country involved. Here, the purpose is only to point out the connections between China's reforms and its historical and revolutionary experience. Analysts in other countries must determine whether China's methods can serve their purposes.

The Decision to Collectivize

Rural society in China before 1949 had much in common with the rural areas of many other Asian nations. The independent family farm dominated the landscape. Measured in terms of land, farms were small, averaging just under two hectares apiece in the north and just over one hectare in the south. Nearly half the land was owned by landlords who rented the land out to peasant families. Landlords tended to be absentee, but even when they lived nearby, they contributed little to production other than their land. Rental contracts tended to be for long periods, even for life, in much of the south, so that tenant farmers did have an incentive to invest in the land, but in the north, one-year tenure was common. Rents were high, typically half of the main crops, and interest rates were usurious, as in most other pre-modern rural societies, averaging more than 30 percent a year in the 1930s.[1] The focus of the village economy was the nearby market town, which in turn was connected to higher levels of the marketing system and, to a degree, even to international markets.

By 1949 this rural system had remained more or less unchanged for several centuries. The system has often been called feudal, but it had few of the compulsory labor features of the European feudal manor. Relations between landlords and tenants and between the state and farmers were based on monetary contracts and were mediated by the market. Scholars still debate how efficient this system was, but, in terms of static efficiency, it appears that Chinese rural society had been able to exploit fully the traditional technology.

Formation of Cooperatives

A land reform program in the 1940s and early 1950s was implemented in areas as they came under Communist control. The purpose of this reform, like land reforms elsewhere, was explicitly political: to consolidate support for the Party among its natural constituency, the tenants and the landless rural laborers.[2] To that end, land was confiscated without compensation, and a major effort was made to ensure that the poorest elements in the village, not the more secure and articulate middle peasants, ended up with the land formerly owned by the landlords. On occasion, land had to be redistributed several times to ensure this result.

The effect of land reform on income redistribution is discussed in a later chapter, and its influence on agricultural production is obscured by the short time during which rural society remained in this particular form. The central point here—and one that will be elaborated in the latter half of this chapter—is that the process of land reform gave the Party a strong rural organizational base that drew its support and leadership from the poorest elements of rural society. Those who sided with the Communists had a very limited stake in the old system and a substantial vested interest in overturning many of its key elements.

There is little point in speculating about what would have happened in the absence of collectivization in China. Experiments with "mutual aid teams" and with various forms of cooperatives began as soon as the land-to-the-tiller program was completed in 1950. There was an active debate within the Party over the pace at which cooperatives were to be formed. But ultimately, Mao was able to induce his colleagues to acquiesce to an accelerated program. The need to consolidate political control in the countryside and to prevent the rise of an independent class of wealthy peasants, however, was widely accepted within the Party. Thus political considerations virtually dictated eventual collectivization, although the decision was made easier by the justification that socializing agriculture would yield economic benefits as well.

The belief that collectivization would increase output was rooted in the notion that mobilizing rural surplus labor would increase rural capital formation and, hence, production. The technological aspects of this issue were discussed in the previous chapter; the connection between this issue and the decision to collectivize is explained here.

Rural public works schemes have typically foundered because it has proved difficult to mobilize idle rural labor voluntarily on any kind of sustained basis. Pilot projects frequently pay wages in the beginning in the often-vain hope that the project will become self-sustaining and the need for wages will be removed once local people discover what can be accomplished on their own without outside assistance. The people doing the work, however, are usually not those who will benefit from the project, and hence they have no incentive to work without wages. The individuals who do benefit are usually landowners whose land will become more productive because of a more reliable water supply or a new road nearby. These landowners are not willing to take over the wage payments, however, because the wages necessary to attract the required labor force are typically higher than the productivity of the labor so employed.

The Party chose to solve this problem by collectivization. In the Soviet Union this method had been used primarily to mobilize the rural agricultural surplus for industrialization and to consolidate Russian Communist Party power in the countryside. The Chinese put it to much the same uses, with political objectives enjoying primacy over economic ones. Compulsory farm delivery quotas were introduced soon after the land reform in late 1953, and, throughout the 1950s and the early 1960s, the transfer of agricultural surplus made an important contribution to industrial development, as was discussed in Chapter 4. But in addition to surplus grain, collectives also provided the state with free labor services during the off-season, similar to the corvee extracted in earlier times, but on a much larger scale.[3]

Mao and others saw collectivization as a way to mobilize rural surplus labor, because the collective could ensure that those who did the work received the benefits, and the state would not have to subsidize wages. The cooperatives were established on a nationwide basis in the winter of 1955–56, and individual family farms were abolished by pooling the land of all the families in a given village. Payment was based solely on the amount of work family members contributed to the cooperative and took the form of work points. An adult who worked a full day might earn ten points and a part-time worker or child a lesser amount. Women generally received fewer work points than men. At the end of the year the number of work points earned by all members of the cooperative would be added up and divided into that part of the co-op's income that was to be distributed to the members (after deductions for taxes, investment, purchased inputs, and the welfare fund). A cooperative family's income, therefore, depended on the number of work points earned by family members and on the average value of each work point. The latter in turn depended on the net production of the cooperative, or basic accounting unit, as a whole.[4] In addition, families received small private plots, about which more will be said below.

Cooperatives also made it comparatively simple to mobilize labor for rural public works. As with the farm work, individuals who participated in such projects received work points on the basis of time spent on the project. Any increase in farm productivity resulting from these efforts went into the co-op's general fund to be shared on the same basis as all other cooperative income. In effect, within each cooperative, operations were much like those of a family farm. Income payments were based on the average product of the cooperative as a whole rather than on the marginal product of individual members. It did not matter if worker productivity on local public works projects was below a subsistence wage as long as productivity was higher than the valuation each worker put on his or her leisure time.

If cooperatives provided a basis for mobilizing more or less voluntary labor for public works projects within the co-op, it was clear by early 1958 that cooperatives had not eliminated the obstacles to mobilizing voluntary labor for larger projects. The problem was really the old one but in a slightly different form. Many large irrigation and road building projects required labor from dozens of individual cooperatives. But typically, most of the benefits from such projects went to a few co-ops, instead of equally to all those who did the work. Co-ops that received few benefits naturally had little interest in diverting their labor force to such efforts.

Formation of Communes

There was an obvious solution to this dilemma. If village-size cooperatives made it feasible to mobilize labor voluntarily within the village, pooling twenty or thirty cooperatives into one large collective unit would make it possible to mobilize labor on a much larger scale. For this reason and out of the desire to promote the socialization of the peasantry, forced draft efforts were begun in 1958 to establish people's communes. Many senior members of the Party felt that the formation of communes was premature, but eventually Mao Zedong prevailed over the opposition, and the Great Leap was set in motion.[5] Initially 26,000 communes were created, and, departing from the system of remuneration used in the cooperatives, payment was according to need as well as labor performed. Between 50 and 80 percent of compensation consisted of subsistence supplies, 20 to 50 percent was in the form of wages differentiated according to the grade of labor, and a small amount was reserved for incentive payments.[6]

A brief history of the early Chinese collectivization movement of course considerably simplifies the reality of this convulsive period. The

formation first of cooperatives and then of communes in the brief period
between 1955 and 1958 was part of a political struggle within the
Chinese leadership over whether to force the pace toward a true communist society or to slow it down. Even in the purely economic sphere,
there were other perceived benefits of collectivization than simply the
possibility of ever larger public works projects. Cooperatives, it was
felt, would make it easier and more efficient to introduce farm machinery, and cooperative cadres would be more willing to experiment with
new techniques than would family farmers, who normally avoid risk.
Still, the ability to mobilize China's rural surplus labor was the main
rationale for collectivization. In addition, there was the desire to eliminate differences in incomes arising from variations in the quality and
size of holdings and to give former poor and landless peasants, who were
loyal to the Party, control over the land rather than leaving it in the
hands of politically unreliable rich and middle peasants.

As pointed out in the previous chapter, however, the results of the
first phase of China's collectivization effort were substantially different
from what was expected. Billions of man-days were mobilized, but
agricultural production fell. The technological reasons that labor mobilization did not lead to large increases in output have been discussed.
But the inappropriateness of applying labor-intensive technologies to
China's water problem was only a part of the problem. The effort to
create an organization that could effectively mobilize surplus labor also
created fundamental problems with internal commune management
and with individual incentives to work.

Internal Commune Organization after 1960

The failure of the Great Leap spurred a reappraisal of the commune
movement. Although communes were not abolished, they were found
to be administratively cumbersome, and, as a first step, existing communes were subdivided, which increased their number to 78,000. The
mode of compensation also drew much criticism, as it provided little
reward for greater effort or higher productivity. Hence, the work point
system was once again used, and throughout the first half of the 1960s,
when economic concerns seemed to dominate political ones, communes
were allowed to experiment with piece rates and work grades to link the
assignment of work points with effort. Alongside the issue of payment,
two other internal issues critically influenced the administrative reforms
introduced in the early 1960s. One concerned the size of the basic

accounting unit, whose income determined the value of the work point. This was also the unit with primary responsibility for managing crop production. The second had to do with the size of private plots allotted to families and the time allowed for working on these plots.

The principal external issues, which are discussed later, were, first, whether higher-level units could direct the activities of the basic accounting unit by administrative means and compulsory quotas or whether control would be exercised indirectly by manipulating market prices; and, second, whether the produce of private plots could be sold on free markets (rural trade fairs) or had to be consumed at home or sold through the state commercial network.

The key decision, made by 1962, was to make the production team, a subunit of the commune consisting of about thirty families, the basic accounting unit. The commune unit of 4,000 to 5,000 families and even the brigade subunit had proved to be too large, as managing more than 10,000 gardeners doing a myriad of different tasks on irregular schedules was a task exceeding the capabilities of even skilled managers.

The incentive problem was also severe on at least two grounds. In a large unit there was little connection between an individual's effort and the value of each work point. The number of work points earned could still be related to effort expended, but the value of each point depended on the net output of the entire unit of 4,000 to 5,000 families. Even if an individual's effort were completely unproductive, the value of his work points would decline by only 0.01 percent. There was a premium on effective supervision, therefore, to prevent loafing on the job because internal motivation based on material gain was not a sufficient discipline. By the same token, however, there was no close supervision by fellow villagers because they too saw little connection between the work of other village members and the value of the work point. Reducing the basic accounting unit improved matters significantly on both counts. At a minimum, villagers had both the ability and incentive to make sure each did his or her share of the work.

The Dazhai System

The problem of relating the allocation of work points on the basis of performance has proven difficult for technical reasons, but its refinement has also been hindered by ideological objections. Beyond a point, a reliance on incentive payments runs counter to egalitarian principles and can threaten a social consensus premised on equality. These and other concerns led to a reliance on time rates or equal sharing from the latter part of the 1960s until after the death of Mao in 1976. The Dazhai approach, which became popular during this period, was meant to simplify the awarding of work points, to stress political and labor attitudes, and to involve the entire team in quality control. The team leader noted the number of days an individual worked, and at a monthly meeting each worker was assigned points based on criteria such as political thought, technical skill, labor intensity, and labor attitude. The assignment was an interactive process, with the individual first evaluating his work and arriving at an estimate of work points he felt were deserved. Following this, other members criticized and adjusted the figure until an agreement was reached.

The Dazhai system functioned well enough in teams with strong leadership, relative equality among households, and a progressive spirit. Elsewhere, the vagueness of the criteria it used and the intense disputes that arose caused much dissatisfaction and generated ideological, cadre, and community pressures in favor of an assessment method based on fixed rates.

The Dazhai system allocates points at meetings where each individual's work over a certain period is assessed and his payment agreed upon by all team members. Under fixed rates, however, a worker is classified according to age and sex and receives a fixed number of points for each day worked. Both systems encourage a clustering of points around a mean. Recent debates over the work point system have revealed that cadres were loath to differentiate allocations at assessment meetings for fear of arousing disputes and spoiling relations among team members. The tendency through much of the 1970s was to give everyone the same for the sake of peace and quiet. But harmony of sorts was attained at some cost in terms of work motivation, and the government's renewed emphasis on growth since 1978 has once again caused a shift to mechanisms of assigning points that discriminate between work effort and quality.[7]

The Responsibility System

The trend that emerged in the less-prosperous communes and spread across the country is toward subdividing the team into smaller production units, often all the way down to the household. Under the so-called "responsibility system," which emerged during 1977 in Sichuan and Anhui before being formally endorsed by the Central Committee in December 1978, the team contracts with work groups to deliver a fixed amount of products grown according to the production plan for land owned by the team. Output above this amount may be retained by the group. The responsibility system has been interpreted in various ways by communes, but there are three main contracts.[8]

CONTRACTS FOR SPECIALIZED TASKS. Specialized contracts are common within affluent and well-diversified production teams. The team management continues to direct production, and accounting is on a unified basis, but the team contracts with a group of its members, a household, or a single individual to accomplish a particular task in areas such as grain production, livestock breeding, or afforestation. The contract requires that the party involved produce an agreed level of output, for which a certain number of work points are assigned. Bonus work points are awarded if the targets are exceeded, and there is a penalty for any shortfall.

OUTPUT CONTRACTS WITH AN INDIVIDUAL OR A GROUP. As in the first case, the team continues to be responsible for most aspects of planning and production, but it subdivides and contracts land to individuals or groups of producers, who promise to meet output goals in return for work points. Rewards and penalties similar to those linked to specialized contracts are used. The peasants' collective income continues to be determined by the team's gross income.

HOUSEHOLD CONTRACTS. Under household contracts, which are the most widely used, the team's productive resources—fields, ponds, orchards, or equipment—are distributed among households that enter into production contracts. Each household is then responsible not only for meeting output quotas assigned by the team leadership, but also for taxes and all other payments to the brigade and the commune. Items such as seed and fertilizers must be financed from the households' own resources, and the families decide how the labor is utilized. Under this system, a household enjoys considerable latitude and is allowed to retain all production in excess of the assigned quotas and mandatory payments, which provides a very powerful incentive for improving productivity.

Thus the responsibility system covers a considerable range of options. However, it definitely excludes the self-assessment and public discussion of work point allocations that characterized the Dazhai system.[9] And mindful of socialist precepts, it stops short of permitting the division of land for individual farming. The commune retains its administrative responsibilities, continues to receive grain output targets from the center, and passes them on to each team leader.[10] But whereas in some respects the situation has been altered only moderately, in other ways the retreat from the socialist ideals enunciated only a few years ago has been quite significant. The swing from moral to material incentives has been much more pronounced than in the early 1960s, even in the prosperous communes where piece rates and allocation of work points according to task are still preferred. In one sense, most peasants have become sharecroppers or tenants, with the agricultural economy of the early 1980s most closely resembling that which emerged soon after the land reform of a little over thirty years ago.

Although the regime has high hopes regarding the recent changes and has been heartened by the experience with the responsibility system now applied by 90 percent of all teams, free rural markets, and enlarged private plots, many problems are being encountered which could eventually force the system to be diluted.[11] The main difficulty with piece rates is monitoring the work done and calculating the labor days due to a person. Similarly, task rates are bedeviled by the absence of any simple method for computing norms. By favoring larger households, these schemes, as well as contracting arrangements, are likely to have serious consequences for income distribution and could give rise to bitterness and tension.[12] Competitive pressures unleashed by the responsibility system have already generated conflicts over the allocation of water, animals, tools, and other inputs. Cadres, faced with an erosion of their considerable authority over the peasants, are reluctant to allow much of their power to slip away and are apprehensive that they may be blamed for allowing peasants too much leeway.

But, arguably, the most serious outcome of this newly gained quasi-autonomy might be the increasing unwillingness (already becoming evident) of farmers to follow plan directives on product mix, volume of output, and transfer of grain to the state when the sale of produce on the free market is so much more profitable. Collective work and capital construction might also suffer. In addition, a weakening of the collective, by limiting the flow of resources into the accumulation fund, is likely to hamper collective activities that are financed through it. The possible effect of the system on the willingness of barefoot doctors to continue their public health activities is discussed in Chapter 7. The authorities clearly do not wish to decentralize so much that plans cannot be implemented and imbalances are created, thus, in their view, damaging the national economy.[13] As has happened in the past, a reinterpretation of official statements to emphasize socialist concerns may become necessary if socialism is to remain the unifying as well as the motivating force in the country. For the immediate future, the dramatic effect of the responsibility system on agricultural production and incomes has partially quieted the critics.

From the very start of collectivization, vegetable production and hog raising were accomplished largely on private plots assigned to families, with work done during spare time. Elimination of private plots in 1958 removed the incentive for families to work in their spare time, and subsidiary production plummeted. The solution was to restore the private plots, so communes distributed from 5 to 7 percent of their marginal land among peasant families for private use. During the Cultural Revolution there were renewed attacks on private plots, but probably only a few plots were actually reduced or eliminated. Since 1979, these plots have been given strong support by the top leadership, as the plots produce almost a quarter of the fruit and vegetable crop and more than 70 percent of agricultural raw materials. In 1979, the land that could legally be allotted to private plots in Sichuan was raised to 15 percent of total arable land, and the actual amount of land in private plots rose from 6.5 percent in 1978 to 9.5 percent in 1980. Other provinces began to follow this lead, and the average amount of land in private plots nationwide rose from 5.7 percent in 1978 to 7.1 percent in 1980.[14]

Relations between the Team and the Government after 1960

Since the restoration of the team as the basic accounting unit, relations between the team and units above it have fluctuated even more than has the internal structure of the team itself.

Agricultural Research

Certain functions, particularly agricultural research, cannot be efficiently managed at the team or even the commune level. The reasons, ranging from the lack of adequate financial resources for personnel at the team level to the inability to appropriate returns for much agricultural research, even in a capitalist society, are well known to students of technological change. These difficulties, however, have not stopped some Chinese leaders from decentralizing research activities as much as possible.

During 1966–76, the prevailing belief that scientific personnel should both learn from the people and assist them directly in solving day-to-day problems compelled agricultural scientists to spend much of their time down on the farm. Although this gave scientists a better understanding of what kinds of research would be most useful, it also deprived them of the time and facilities needed for sustained, high-level research. Several delegations of plant scientists who visited China in the early 1970s reported that China's rural extension system enabled new ideas to be transferred quickly to the farmers who would use them. The research needed to provide these new techniques had lagged far behind, however, and the institutions of higher learning could not produce the needed manpower, as is discussed further in Chapter 8.

By 1979 the responsibility for agricultural research and for the training of research personnel had been centralized once again. Basic research was concentrated under the Chinese Academy of Agricultural Sciences, the Peking Agricultural College, and a few key research institutes, while colleges were once again expected to devote most of their time to training rather than to communication with the masses at the commune level and below. In contrast, the agro-technical personnel at the county level and below were explicitly directed only to popularize advanced techniques rather than to do research and to develop the techniques themselves.

Crop Quotas

Communication between the central government and farmers at the team or commune level were not confined to the propagation of new techniques. Of more immediate importance to the daily lives of team members has been how the state has handled the issues of who is to decide what crops will be raised in which areas. When collectivization was first completed in the winter of 1955–56, some senior officials apparently felt that agricultural planning could generally follow the pattern of the Soviet system, which was being adopted by the industrial sector. Under this system of planning, the center provides guidelines, which are passed down through the provinces and localities, eventually reaching the cooperatives. The cooperatives adjust production and other targets to local conditions and send their suggestions for revision back up to the center, which then decides on the final targets, which are sent down with the force of law behind them. By late 1956 most of China's leadership realized that this system was completely unworkable when applied to the agricultural sector.

Market Forces versus Administrative Control

Ever since the mid-1950s Chinese agricultural planners have struggled over how to implement the broad goals of their agricultural plans. The key issue has been whether to rely on administrative commands to accomplish the principal goals or to depend instead on the manipulation of rural purchase prices to achieve desired aims.

For prices to work, however, cooperatives, and later production teams, had to be allowed to maximize their income, but a nation full of income-maximizing basic accounting units had strong unfavorable ideological overtones. Could leaders who were attempting to educate the population to work for the good of society regardless of personal gain live with a system in which the main criteria for success for 80 percent of the people was income maximization? The answer of those who dominated the political debate during 1966–75 was no.

There was more to the problem than ideology, however. High-level cadres with no political allegiance to the Cultural Revolution still wanted to accomplish certain specific goals quickly, and what quicker way was there than to simply give an order, which was to be passed down through the Party or government administrative structure? Such orders, in most developing societies, would have little effect because lower levels would not be able to implement them, but such was not the case in China for reasons that are explained in the latter half of this chapter.

In principle, prices could be set to accomplish most or all goals of the national or even provincial plans. In practice, the issue was not so simple and can be illustrated by the conflict over the scope of the free market, the size of the private plot, and the amount of time farmers had to contribute to collective labor. Leadership cadres at the local level have had a vested interest in maximizing collective labor time and restricting the scope of the private plots and the free market. These cadres were charged with meeting certain goals for grain or cash crop deliveries to the state and did not want their labor force diverted to other tasks that would reduce the chance of meeting these deliveries. Team members would also suffer if deliveries were not met, but, unlike the cadres, team members would be compensated with higher private incomes and would not, in any case, bear the brunt of criticism from their superiors. Given their authority over the scope and procedures of free markets, therefore, the instinct of most rural cadres was to limit that market's vitality. Thus, ideological pressure simply reinforced tendencies already inherent in the system.

The same kind of problem existed with the decision whether to emphasize grain or cash crops. On the one hand, in administrative and Party channels grain was seen as the "key link" and hence a fundamental basis for determining the success or failure of a cadre. On the other hand, periodic shortages of important cash crops have occurred, and the state has responded by raising the prices of these crops to encourage their production. Both grain and major cash crops are produced within the collective sector, so the issue was not over the scope of the private sector. The issue instead was whether cadres would be judged on their success in maximizing collective income or in meeting their grain delivery quotas. Increasing income might have a bigger effect on the welfare of team members, but failure to meet delivery quotas was more apt to be noticed by high-level officials.

If enough data were available, a study of variations in the price responsiveness of production teams would be a good test of the relative importance of markets versus administrative channels at any given time. As it is, only a few scattered bits of information are available. In 1956 and early 1957, for example, the state instituted large increases in the prices of rapeseed, tea, cocoons, and several other crops. The production of grain, whose price was not increased, rose slightly in 1957, but production decreased for every crop whose price was raised.[15] In 1971 the state raised the purchase prices of bast fibers, oil seeds, and sugar, and in 1972, despite what was generally a poor harvest, output of bast fiber rose 40 percent and that of rapeseed rose 20 percent above the output of sugar.[16] Thus, even during the early 1970s, when the spirit of the Cultural Revolution still had considerable influence, many teams appear to have been attempting to maximize their income.

Throughout 1966–76 higher-level cadres constantly interfered in team decisions, and although rural trade fairs or free markets did exist, their scope was severely restricted. It is clear, though, that since 1977 in rural areas higher-level interference has lessened dramatically, and the role of the market has expanded.

The principles underlying the recent changes are straightforward. In essence, production teams are now free to concentrate on raising income, subject to paying their taxes and meeting moderate delivery quotas. The price of grain within the quota was raised 20 percent in 1979 and that for grain above the quota another 50 percent, and the prices of numerous other crops have also been increased.[17] Restrictions on the free market have also been removed, with results apparent to any visitor traveling through the Chinese countryside in the early morning. Production team members participate in commune and higher-level projects voluntarily, and compensation is paid for such voluntary participation where necessary.

Although the principles are reasonably clear, the reality is less so. Complaints in the Chinese press about the behavior of cadres in Liucin Commune of Hebei Province illustrate the problem. The Nanzhuang Brigade of this commune had committed several acres of land to growing melons, an apparently lucrative crop, only to be accused by commune cadres of taking the capitalist road and then ordered to destroy the crop. These press reports make the Liucin cadres out to be unreconstructed followers of the Gang of Four, but whether or not ideology was the motive, there is ample reason to doubt the enthusiasm with which many cadres have greeted the replacement of their authority with the more indirect controls of market forces.

Furthermore, there are substantial grounds for doubting the commitment of many of the top national leaders to using market methods of control in the countryside. The government, for example, is currently pushing for a nationwide effort toward specialized agriculture, whereby regions with particular conditions will concentrate on crops suitable to those conditions. But what if the production teams are unresponsive? Will the top leadership simply manipulate prices to achieve the desired goal, or will it use more direct action, such as raising delivery quotas for the desired crops?[18] If emphasis on market forces continues to be as successful as it appears to have been between 1978 and 1982, that role may well continue to expand. But if the underlying poor agricultural endowment once again slows growth, as the analysis in the previous chapter suggests is probable, then China's leaders may be tempted once again to resort to direct action even in the absence of any evidence that direct action will improve performance.

The Sources of China's Implementation Capacity

To understand how the Chinese were able to make so many fundamental changes in the institutions governing the rural sector and how direct administrative controls could be implemented on such a massive scale, a host of considerations that influenced the choices must be examined, among them: ideological convictions, external relations, and beliefs engendered during the protracted guerrilla campaign before the Communist takeover in 1949; the strength of the organizational instruments, in particular the bureaucracy and the Party, which have been relied upon to implement policies; the desire to wrest the peasantry from the grip of traditional, kin-related communities and the impossibility of disavowing the many facets of tradition altogether; a deep suspicion of foreigners (nurtured during the preceding century and more), combined with a fierce national pride, which made it imperative to "walk on two legs"; and, finally, the leadership's authoritarian bent of mind, which placed both democratic socialism and market-related decentralization on the fringes of possibility.

It is perhaps worth reiterating at this stage one of the economic tenets of Communist ideology, since it has had an important influence on how Chinese organization has evolved and how social pressure has been combined with material benefits to motivate a peasantry lacking the spur of individual gain. There is a strong egalitarian cast to Maoist ideology. Differences in status and in material possessions, it is believed, can create divisions among the populace, weakening political solidarity and the willingness to make extraordinary sacrifices for the sake of national development. There is a pragmatic underside to this ideological standpoint. By downplaying material rewards the regime is able to divert resources to investment and detract attention from the low overall level of income.

Recently the regime has seen the disadvantages of pushing its egalitarian ideals too far, but the fact still remains that the Chinese are unique in the determination with which they have tried to disassociate the motivation to work from immediate pecuniary benefits. Nor is it possible to ignore their success in keying the motivation of the labor force to moral exhortation, nationalist pleas, the achievements of model workers, as well as a range of nonpecuniary incentives, which are very different from those found in most other countries.

Emergence of the Communist System

The development strategy pursued by the Communist regime has not been dictated by economic exigencies alone. Not only is labor the most abundant economic resource, it is also the basis for the regime's power. In the course of nearly two decades of skillful guerrilla campaigning in the 1930s and 1940s, the Communists became adept at organizing and leading the peasantry. The possession of these organizational skills encouraged the leadership to support labor-intensive production techniques, and it reinforced the ideological predispositions toward an authoritarian, centrally controlled socialist system, in which market prices and individual initiative were deemphasized.

To organize the people, the regime needed instruments, the most important of which were the Communist Party and the state bureaucracy. The government also needed to change the rural institutions so as to weaken potential sources of opposition to its policies, to suppress traditional elites, to sever the peasantry's traditional allegiances, and to create a political as well as an attitudinal orientation, which would strengthen its grip on the populace and facilitate embedding new modes of thought and action. The regime quickly realized, however, that a revolutionary organizational structure had to come to terms with the cultural inheritance of the peasantry. Traditional institutions could be dismantled and replaced by a new species, but the new institutions had to be built on the foundations of the old. For this reason, it is necessary, when studying the Chinese efforts to mobilize the masses, to note how some of the existing institutions were accommodated and utilized, how others were outflanked, and how still others were effectively demolished.

Rural manpower could be organized and the institutional environment modified, but by itself this was not quite enough to call forth the effort required. And the regime learned that organizational pressure and ideological exhortations had to be blended with material incentives to sharpen the peasantry's desire to cultivate the land assiduously.

Rural Society before the Communist Takeover

As a start it is useful to sketch the socioeconomic axes of traditional village society from the late nineteenth century until the early 1930s. The vital elements of a peasant's life were the ties of kinship and community. They regulated not only social interaction, but also the circulation of labor and capital within the village. A cluster of hamlets, frequently linked by many levels of family connections and economic exchange, were often arrayed around a market town. Such a marketplace was the focus of local trade, but it could be the site of the largest temple and support an active marriage bourse as well. By serving as the crossroads at which marriages were negotiated and by being the center of religious activity, the market town created its own rural planetary system.

The society was markedly hierarchical with many gradations of wealth, status, and power. Leadership was the prerogative of the gentry and the landowning class, which were usually allied with the local representative of the imperial bureaucracy.[19] Often the power of the rural elites and their close association with the state led to a cruel exploitation of the peasantry. Even where there was no oppression, the life of the peasant was more closely regulated than is (or was) common in other developing countries. It is a testimony to the power of tradition that several of the mechanisms through which lineage heads and magistrates exercised control have survived, albeit in new guises, down to the present day.[20] The Communists also found it expedient to come to terms with the local marketing systems, after making a determined effort to destroy the institutional arrangements they represented.[21]

Transformation of Rural Institutions in the 1950s

There were many sources of friction in the rural society: within and between lineages, between tenants and landlords, between secret societies and other social groupings, and between farmers who were forced to pay taxes and the officials who collected them. The Communists profited from such tensions and manipulated them to arouse class consciousness among the peasantry and to ignite class struggle. The initial efforts in Kiangsi were a failure, but the lessons learned there were later translated into an effective strategy for mobilizing peasants in the northern parts of the country.[22]

Kiangsi had been a disaster because of the heavy-handed attempts to incite the peasants combined with the brutal methods used to eliminate the wealthier elements. There had been little attempt to understand the rural social relations and the existing sources of friction. Most serious of all, the Communist cadres had not listened to the peasants or tried to create a rapport with the villagers through face-to-face contacts.

Once the Party was ensconced in Yenan and in numerous bases behind the Japanese lines, however, it attempted a different tack, using newly trained cadres to mesh the Communist organization with the rural communities as tightly as institutional realities permitted. This time, there was no move to destroy the local leaders and the rich peasants; on the contrary, the Communists, while pressing ahead with some of their social reforms, attempted to forge alliances with local leaders.

In Kiangsi, priority had been given to destroying rural elites, and the Party fueled the peasants' sense of being an exploited class. It realized, however, that the masses would not relinquish their traditional alliances and institutions unless the Communists promised them some immediate and tangible benefits. Hence, during the 1940s, the Party devoted much of its energy to building up the economy of the base areas, improving the administration, encouraging cooperative activity, and assisting the poor, by reducing rent and interest payments.

But the goal of revolutionary change was not neglected. Cadres were instructed to immerse themselves in village communities so as to know the peasants on their terms and to see their problems, their relations with landlords, with neighbors, and with kinfolk through the eyes of the villagers themselves. To wean them away from traditional institutions and the network of social relations, which placed the lineage at the center of the peasants' world and the gentry at the apex of the social hierarchy, the cracks and fissures had to be seen from the inside. Then the susceptibilities of the people were diligently preyed upon until the cracks expanded to the point where the entire structure collapsed in a welter of contradictions, lineage rivalries, class animosities, tenancy disputes, and all the rest.

Thus waves of cadres began patiently to undo the entire social and economic fabric of communities in Communist-held areas and then to reweave and tie them into the infrastructure of the base. "How deep the communist forces set their roots in the soil of the North was a testimony to their experiences in Kiangsi."[23]

While they struggled to build a mass base, the Communists benefited in no small part from the war against Japan, which weakened the Nationalist government and at the same time induced many of those wishing to fight the invaders to join forces with the Communists. In the early 1940s the Communists also began to experiment with rural policies, which they were to introduce after taking over the government.[24]

Once the Communists were in the saddle, the organization of rural manpower and the transformation of rural institutions began in earnest. The new government, which in those days was heavily influenced by the Soviet model, had three objectives.

The first objective was to enlarge the organizational apparatus of the state and to envelop the peasantry within an administrative structure that gave the regime control over all social and economic decisions. In 1949, the regime had 720,000 cadres at its disposal, not including those in the military. New cadres were recruited from among peasants and workers who had distinguished themselves in mass campaigns, from among college students who had been trained and indoctrinated, and from among administrators belonging to the old regime who were willing to embrace the Communist value system. Within three years, the number of personnel at the Party's disposal had risen to 2.75 million (it now exceeds 36 million). From this number, the most trusted cadres were sent to the villages to learn about the problems of the peasants through personal contact and to establish the framework of communication and control, which the regime could then use for the task of development.

A second, and related, objective was to consolidate political power by broadening the base of support among the peasantry and by dislodging the traditional elites. Land reform, spearheaded by special work teams of between three and thirty members, was the first step.[25] It commenced in 1947 amid much violence directed against the 20 million members of the landlord class, and as many as 800,000 of them were eventually executed.[26] By 1950, the government felt that the expropriation of land from the better-off peasants had progressed to the point where production was being affected. It therefore slowed down and systematized the pace of socialization, but the destruction of the landlord class and the confiscation of their property continued. From land reform to communization involved four additional steps. At first, mutual aid teams modeled on traditional community arrangements were set up, to be followed by producer cooperatives and then advanced producer cooperatives (APC). Under the APC, most land implements and labor were pooled, but some residual ownership rights and decisionmaking autonomy was retained. The APC, however, did not offer the degree of control over the populace that the leadership desired, and, in 1958, Mao overrode all opposition and signaled the start of communization. Within a year 26,000 vast communes had subsumed earlier administrative structures, had eliminated the old marketing systems, and had challenged even such well-entrenched institutions as the family.[27] The number of communes has since risen to 52,000 (see Table 5–1).

As already indicated, the Great Leap caused intense disruption. Less than two years later the regime found it expedient to reduce the size of the communes for the sake of administrative convenience and to realign them, where possible, with the traditional market systems. Revolutionary change slowed down in the first half of the 1960s. It was a period of bureaucratic consolidation. Administrative procedures were formalized, and the decentralizing measures introduced in the latter part of the previous decade were partially reversed. The structure that was emplaced in the early 1960s still remains, although the mechanics of management have changed.

The regime's third objective was to use the political power and administrative leverage at its disposal to mobilize agricultural labor for development purposes, to increase investment, to improve agricultural

Table 5-1. *The Structure of Communes, Brigades, and Teams*

Item	Nationwide (1980)	Shaanxi (1978)
Number of communes	52,000	2,250
Number of brigades	700,000	29,912
Number of teams	5,150,000	139,396
Households per commune	2,600	1,922
Households per brigade	195	162
Households per team	26[a]	35
Population per commune	13,000	9,436
Population per brigade	(1,148)	795
Population per team	(172)	171

Note: Figures in parentheses were derived by the authors and are subject to substantial error because of rounding in the underlying data.

a. This can be as high as 90.

Sources: The nationwide figures are from the Ministry of Health, Statistics, and Finance Bureau, *China Encyclopedia, 1980* (Beijing, 1980). The Shaanxi figures are from a briefing to the American Economics Delegation (1978).

extension, and to extract surplus grain for urban consumers and for export. Five policies are suggested to have been especially important in mobilizing resources:

a. Decentralization

b. Politicization of the rural populace

c. Mass campaigns

d. Suppression of lineages and traditional social linkages between communities

e. Creation of the work point system and the blending of material with other incentives.

Each of these policies is analyzed briefly in the following sections, except for the last, which was discussed earlier.

DECENTRALIZATION. The administrative structure in the rural sector is rigidly hierarchical. It is divided into several tiers: province, county, commune, brigade, and production team, with the last being the basic accounting unit in the system. Decisionmaking power is highly concentrated, but the center has encouraged feedback from lower level units and delegated routine decisions. However, the impression of power concentrated at the center is counterbalanced by a sense of its tenuousness. The Chinese regime is poorly equipped to run such a huge economy from Beijing, since it lacks the apparatus to gather and process the information needed to do so. A centralized economy depends heavily on the collection and processing of information, and this requires a large staff of technicians, both to devise the procedures for gathering the data and to make it usable for decisionmakers. China lacks both the educated manpower and the administrative channels to mount a massive planning operation and cope with extensive and detailed monitoring (see Chapter 8). Before the Communist takeover, the collection of statistics, especially agricultural ones, had been sporadic at best. In 1951, a Bureau of Statistics was established, but the information that began trickling through these newly created channels was deficient in quantity as well as quality. The system was twice exposed to a severe battering: once during the Great Leap Forward and again in the course of the Cultural Revolution. A renewed interest in statistical reporting emerged with the passing of the Gang of Four era, and the government is making strenuous efforts to create additional channels of information and to refurbish existing ones, but there is still a very long way to go before the quality and volume of information is adequate for the needs of such a large, centrally managed economy.[28] The leadership is well aware of these deficiencies and has attempted to maintain its hold by making the economy, as far as possible, self-policing, through institutions such as the commune, through the moral values of selflessness and commitment, and, most recently, through the use of market forces. The important policies emanate from Beijing, but the center makes little effort to monitor and direct on a day-to-day basis. Its power is dramatized by its control over all the major policy initiatives; its weaknesses are rarely apparent because it has contrived, by dint of indoctrination and institutional means, to make the economic units respond to its directives and monitor their own progress. This approach is called "putting politics in command," and it is a crucial part of the Chinese control mechanism.

POLITICS IN COMMAND. The Chinese have proclaimed repeatedly that rural development rests upon effective local leadership and a dynamic interplay between the Party cadres and the masses—the so-called "mass line." Thus, at the interface between the state organization and the populace, control is not an administrative process but a political one. The masses are not so much commanded as led. They are encouraged to see themselves as participants in a political system that is responsive to their needs. Control, then, is a matter of winning commitment to the policies of the center by forcing political awareness on the populace, making them appreciate their stake in the country's development, and thereby engendering a willingness to acquiesce to the regime's policies. Every policy, whether its objectives are social or economic, has a political dimension. It is never presented as a hard and fast directive, but demands a response from the masses; it asks of them to enter into a kind of collaborative venture with the Party leadership and to view the local cadres as their spokesmen.

The Communist regime concluded at an early stage that detailed management of the economy from one or even several centers was beyond its administrative capability. It nevertheless went ahead with administrative centralization, avoiding as far as possible the delegation of power to subordinate units. Flexibility was injected into policies, not through administrative design, but by making the interpretation of policies an intensely political effort involving mass participation.[29]

A highly politicized populace is a volatile body, but three significant checks have been built into the system to help keep all the pieces together. The Party, of course, is the vehicle for politicizing the masses, but to stay in command it must retain an exclusive right to the political dialogue with the masses. This it does by exercising its power to screen all appointments to positions of authority, thus ensuring that only those with the correct ideological views earn the right to lead or administer.

The sheer mass of the state machinery is a second check on any turbulence that may arise in the lower reaches of the administrative hierarchy as a result of grass roots political activity and the impossibility of detailed regulation. Bureaucratic inertia has regularly been decried, but by minimizing changes and encouraging the persistence of old routines, it stifles the destructive as well as the beneficent changes. Local autonomy in the Chinese system can never go very far unless the center wills it or unless Beijing dismantles the bureaucracy, as was attempted during the Cultural Revolution.

The third corrective, which is really a means of keeping cadres on a tight leash, is the manner in which policies are enunciated and filtered down the administrative and Party hierarchies. Most often, the leadership only defines broad goals and leaves it to cadres to proceed in the most appropriate manner at their own discretion.[30]

The general terms in which policies are presented allow for local variations. A policy's frame of reference, however, is determined by an ideological code. A cadre must interpret and act or else he will be attacked for quietism, but if he is misinformed about recent changes in the code, he is likely to err in his interpretation and be vulnerable to a purge. The most unsettling feature of the entire process is that the code keeps changing, and past interpretations can be branded as erroneous at a later date, with unfortunate consequences for the cadres concerned.

Although this approach can, on occasion, demoralize the lower ranks, it has numerous advantages for the leadership. It gives flexibility to administrators in the field. More important, perhaps, it puts cadres in a perpetual state of vulnerability. Local influence is no guarantee against a purge in the next campaign. The Party dominates the country's politics, but each cadre is at the mercy of Beijing.

Finally, since every ripple in the ideological current must be noted with care, those who govern the country are constantly observing the actions of the Party leaders and weighing each utterance with a sensitivity honed by the memory of many rectification campaigns. Being the ideological center of the country enormously reinforces Beijing's importance as the administrative center. It could not be otherwise in a country where the regime's power and its ability to mobilize resources depend so much on ideology and the political reflexes of the populace.

MASS CAMPAIGNS. For decades the Communists have firmly believed in the political and economic efficacy of mass campaigns.[31] Such campaigns have been used to galvanize the populace into undertaking particular projects requiring very large inputs of labor. They have also been a part of the continuing effort to suppress deviancy, which in China can mean actual or suspected infringement of the Party line being enunciated around the time of the campaign. A campaign of this sort is directed not only against politically (or morally) untrustworthy elements of the masses, but also against cadres whose behavior is considered less than impeccable by the prevailing standards.

Mass campaigns are exhausting. If a campaign is pressed too long, people become restless, and the enthusiasm of the cadres also begins to flag in the face of a rising crescendo of criticisms. Hence campaigns are necessarily periodic and relatively short-lived occurrences. To supervise—and, one might add, to politically indoctrinate—the peasantry on a more continuous and low-keyed basis, the regime has relied on group discussions and pressure. The working population has been divided into study groups of perhaps twelve to twenty individuals each, guided by politically reliable cadres or local activists who have been screened by the Party.[32] The study groups, which resemble in some ways the village institutions that existed in imperial times, are a vehicle for quickly communicating the regime's policies to the people at large. Group discussions also keep the Party abreast of reactions to these

policies and the general mood of the rural populace. The most important function of these small groups, however, is to constantly evaluate
the behavior of each member according to criteria set by the Party.
Enforced participation, searching criticism, and unending political indoctrination are notably effective in achieving conformity and contain-
ing protest.

SUPPRESSION OF SOCIAL LINKAGES AND INSTITUTIONS. The system of
politically oriented groups that is built on earlier foundations is one of
the positive institutional measures for controlling the masses. There are
also several others, whose purpose has been quite the reverse.

Confiscation of property during the land reform and active persecu-
tion of gentry thereafter went a long way toward extinguishing the
power of the rural elite. With the landowning class in disarray, the
lineages quickly began to lose their social significance. The Communists, however, were not satisfied with removing the gentry from the
role of community leadership. As long as lineage connections remained
alive, they could serve as a focus for future rural resistance. Hence, the
family, which was the building block of lineage organization, came
under sustained attack.[32] The regime has not attempted to eliminate the
nuclear family, a social unit involved with rearing children, providing
support for the elderly, and producing foodstuffs.[33] The Communists
have tried to prevent the coalescence of families into social entities that
resist penetration by the state and can become a source of political
resistance. To neutralize the political potential of the family, the state
has moved against the institution of arranged marriages, through which
alliances were cemented and lineages gained power. In the past, a
suitable spouse was chosen by an individual's parents in collaboration
with lineage elders. It was the parents, with some support from kinfolk,
who paid for the dowry and wedding ceremonies. The Marriage Law,
passed in 1950, disallowed the arrangement of marriages or the giving of
dowries. Extravagant wedding functions, which injected vigor into
social relations, have also been frowned upon by the Party as a waste of
time and savings.[35] Thus, the nuclear family has been carefully preserved as a social unit, but its functions have become rather petrified. It
has been forced into becoming inward-looking and has been disassoci-
ated from the lineage; it is politically quite defenseless and at the mercy
of the state. Whether the partial rehabilitation of market towns will
breathe new life into dormant lineage relations remains to be seen.
Much depends on the success of experiments with producer autonomy
and the price mechanism, the willingness of Chinese leaders to modify

socialist ideals, and the political repercussions of widening differences in rural income.

Mao believed that religion was one of the four thick ropes binding a peasant to the old order—the other three being the marital system, the authority of clan leaders, and the many levels of influence in the political system. The effective penetration of rural society, therefore, could not be complete so long as the religious institutions remained untouched. In the early 1950s the Party began to close down monasteries and to disband the monastic orders. Ancestor worship and the keeping of tablets were banned, ancestor halls were closed, and the peasants were pressured to substitute new secular functions for traditional religious festivals. The campaign to dislodge religious institutions has been quite successful. Organized religion has ceased to be a living force in China.[36]

The Chinese Experience as a Model of Development

Rural development is very often viewed almost exclusively in terms of increased production resulting from the effective use of technological factors, with a salaried bureaucracy providing inputs, supporting research centers, and manipulating prices. It is thought that all this can be achieved without touching the institutional framework. The strategy favored, according to Ashok Rudra, is one which "aims at changing the forces of production, without aiming at any concomitant changes in the relations of production."[37]

Successes and Strengths

On this point at least the Chinese experience is unequivocal. Institutional changes, sometimes of a very far-reaching sort, are unavoidable for a country that is both making the transition from a "feudal-capitalist" agrarian structure to a socialistic one, and attempting to modernize the rural economy at the same time. But the Chinese experience also points out the limits of deliberate social engineering. Old institutional furniture cannot be totally rearranged, nor is it possible for reformers to introduce whatever institutional arrangement catches their fancy. As Fairbank has pointed out, Chinese Communist organization has not been simply imposed on the populace by the leadership, but has required the extensive participation of the masses as well as the "millions of cadres who may be most conscious of the new ideology, but whose available options of language and style still lie within the old social matrix surrounding them. In fine, revolutionary organization must be achieved among the people and therefore largely within the limits set by their inheritance."[38]

The need for institutional change and the limits to this change are the first two generalizations that can be derived from a study of Chinese rural development. The far-reaching involvement of the masses in the processes of making and implementing decisions is a third lesson of some universality. In developing the mass line, the Communists devised an organization that reached down to the grass roots and that would lead the peasantry, but they also saw the necessity of interacting closely with the rural populace—to hear their problems, to understand their points of view, and to ensure that any new policies mirrored these realities.

The modernization of a socialist system such as that in China is inconceivable without a large and powerful organization. It is not easy, however, to state exactly how such an organization can be created and tempered so as to make it into an efficient instrument. The Chinese Communist Party emerged from the chaos that followed the collapse of the Qing dynasty. It benefited from the nationalist sentiments aroused by the presence of Europeans in the treaty ports and later by the Japanese invaders. The Party's organizational structure and techniques for controlling the peasantry matured during the decades of guerrilla warfare against the Nationalist forces. Finally the Party derived its inspiration, its dedication, and much of its resilience from the remarkable group of men who provided leadership and wove a compelling ideology out of their experience and convictions.

Abstracting from this historical sequence and ignoring the personalities of the men who led the movement leaves something less than a recipe for molding an efficient organization. Some of the ingredients are known: a dedicated group of leaders, a dynamic ideology that promised to end suffering, a committed band of followers, and a disaffected peasantry. But very little can be said about the temporal process by which all these are brought together or about the ability of a few able men to bring about a revolution, and, having dislodged the old order, to fulfill many of the promises that induced a multitude of people to accept suffering and upheaval.

Although it is difficult to be very concrete about the design of a successful revolutionary organization, it is possible to be more precise about the mechanism that enabled the Communists to exert irresistible pressure on the peasants and force them to adopt very frugal consumption norms and to work long hours on communally owned lands. The destruction of traditional lineage associations and the subsequent incorporation of the peasants into small discussion groups supervised by the Party is one of the ways in which earlier links were severed and the individual made to comply with state directives. But the effectiveness of this policy depended in turn on other regulations that kept communities intact by drastically curtailing both job mobility and emigration. By maintaining the stability of rural communities, the Communists ensured that the individual could not evade social pressure or sidestep social norms.

Organizational Problems

These observations can be instructive for a country considering a system for development based on a centralized organization, but of equal significance are certain problems with this strategy. These have become increasingly obtrusive in China as the size of the bureaucracy has grown and as revolutionary convictions have been overshadowed by administrative routines. Five are worth noting: (a) bureaucratism; (b) the emergence within the Party and the state apparatus of a new ruling elite that is increasingly remote from the people; (c) the difficulties of centralized management, particularly in the rural sector, in a system where the machinery to generate and communicate information to the leadership is poorly developed; (d) the importance of experts whose skills are indispensable, but whose ideological motivation tends to be weak; and (e) the disaffection of rural cadres, who actually implement the regime's policies.

None of these is peculiar to China. Any country attempting to manage a large and complex economy through a centralized bureaucracy is likely to encounter the very same difficulties. Further, the Chinese do not appear to have discovered a cure to these bureaucratic failings, but the recent history of the country does indicate how the frailties of a state organization may be contained by vigilance, criticism, and institutional reforms.[39]

Notes to Chapter 5

1. See R. Thaxton, *China Turned Right Side Up* (New Haven, Conn.: Yale University Press, 1983), pp. 38–39; and V. Lippit, *Land Reform and Economic Development in China* (White Plains, N.Y.: International Arts and Science Press, 1974), pp. 45–65.

2. S. Pepper, *Civil War in China: The Political Struggle, 1945–49* (Berkeley: University of California Press, 1978), chap. 7; and C. K. Yang, *Chinese Communist Society: The Family and the*

Village (Cambridge, Mass.: M.I.T. Press, 1959), chaps. 9 and 10; J. Gray, "The High Tide of Socialism in the Chinese Countryside," in J. Chen and N. Tarling, eds., *Studies in the Social History of China and Southeast Asia* (Cambridge: Cambridge University Press, 1970).

3. Corvee was a tax paid in the form of labor services.

4. Computing work points from standard labor days was a tedious business and encouraged experimentation with other forms of compensation such as seasonal contracting and the care of specific parcels of land, which resurfaced in the 1960s and are now, once again, in vogue. Peter Schran, *The Development of Chinese Agriculture, 1950–59* (Champaign: University of Illinois Press, 1969), pp. 29–31.

5. The political debate and maneuvering before the Great Leap are discussed by P. H. Chang, *Power and Policy in China*, 2nd ed. (University Park: Pennsylvania State University Press, 1978), pp. 65–121; while MacFarquhar has provided a remarkable account of intra-Party politics during 1958–60. See Roderick MacFarquhar, *The Origins of the Cultural Revolution*, vol. 2, *The Great Leap Forward, 1958–60* (New York: Columbia University Press, 1983).

6. Schran, *The Development of Chinese Agriculture*, p. 36.

7. An account of one community's experience with the Dazhai system is given in A. Chan, R. Madsen, and J. Unger, *Chen Village* (Berkeley: University of California Press, 1984), pp. 90–93 and 247–49.

8. The many forms of the responsibility system are described by: Zhang Yulin, "Readjustment and Reform in Agriculture," in Lin Wei and A. Chao, eds., *China's Economic Reforms* (Philadelphia: University of Pennsylvania Press, 1982), pp. 131–37; Kuan-I Chen, "China's Changing Agricultural System," *Current History*, vol. 82, no. 485 (September 1983), pp. 259–62; D. Zweig, "Opposition to Change in Rural China," *Asian Survey*, vol. 23, no. 7 (July 1983), pp. 883–84; and G. O'Leary and A. Watson, "The Role of the People's Commune in Rural Development in China," *Pacific Affairs*, vol. 55, no. 4 (Winter 1982–83), pp. 607–11. See also Liu Xumao, "A Brief Introduction to Several Important Kinds of Production Responsibility Systems Currently in Use in Our Country," *Jingji Guanli*, no. 9 (September 15, 1981), pp. ix–12–14; T. Tsou, M. Blecher, and M. Meisner, "The Responsibility System in Agriculture," *Modern China*, vol. 8, no. 1 (January 1982), pp. 41–103; N. L. Gonzales, "The Organization of Work in China's Communes," *Science*, vol. 218 (September 3, 1982), pp. 898–903; and K. Hama, "China's Agricultural Production Responsibility System," *China Newsletter*, no. 40 (1982), p. 2–11.

9. See "Team Leader on New Contract System," *China Reconstructs* (November 1981), pp. 50–51; and *Renmin Ribao Beijing*, "Editorial on Rural Responsibility System" (January 22, 1983) (in *FBIS, China*, January 22, 1983, pp. K6–K9).

10. See L. M. Wortzel, "Incentive Mechanisms and Remuneration in China: Policies of the Eleventh Central Committee," *Asian Survey*, vol. 21, no. 9 (September 1981), pp. 961–76; and V. Nee, "Post-Mao Changes in a South China Production Brigade," *Bulletin of Concerned Asian Scholars*, vol. 13, no. 2 (April–June 1981).

11. On the favorable effects of the responsibility system on production, see Kuan-I Chen, "China's Changing Agricultural System," p. 259; G. Johnson, "Responsibility Reaps Reward," *Far Eastern Economic Review* (October 6, 1983), p. 55; *Xinhua Beijing*, "Specialized Households Are Boon to Rural Economy" (September 26, 1983) (in *FBIS, China*, September 28, 1983, pp. K2–K4); and *Renmin Ribao*, "Wan Li's Speech of November 5" (December 23, 1982) (in *FBIS, China*, January 4, 1983, pp. K2–K3).

12. J. Domes, "New Policies in the Communes: Notes on Rural Social Structures in China, 1976–1981," *Journal of Asian Studies*, vol. 41 (February 1982), p. 264; and Zweig, "Opposition to Change in Rural China," p. 886.

13. Several articles expressing such concern have been carried by the Chinese Press: *Dazhong Ribao*, "Talks on Rural Work" (June 28, 1982) (in *FBIS, China*, July 9, 1982, p. O.5); "Further Sum-up, Perfect and Stabilize the Agricultural Production Responsibility System,"

Sichuan Ribao China (July 8, 1982) (in *FBIS*, July 14, 1982, p. Q1); *Renmin Ribao*, "Wan Li's Speech of November 5," pp. K5–K8; and Zweig, "Opposition to Change in Rural China," pp. 889–90.

14. Li Bingkun, "Rural Commune Family Sideline Occupations in China," *Zhongguo jingji nianjian* (1982), p. v–20.

15. This is discussed in Dwight H. Perkins, *Market Control and Planning in Communist China* (Cambridge, Mass.: Harvard University Press, 1966), pp. 70–71.

16. New China News Agency releases of December 31, 1971, and December 26, 1972. Sown acreage of these crops also rose sharply in 1972 as reported in State Statistical Bureau, *Statistical Yearbook of China, 1981* (Hong Kong: Economic Information Agency, 1982), pp. 140–42.

17. By 1981 the average purchase price of grain was 26 percent above that in 1978.

18. There is a large literature on the appropriate role of prices in China and the role of the market, particularly in various issues of *jingji yanjiu* (Economic Research). The best and most current work in the Western literature on China dealing with this subject is Nicholas Lardy, *Agriculture in China's Modern Economic Development* (Cambridge: Cambridge University Press, 1983), chaps. 2 and 3.

19. On the leadership of lineages by the gentry, see J. K. Fairbank, "Introduction: The Old Order," in J. K. Fairbank, ed., *The Cambridge History of China*, vol. 4, *Late Ching, 1800–1911*, Part 1 (Cambridge: Cambridge University Press, 1978), p. 13. Throughout imperial times, local government rested upon an alliance between magistrates and the gentry. See P. A. Kuhn, *Rebellion and Its Enemies in Late Imperial China* (Cambridge, Mass.: Harvard University Press, 1970), pp. 3–4. In many instances specialized local bureaus served as the vehicles for such cooperation. J. M. Meskill, *A Chinese Pioneer Family* (Princeton, N.J.: Princeton University Press, 1979), p. 208.

20. To govern the country through bureaucratic instruments of modest dimensions, Chinese emperors had to settle for a fairly extensive delegation of authority. Fortunately for the imperial government Confucianism allied with social institutions made it possible to compartmentalize society into more or less self-regulating units. Through the judicious infusion of the principle of collective responsibility, these units could be relied upon to administer themselves and pay taxes when the dynasty was strong. Institutions such as the pao-chia and the li-chia, which made collective responsibility into a bureaucratically super-vised reality, are described in Kuhn, *Rebellion and Its Enemies in Late Imperial China*, p. 60; P. A. Kuhn, "Local Self-Government under the Republic: Problems of Control, Autonomy, and Mobilization," in F. Wakeman, Jr., and C. Grant, eds., *Conflict and Control in Late Imperial China* (Berkeley: University of California Press, 1975), p. 258; and Hsiao, Kung-Chuan, *Rural China* (Seattle: University of Washington Press, 1960), chaps. 3 and 4.

21. G. William Skinner, "Marketing and Social Structure in Rural China, Part 3," *Journal of Asian Studies*, vol. 24 (May 1965), pp. 382–85 and 397–98; and A. Donnithorne, *China's Economic System* (New York: Praeger, 1967), p. 49.

22. See R. Hofheinz, "The Ecology of Chinese Communist Success: Rural Influence Patterns, 1923–45," in A. Doak Barnett, ed., *Chinese Communist Politics in Action* (Seattle: University of Washington Press, 1969); T. Kataoka, "Communist Power in a War of National Liberation: The Case of China," *World Politics*, vol. 24, no. 3 (April 1972), pp. 410–27; and C. E. Dorris, "Peasant Mobilization in North China and the Origin of Yenan Communism," *China Quarterly* no. 68 (December 1976), pp. 697–719.

23. Kataoka, "Communist Power in a War of National Liberation," p. 425.

24. The basic strategy was to serve the immediate interests of the peasants. "If we want to win," wrote Mao, "we must lead the peasants' struggle for land and distribute land to them, heighten their labor enthusiasm and increase agricultural production, establish crops, develop trade, and solve the problems facing the masses." P. Schran, "On the Yenan Origins of

Current Economic Policies," in Dwight H. Perkins, ed., *China's Modern Economy in Historical Perspective* (Stanford, Calif.: Stanford University Press, 1975), pp. 289–90; F. Schurmann, *Ideology and Organization in Communist China* (Berkeley: University of California Press, 1968), p. 416.

25. V. Shue, *Peasant China in Transition* (Berkeley, University of California Press, 1980), pp. 67–69.

26. Mao is reported to have given a figure of half million; Zhou-enlai, of 830,000; see Benedict Stavis, *Politics of Agricultural Mechanization in China* (Ithaca, N.Y.: Cornell University Press, 1978), p. 29.

27. The background to this landmark decision is provided by Parris Chang. See Chang, *Power and Policy in China*, pp. 84–85. On the number of communes, see P. Schran, "Economic Management," in J. M. H. Lindbeck, ed., *China: Management of a Revolutionary Society* (Seattle: University of Washington Press, 1971), p. 204.

28. Problems with Chinese statistical reporting are discussed by H. Egawa, "Chinese Statistics: How Reliable?" *China Newsletter*, no. 33 (1982), pp. 12–15.

29. For a discussion of mass participation, including some of its drawbacks, see L. W. Pye, "Mass Participation in Communist China: Its Limitations and the Continuity of Culture," in Lindbeck, *China: Management of a Revolutionary Society*, note 27; and J. Sigurdson, *Rural Industrialization in China* (Cambridge, Mass.: Harvard University Press, 1977), pp. 116 and 120.

30. Chang, *Power and Policy in China*, p. 180.

31. See S. L. Greenblatt, "Campaigns and the Manufacture of Deviance in Chinese Society," in A. Auerbacher Wilson and others, eds., *Deviance and Social Control in Chinese Society* (New York: Praeger, 1977); and Alan. P. L. Liu, *Communications and National Integration in Communist China* (Berkeley: University of California Press, 1975), pp. 88–89, 113. For an account of how the Four Cleanups Campaign affected village life, see Chan, Madsen, and Unger, *Chen Village*, chaps. 2 and 3.

32. In "augmenting formal organizational structures with semi-official groupings of ordinary citizens and in assigning collective responsibility for reporting deviance to higher authorities, the small group captures the essence of the pao-chia system." The manner in which the study group conducts its sessions is reminiscent of the hsiang-yueh lecture system dating back to Sung times, which arranged for bi-monthly speeches to be given to the populace, throughout the empire, "stressing conformity with Confucian virtues and advocating an orderly industrious life." M. K. Whyte, *Small Groups and Political Rituals in China* (Berkeley: University of California Press, 1971), p. 20; and G. S. Alitto, *The Last Confucian* (Berkeley: University of California Press, 1979), pp. 209–10.

33. As Freedman has observed, "Bureaucratic influence [reaches] down right into the affairs of the smallest units of society. [The family] now lies open to the state. It has little property to hold it together. Its ritual bond has been removed. Its head can call on few sanctions to support him in the exercise of authority—his wife can divorce him, his children defy him." M. Freedman, *The Study of Chinese Society* (Stanford, Calif.: Stanford University Press, 1979), p. 250.

34. See P. Printz and P. Steinle, *Commune: Life in Rural China* (New York: Dodd, Mead and Co., 1973), p. 111; W. Parish and M. K. Whyte, *Village and Family in Contemporary China* (Chicago: University of Chicago Press, 1978), pp. 74, 321; and Article 13 of the Marriage Law, in D. C. Buxbaum, ed., *Chinese Family Law and Social Change* (Seattle: University of Washington Press, 1978), p. 479.

35. These persist though in a much attenuated form. See D. C. Buxbaum, "A Case Study of the Dynamics of Family Law and Social Change in Rural China," in Buxbaum, *Chinese Family Law and Social Change*, pp. 181, 186–87.

36. See H. Welch, "The Fate of the Religion," in R. Terrill, ed., *The China Difference* (New

York: Harper and Row, 1979); H. Welch, *Buddhism under Mao* (Cambridge, Mass.: Harvard University Press, 1972); Parish and Whyte, *Village and Family in Contemporary China*, pp. 249–51; and Chan, Madsen, and Unger, *Chen Village*, p. 87.

37. A. Rudra, "Organization of Agriculture for Rural Development: The Indian Case," *Cambridge Journal of Economics*, vol. 2 (December 1978), p. 383.

38. J. K. Fairbank, "The State That Mao Built," *World Politics*, vol. 19 (July 1967), p. 676.

39. For instance, competitive elections and the strengthening of the people's congress system provide influence over officeholders and increase the prominence of elected officials. B. Womack, "Modernization and Democratic Reform in China," *Journal of Asian Studies*, vol. 43, no. 3 (May 1984), pp. 428, 433–43.

Chapter 6

~~~~~~

Income Distribution

CHINA IS FREQUENTLY CITED as an example of a country that eliminated rural poverty by using programs that affected poor peasants directly. Even without industrialization and urbanization, it is sometimes argued, a nation willing to follow China's path of radical reform and direct action can often accomplish more than decades of economic development that relies on trickle-down effects to reach the poor.

Previous chapters showed that agricultural production did not begin to increase steadily until it began to use inputs from the rapidly growing industrial sector. This fact leads to the question of whether the same rapid industrial growth was necessary to meet the basic needs of the rural poor. Or was China able to eliminate the worst forms of poverty by imaginative changes in organization and by ways of redistributing income that did not depend on the modern sector or even on rapid increases in agricultural production?

Two key ingredients of a direct action or basic needs program to help the poor are the political will to push for such programs and the capacity to implement them once they are approved. In a very real sense, China after 1949 was a nation run in the interests of poor peasants by people who, in many instances, had themselves been members of the rural poor. China had also acquired a formidable capacity to implement programs in the rural areas.

Possessing both the will and the capacity to implement, China carried out wide-ranging programs designed to eliminate rural poverty or, at least, its worst effects on the quality of rural life. A key feature of many (but not all) of these programs was that they mobilized resources already in the rural areas, rather than drawing large amounts away from programs to develop the modern sector. The income of the poorest peasants was not raised as much by massive investments of concrete and steel in rural infrastructure in poor areas, as by redistribution of the former landlords' income.

China, therefore, is a test case of at least several kinds of rural direct-action programs to eliminate the worst forms of deprivation. In China it cannot be argued that a particular program would have worked only if it had been really tried. China did try many of the programs described as being desirable elsewhere. In fact, China has sometimes been the inspiration for such programs.

Behind the rhetoric, however, there are some surprises about the actual performance of China's programs directed at the rural poor. Rural incomes were redistributed significantly after 1949, but much of this redistribution occurred in the late 1940s and early 1950s. Rural inequality since the early 1950s has proved stubbornly resistant to efforts to reduce it further.

This chapter begins with an analysis of these quantitative trends in inequality within rural China from the 1930s to 1980. Some systematic work on this subject was done earlier, but most discussion of inequality in China was dominated until recently by the superficial impressions of the typical trip report.[1] Data published beginning in 1980, however, make possible serious quantitative analysis, although there are still many aspects of the distribution of income in China for which relevant data are not available.[2]

The latter part of the chapter expands the discussion to include what is known about trends in inequality between the urban and rural sectors. Throughout, an effort is made, first, to discern the extent of inequality and whether it was rising or falling over time and, second, to explain the sources of the remaining inequality and to analyze how government policy has ameliorated or, in some cases, exacerbated these remaining inequalities.

Definition of Terms

Economists with direct access to surveys of income distribution would usually look at the distribution of family income. Changing family structures during development complicate comparisons of distributions over time and between countries, but the distribution of family income is still a more useful measure of welfare than is the distribution of individual income.

Economists outside of China, however, do not have access to surveys of income distribution by family except for a few individual communes. Instead, they must work with the average per capita income of regions. The most complete data, for example, are for average incomes for entire provinces. There are also a few figures on the distribution of average per capita brigade income both on a nationwide basis and for a few individual provinces. The more disaggregated these data are, the closer they tend to approximate the size distribution of family income. Provincial averages in the Chinese context, in contrast, obscure differences in income within provinces that are far greater than differences between provinces.

Several different definitions of income and product can be used.

GROSS VALUE OF OUTPUT PER CAPITA. Output figures are available on a provincial basis for a few select years (notably 1957 and 1979), but are flawed measures of family welfare since they include intermediate inputs that are used up in the course of production. If intermediate inputs were a similar share of gross value throughout the country, gross value distributions could be used as a proxy for income or value added. But value added shares vary, particularly when commune output includes a substantial amount of rural industry where the share of intermediate inputs in gross value is typically much higher than with agriculture.

DISPOSABLE FARM FAMILY INCOME. The concept of family income includes income from both collective and private sources and ideally would include the income of family members who reside in the rural areas but work in state enterprises in the city or elsewhere. Data to fit this definition, however, are simply not available on a nationwide basis. The most serious problem is the fragmentary nature of much of the data on private income. There are no data on income of state enterprise employees residing in communes.

COLLECTIVE DISTRIBUTED INCOME. All sources of rural collective income actually distributed to farm families for their personal use include income in kind as well as in cash and the distributed profits of commune enterprises as well as income from agriculture. Excluded are all private sources of income and the income of family members who work in state enterprises. Commune accounting procedures make it easy to calculate collective distributed income, and it is these figures that Chinese analysts use to discuss problems of income distribution in rural areas. Much of the analysis in this chapter also relies on these data, but they are subject to probable biases that must be considered.

Income Distribution within Rural Areas

Data on income distribution for the 1930s and the 1950s contain many problems and possible sources of bias, but their message is clear. China's land reform in the late 1940s and early 1950s had a significant effect on the rural distribution of income (see Table 6-1). The income of the poorest 10 percent of China's rural population doubled, and that of the poorest 20 percent rose nearly 90 percent. In a matter of a few short years, the income of these very poor people rose by an amount that would have taken several decades to accomplish by general increases in farm output.[3] And general increases in output would have benefited these poor only if they had shared proportionately in the increase in output, something that may or may not have occurred.

At the upper end of the distribution, the top 20 percent of the population lost 17 percent of their income on average, and the next 20 percent, 11 percent. Actually, these figures are misleading. Landlords,

Table 6-1. *Distribution of Rural Income before and after Land Reform*

	Income share (percent)		
Decile	*1930s (before land reform)*	*1952 (after land reform)*	*Change in share*
Top 10	24.4	21.6	− 2.8
Top 20	42.0	35.0	− 7.0
Second 20	23.9	21.3	− 2.6
Third 20	14.9	17.4	+ 2.5
Fourth 20	13.2	15.0	+ 1.8
Bottom 20	6.0	11.3	+ 5.3
Bottom 10	2.5	5.1	+ 2.6

Sources: C. Robert Roll, "The Distribution of Rural Income in China: A Comparison of the 1930s and the 1950s," Ph.D. dissertation, Harvard University, Cambridge, Mass., 1974, p. 76. Income as used here includes income from all sources, not just farm income. Roll's data for the 1930s are based on several surveys taken in that period, but the main source is a large national land survey taken in early 1935 under the direction of the National Land Committee. The data for the 1950s are also based on sample surveys of the period and are reported in various sources, notably Li Chengrui, *Zhonghua renmin gongheguo nongye shui shigao* (1962).

constituting roughly 3 to 4 percent of the total population, lost most of their income (they were reduced to the level of poor peasants, when allowed to live at all), while the remaining people in the top 40 percent retained most of their land and income. Since some landlords were not as well-off as many rich and even middle peasants, reducing their income affected the top four deciles, not just the first.

Land reforms do not always lead to such a large transfer of incomes from the rich to the poor. If landlords had been fully compensated for their lost land, less income would have been redistributed, particularly if those receiving the former landlord's property directly or indirectly paid that compensation. There was also nothing automatic about the poorest rural families receiving the land formerly held in tenancy. If the land had gone only to those who had formerly been renters, many rich and middle peasants would have received some land, while landless laborers, among the poorest people in any village, would have received none. As it was, Communist Party activists often had to come into a village and order land redistributed a second time to ensure that the poor rather than the politically more astute middle peasants received most of what was taken from the landlords. This extra effort was motivated by the belief that poor peasants constituted the natural base of rural support for the Party.[4]

The effect on agricultural production of collectivization in 1955–56 and of the formation of communes in 1958 has already been discussed. It is widely believed that the communes caused the differences in rural incomes to narrow even further. Although the limitations of the data make a definitive statement impossible, the available figures suggest, contrary to popular belief, that income differences narrowed little, if at all, between 1957 and the late 1970s or early 1980s.

The formation of cooperatives and communes did eliminate differences in incomes within a single cooperative or production team, when the difference resulted from variations in the amount of land owned by each family. The differences that remained within teams resulted from some families having more adult workers than others. A widow with three children under the age of twelve, for example, would have a lower income than a family headed by a forty-five-year-old couple with three sons in their late teens or early twenties.

The largest gaps in income in China, however, resulted from differences in income between regions, and the formation of communes did nothing to reduce these disparities. The effect of collectivization on the distribution of rural income within regions can be simulated, as shown in Table 6-2. These data give the average income of three classes of

Table 6-2. *Distribution of Income before and after Collectivization*
(percent)

Group	Before collectivization		Region	After collectivization (simulated)	
	Population share	Income share		Population share	Income share
1	3.84	10.79	1	3.00	8.47
2	6.61	11.98	2	5.67	10.70
3	16.29	20.81	3	11.13	14.91
4	20.28	19.60	4	24.43	25.42
5	39.34	29.57	5	41.41	32.53
6	13.63	7.19	6	14.35	7.91
Gini coefficient[a]	—	0.227	Gini coefficient	—	0.211

Note: The method of simulating collectivization used here was very simple. All peasant income within a given geographic region was assumed to be either raised or lowered to the average income of that region. Thus, the share of income was simply the total income of all rich, middle, and poor peasants of that region.

In contrast, in the figures for the period before collectivization, the incomes of classes from different regions were pooled to form the size groups. Thus, group 1 includes the richest groups, that is, rich peasants in regions 1, 2, and 3, plus middle and poor peasants in region 1, and so forth.

The regions are not single attached geographic areas, but are collections of regions from all over the country. Thus, region 1 includes the richer districts of the far northwest, but also certain districts along the Yangtze River.

— Not applicable.

a. Because these gini coefficients were calculated from grouped data, they probably slightly understate the degree of inequality.

Sources: Derived from data similar to, but somewhat more precise than, the data in Table 6-1. See Roll, "The Distribution of Rural Income in China," p. 72, table 19.

peasants (rich, middle, and poor). Collectivization changed the names of those in the bottom and top decile, but it did not reduce the four-to-one ratio between those in the higher and lower groups. In rich regions and poor, those with above average incomes were brought down to the average, and those below it were raised up. Thus, rich farmers in poor regions who might have made the fourth or fifth decile nationally were reduced to the tenth decile, and poor farmers in better-off regions were raised from the tenth to the fourth or fifth decile. Gini coefficients show that regrouping in this way left nationwide measures of inequality essentially unchanged. To oversimplify, collectivization gave all peasants the income of middle peasants within a region, but did nothing to eliminate the differences between regions.

This simulation makes clear that there was no necessary progression from the formation of communes to a reduction in rural inequality, but do recently published data indicate what actually happened to the distribution of rural income during the past quarter century? Averages of per capita gross value of agricultural output and collective distributed income for each province are presented in Table 6-3. If the suburban areas of the three directly administered cities (Shanghai, Tianjin, and Beijing) are excluded, the average per capita income or product in the richest provinces is about double that in the poorest, a rather narrow difference given the great size and diversity of the Chinese countryside. The crudeness of the per capita figures for 1957 makes it difficult to say anything about trends over time in the level of inequality. If the 1957 figures are reasonably accurate, however, interprovincial inequality as measured by the standard deviation of the subsample of nineteen provinces appears to have declined.

But do provincial averages capture most of the interregional inequality in China? Data on differences in income within provinces give a clear negative answer to this question. Data for Hebei and Gwangdong, presented in Table 6-4, show that within these two provinces the income of the richest 10 percent of the teams is around four times that of the poorest 10 percent, or roughly double the interprovincial difference. Less complete data for Jiangsu and Shaanxi provinces also indicate a range within each province of around four to one.[5] The Hebei data indicate that, at least for that one province, even the use of county data would seriously understate regional inequality.

One final set of data needs to be considered. Data published for 1979, based on an unpublished survey, indicate that 9.9 percent of all rural production brigades had average collective distributed incomes of more than 150 yuan a year (2.3 percent were more than 300 yuan), and 8.2 percent received average incomes of under 40 yuan. Similar data broken down into seven groups are available for 1980 and 1981. These figures also suggest that the ratio of the top to the bottom 10 percent was at least four to one. In fact, the somewhat hypothetical calculations in Table 6-5 suggest that the difference may have been more like five to one. The methodology used to construct these hypothetical distributions is explained in the notes to the table. The fit of the regression line used to estimate these distributions, however, is so poor that slightly different assumptions would have produced significantly altered results. Table 6-5 is at best a crude indication of trends over time, therefore.

What, then, can one conclude about trends in inequality in rural China between the 1950s and 1979 or 1980? Some figures indicate a

Table 6-3. *Income and Product per Capita, by Province*

Province (city)	Gross value of agricultural output (1970 prices in yuan)		Distributed collective income (current 1980 prices in yuan)
	1957 (approx.)	1979	
Shanghai	n.a.	516	197.2
Tianjin	n.a.	370	151.4
Beijing	n.a.	320	181.5
Xizang	n.a.	n.a.	127.5
Jiangsu	134	271	94.6
Heilongjiang	248	257	115.8
Zhejiang	168[a]	245	102.2
Jilin	319	241	117.5
Liaoning	197	234	122.6
Hubei	n.a.	234	87.5
Xinjiang	256	208	107.0
Hebei	n.a.	205	83.6
Nei Monggol	213	202	66.2
Qinghai	219[a]	198	108.0
Hunan	n.a.	197	91.9
Shanxi	172[a]	191	82.2
Shandong	123	188	101.6
Jiangxi	167	183	83.7
Fujian	131[a]	175	71.9
Shaanxi	n.a.	165	65.8
Guangdong	143	157	104.9
Henan	127[a]	156	73.1
Anhui	92[a]	156	66.4
Guangxi	n.a.	154	75.2
Sichuan	126	152	72.1
Yunnan	137[a]	134	68.3
Gansu	131	131	62.2
Guizhou	91[a]	117	50.4
Ningxia	n.a.	n.a.	77.3
Standard deviation ÷ mean (unweighted)			
Truncated sample[b]	0.348	0.231	0.241
All provinces	n.a.	0.384	0.350

Note: The 1957 estimates are a crude approximation obtained by converting provincial gross value of agricultural output in 1952 or 1957 prices into 1970 prices and then dividing by 86 percent of the provinces' total population, since data on rural population for each province were not available. The trends in individual provinces between 1957 and 1979 should not be used without further work to establish their validity. The figures used here are for commune output and population plus family sideline income, but excluding state farms.

n.a. Not available.

a. Figures are for 1954.

b. Refers to those provinces for which estimates for 1950 are available.

Sources: For 1979, Ministry of Agriculture, *Zhongguo nongye nianjian, 1980*, pp. 6 and 131. For 1957, derived from data in N. R. Chen, *Chinese Economic Statistics* (Chicago: Aldine, 1967). For 1980, *Zhongguo baike nianjian, 1981*, p. 70.

Table 6-4. *Differences in Rural Income within Provinces*

Per capita collective income (yuan)	Hebei		Guangdong, percentage of teams
	Percentage of teams	Percentage of counties	
0–40	13.9	1.4	18.7
41–50	14.1	10.1	14.6
51–100	54.8	75.6	50.7
101–150	14.8	11.5	11.1
150+	2.4	1.4	4.9

Source: Keith Griffin and Ashwani Saith, *Growth and Equality in Rural China* (Singapore: ILO Asian Employment Programme, 1981), pp. 19–20.

slight decline in inequality, others a slight increase. When all the evidence is put together, the most reasonable conclusion appears to be that there was not much change in rural inequality as a result of collectivization or of other policies pursued by the government after collectivization.

The figures we have used here, however, have excluded income from private sources. In the early 1980s the Chinese once again began to publish data on private as well as collective income. Between 1978 and 1981, private (domestic sideline) income rose from 27 to 38 percent of total household disposable income.[6] A survey of more than 4,000 households in 1958 indicated that private income in 1957 was also 27 percent of total household income, and a nonrandom sample of ten communes in 1965 yielded a 20 percent average from private sources.[7] Thus, the rise in 1981 to 38 percent appears to be a major departure from past patterns.

Given the size of private income, knowledge of how it is distributed is crucial to making any kind of definitive statement about the level of inequality in rural China. The rising share of private income also indicates that its distribution must be known before attempting to appraise the effect of reforms after 1978 on the overall distribution of income. Presumably, the poorest regions have limited access to the more profitable private activities. But do rich suburban communes have the highest level of private activity, or is collective work in these areas so profitable that it crowds out private work? The answer will have to await the publication of more data.

Table 6-5. *Hypothetical Distribution of Rural Income*
(percent)

	Income share		
Decile	1952 (after land reform)	1979 (hypo-thetical)	1981 (hypo-thetical)
Top 10	21.6	28–30	24
Top 20	35.0	43–45	44
Second 20	21.3	18–20	22
Third 20	17.4	15±	14.5
Fourth 20	15.0	12±	11
Bottom 20	11.3	10±	9
Bottom 10	5.1	5±	4

Note: The 1952 data are from Table 6-1. The 1979 estimates were reconstructed from information that in 1979 2.3 percent of rural brigades had a collective distributed income of more than 300 yuan, 7.6 percent averaged more than 150 yuan, 27.7 percent received less than 50 yuan, and of those 8.2 percent received less than 40 yuan. *Beijing Review* (January 19, 1981), p. 22. The 1981 data are from State Statistical Bureau, *Statistical Yearbook of China, 1981* (Hong Kong: Economic Information Agency, 1982), p. 203.

To obtain the 1979 estimates, a simple regression was used to estimate the parameters of a Pareto distribution, $\ln N = \ln A - \beta \ln Y$, where N = number of brigades with income above Y, and Y = per capita income of the brigade. The estimated parameters were for 1979: $\beta = -1.8834$, $\ln A = 13.8417$, and $r = 0.502$. The parameters for 1981 were: $\beta = -1.2909$, $\ln A = 11.74$, and $r = 0.189$.

The fit in the case of the 1981 data is particularly poor and one of several reasons for using these hypothetical distributions with great caution. This produced the following reconstructed distribution:

N	*Y* (yuan per capita)		N	*Y* (yuan per capita)	
	1979	1981		1979	1981
(23)	(300.0)	—	600	52.1	62.7
(76)	(150.0)	—	700	48.1	55.7
100	134.9	251.4	(723)	(50.0)	—
200	93.3	147.0	800	44.7	50.2
300	75.3	107.3	900	42.0	45.8
400	64.6	85.9	(918)	(40.0)	—
500	57.4	72.2			

Figures in parentheses are the actual published figures for 1979. The actual 1981 figures are not included for reasons of clarity and simplicity.

To convert these figures into the share of each decile in total income, the average distributed income for all brigades of 83.4 yuan per capita for 1979 and 101.32 yuan for 1981 was used to derive total income. Average income of each decile, except for the bottom and top decile, was assumed to be the average of the top and bottom income figure for the decile. The bottom decile was assumed to have an average income of 40 yuan, which may be high because 8.3 percent had an income of 40 yuan or below. The top decile was derived as a residual and hence was influenced by whatever errors existed in the other deciles. The second decile was assumed to have either an average income halfway between the top and bottom figure, as with the other deciles, or, in the 1979 case, an average income of 120 yuan. The latter figure was used to see how sensitive the final estimates were to possible errors in the parameters and average incomes assumed per decile.

Income Differences between Rural Areas

Although the data base for this study is imperfect, it is adequate enough to clearly establish the persistence of regional differences in income. Therefore it is possible to attempt to explain why these differences persist.

The first step in analyzing the determinants of rural income differences between regions is to plot income data on a map of China. Average per capita collective distributed income by province in 1980 is shown on Map 2, as is the location of all counties with an average per capita income below 50 yuan in 1979. As the map makes clear, most provinces with a per capita collective distributed income below 80 yuan per year were in China's interior. Of the 221 poor counties whose income remained below 50 yuan for three years running (1977–79), 103 were in the four western provinces of Guizhou, Gansu, Yunnan, and Shaanxi.[8] The richest provinces were either on the coast (except for Fujian) or in the comparatively sparsely populated regions of the far west or the northeast. The one major pocket of poverty not deep in the interior was on a part of the North China Plain. Roughly sixty poor counties were clustered together in an area about 500 kilometers long and 200 wide, overlapping parts of four provinces.

The data on the location of rich counties, those with per capita collective distributed incomes of more than 150 yuan in 1980, presented in Map 3 tell much the same story. If one excludes the lightly populated regions of Tibet, Qinghai, and Xinjiang, whose data are difficult to interpret, most of the remaining areas with high average farm incomes are near the coast and close to major urban centers. In fact more than 40 percent of the richest farm areas are those formally within urban districts (x's in Map 3). If rural counties located near urban areas are included, the figure rises well above 60 percent.

One significant source of differences in farm family income throughout the world is the fact that some families have more and better land than others. The first question to ask about China, therefore, is whether similar differences in land endowment per capita explain much of the variation in Chinese rural incomes. The presence of so much poverty in China's interior, however, suggests other explanations as well. Most of the poor interior counties are in mountainous regions where transport is poor and access to rich urban markets limited. Opportunities to set up subsidiary enterprises to supply urban factories with key parts or urban consumers with special products are thus also limited, and subsidiary

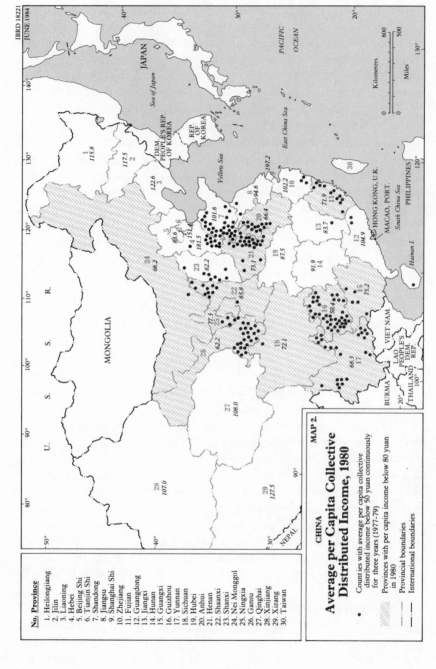

MAP 2.

CHINA

Average per Capita Collective Distributed Income, 1980

• Counties with average per capita collective distributed income below 50 yuan continuously for three years (1977-79)

▨ Provinces with per capita income below 80 yuan in 1980

--- Provincial boundaries

—·— International boundaries

No.	Province
1.	Heilongjiang
2.	Jilin
3.	Liaoning
4.	Hebei
5.	Beijing Shi
6.	Tianjin Shi
7.	Shandong
8.	Jiangsu
9.	Shanghai Shi
10.	Zhejiang
11.	Fujian
12.	Guangdong
13.	Jiangxi
14.	Hunan
15.	Guangxi
16.	Guizhou
17.	Yunnan
18.	Sichuan
19.	Hubei
20.	Anhui
21.	Henan
22.	Shaanxi
23.	Shanxi
24.	Nei Monggol
25.	Ningxia
26.	Gansu
27.	Qinghai
28.	Xinjiang
29.	Xizang
30.	Taiwan

IBRD 18221
JUNE 1984

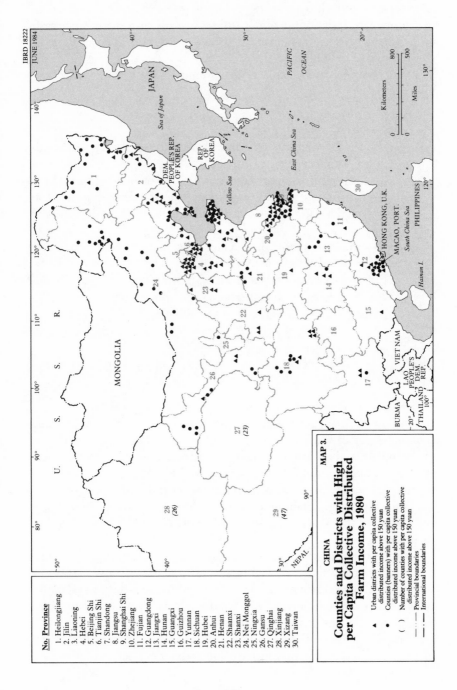

No.	Province
1.	Heilongjiang
2.	Jilin
3.	Liaoning
4.	Hebei
5.	Beijing Shi
6.	Tianjin Shi
7.	Shandong
8.	Jiangsu
9.	Shanghai Shi
10.	Zhejiang
11.	Fujian
12.	Guangdong
13.	Jiangxi
14.	Hunan
15.	Guangxi
16.	Guizhou
17.	Yunnan
18.	Sichuan
19.	Hubei
20.	Anhui
21.	Henan
22.	Shaanxi
23.	Shanxi
24.	Nei Monggol
25.	Ningxia
26.	Gansu
27.	Qinghai
28.	Xinjiang
29.	Xizang
30.	Taiwan

CHINA

MAP 3.

**Counties and Districts with High
per Capita Collective Distributed
Farm Income, 1980**

▲ Urban districts with per capita collective
   distributed income above 150 yuan

● Counties (banners) with per capita collective
   distributed income above 150 yuan

( ) Number of counties with per capita collective
   distributed income above 150 yuan

----- Provincial boundaries
—·— International boundaries

117

output would be expected to be a smaller share of the total than in areas nearer cities and cheap transport. Other possible sources of income differences are variations in opportunities to grow cash crops, since cash crops normally give a higher return per acre than grain, and variations in the amount of grazing land.

These relations can be explored in a preliminary way with the following equation:

$$y_i = a + b_1 x_{1i} + b_2 x_{2i} + b_3 x_{3i} + b_4 x_{4i}$$

where y_i = gross value of agricultural output per capita in the ith province

x_{1i} = per capita arable acreage in the ith province adjusted for quality by multiplying by an index representing the ratio of that province's grain yield per hectare to the national average

x_{2i} = the share of the ith province's income obtained from collective subsidiary activities

x_{3i} = the share of output from cash crops

x_{4i} = the share of output from animal husbandry

a, b_1, b_2, b_3, b_4 = parameters to be estimated.

Using 1979 data, the equation becomes

$$y_i = -112.8 + 58.8x_{1i} + 6.06x_{2i} + 0.185x_{3i} + 3.28x_{4i}$$
$$(-4.41) \quad (8.09) \quad (11.56) \quad (0.20) \quad (4.63)$$

t statistics are in parentheses, and R^2 (adjusted) = 0.901.

This equation suggests that two-thirds and more of the variation in provincial per capita output can be "explained" by variations in per capita arable land adjusted for quality, and that much of the rest of the variance results from different opportunities to develop subsidiary industries or, mainly in the far western provinces and Inner Mongolia, the availability of large amounts of land suitable for grazing. Somewhat surprisingly, the share of cash crops explains little or none of the variation.

Although these basic conclusions are likely to stand up to further analysis, the equation is flawed in several important ways. To begin with, it is presented as if it were a production function, but several of the independent variables on the right-hand side are not inputs into production in any conventional sense. Ideally, instead of the share of subsidiary output, one would use a measure of the distance to a major urban market, access to adequate supplies of electricity or coal, and other key inputs. Unfortunately, no such data exist in appropriate form. Similarly, rather than the share of income from animal husbandry, it would be better to use a measure of grazing land of a given quality per capita, but again the data are not available.

The land variable using 1979 data really includes inputs other than land alone because of the use of yield data to adjust for quality. Part of the difference in yields between provinces is presumably the result of variations in investment in irrigation systems or in the availability of fertilizer. One way around this problem would be to use yield figures from 1957 rather than 1979 to adjust for differences in the quality of land.[9] The advantage of doing this is that in 1957 the large-scale use of modern inputs, such as chemical fertilizer, had not begun. The disadvantage is that data for 1957 are less complete than those for 1979.

The main point of going through this flawed regression exercise is to show how locational advantages account for most of the differences in per capita output. Households that live in less densely populated regions with good soil or near cities where subsidiary activities are greater and more profitable, or both, have considerably higher incomes than households that do not enjoy these advantages. Households that live in densely populated, mountainous regions far from large cities and where rainfall is problematic are poor—often very poor. A collective income of 40 yuan per person per year in 1979, for example, would just pay for 150 kilograms of grain with nothing left over for anything else.[10] And 150 kilograms is not enough to meet the minimum calorie requirements of an adult farm worker. Since collective income must be spent on items other than grain, it is clear that neither 40 nor 50 yuan per capita, even after allowing for the lower requirements of children, would be enough to meet minimum calorie and nutrition requirements. It is presumably people with these levels of income that Li Xiannian was referring to when he spoke of 100 million people living at semi-starvation levels and of the tens of millions of people who must rely on government-supplied emergency rations to survive.[11]

Policy Tools to Redistribute Income

Has the Chinese government done everything in its power to eliminate these differences in income within the rural areas? Direct welfare measures, such as the supply of relief grain, undoubtedly eliminate the worst forms of deprivation except during periods of disorder or nationwide shortages, as in 1959–61. But what has been, or could be, done to

reduce inequality in income or production per capita other than providing relief for the desperately poor? Leaving aside rural-urban migration
for the moment, the government could have reduced inequalities by
moving the rural population around to equalize land endowments, by
instituting a progressive system of rural taxation, or by allocating state
expenditures on agriculture and state-controlled inputs to agriculture in
a progressive manner.

Relocation of Farmers

Given the fixed nature of China's arable land endowment, however,
there is little opportunity for moving farmers in poorly endowed regions
to areas with a more ample endowment. Poor farmers would have to be
resettled in regions already highly populated by international standards, and it is difficult to imagine an economically and politically more
disruptive process. No government interested in staying in power
would seriously contemplate such a measure. Even the limited attempts
to settle urban youth in the countryside created great tension. Most
urban youth, as a result, were sent off to state farms in the northwest
and northeast, where they helped to open up new land. Although the
state farms could handle a large portion of the millions of youth taken
out of the cities, these farms were much too small to skim off the surplus
rural population, which was growing at more than 10 million people a
year.

Taxes on Consumer Goods and Agriculture

With relocation eliminated as a policy tool for redistributing rural
incomes, the two remaining tools were taxes and state investment.
Basically, however, there are two kinds of taxes paid by farmers in
China, and neither is very progressive. By far the largest tax is that
represented by "industrial and commercial" (that is, sales or turnover)
taxes and taxes on the profits from selling industrial consumer goods in
rural areas. In the 1950s the average markup above cost on industrial
products was 47 percent, and most of this markup ended up in the
coffers of the state.[12] In principle, the markup on consumer goods could
have been calculated to introduce progressivity. In practice, however,
the prices were frozen at the levels prevailing in the early 1950s, and
prices for only a few items have been adjusted significantly since. The
markup on any given commodity, therefore, is a product of market
conditions in the early 1950s and subsequent changes in the cost per unit

in production. Notable exceptions include medicines and producer goods sold to rural areas where prices have been sharply reduced, but it is unlikely that these reductions had any noticeable effect on the progressivity of the tax. The only progressivity in these taxes, therefore, arises from the fact that poorer farmers provide a higher percentage of their own consumption on which no taxes are paid.[13]

China also has an "agricultural tax," which is, in effect, a land tax. Nominally, the tax is a percentage of the yield from a given piece of land. In practice, the yield figure used was the normal yield of the land, and the normal yield was fixed for long periods. In fact, there is little evidence of much change in the amount of tax on a given piece of land anytime during the past twenty years. What progressivity there is, therefore, depends on whatever existed when taxes were first set in the 1950s.

While individual peasant agriculture continued to exist, taxes were quite progressive, ranging from commutation for those with very low incomes to 30 percent of income for the top income group.[14] With the formation of cooperatives, however, calculation was based on normal yield, and progressivity was reduced. Basically, the state set an average rate for each province and then allowed local authorities to adjust the rate for specific areas within certain limits (not to exceed 25 percent). The lowest provincial rate was 13 to 13.5 percent for the areas of Xinjiang, Gansu, and Qinghai. The highest rates were for the land-rich northeast: 19 percent in Heilongjiang, 18.5 percent in Jilin, and 18 percent in Liaoning. Most other provinces were set at 15 or 16 percent.[15] In short, the degree of progressivity in the rate was substantially less than the differences in average provincial incomes.

What has reduced the redistributive effect of the agricultural tax even further is the small size of the tax overall. A rate of 15 to 16 percent of normal yield translated into only 11.5 percent of crop output in 1953–57 and a substantially lower percentage of gross agricultural output. By 1970 the actual rate had dropped to 6 percent and by 1978 to 5 percent.[16] As a percentage of total rural industrial and agricultural output, all rural taxes, including industrial and commercial taxes on rural industry, amounted to only 3.35 percent.[17] Provinces were allowed to exempt poor areas from the tax altogether, but given the low level of the tax in the first place, the redistributive effect of this measure could not have been great.

The original reason for setting the agricultural tax on the basis of normal rather than actual yield was administrative convenience. Once the commune structure was well established, however, administrative

122

convenience could not have been the major consideration. Communes had to keep elaborate accounts anyway, and a tax rate based on actual income would not have created many additional administrative problems. The continued use of normal yield appears instead to have resulted from a desire to remove any disincentives to increased productivity. In short, it was a choice in favor of growth over equity, at least in the short run.

Investment by the State

The redistributive effect of the central government budget overall may have been somewhat greater than that of the taxes on agriculture and consumer goods. In discussing this issue it is important to distinguish between redistribution from richer to poorer regions in general, and redistribution from richer to poorer rural areas. There is no doubt at all about the regionally redistributive effect of the government budget at a general level. Most profits and industrial and commercial tax revenues are collected by provincial governments, a portion of that revenue is turned over to the central government, and the remainder is used within the province. The central government revenues are then allocated to investment projects in the various regions. In Shaanxi, a poorer than average province, for example, only 8 percent of a total provincial revenue of 1,877 million yuan in 1978 was turned over to the center. In Jiangsu, one of the richest provinces, in contrast, 60 percent of all revenue was turned over to the center, while for Shanghai the figure for 1978 was 85 percent.[18]

For government expenditures on the rural sector, however, the redistributive effect on that sector may be substantial, but further work is required before definitive conclusions are made. The 1979 government budget called for the largest expenditure on the rural sector in Chinese history. Out of a total budget of 112 billion yuan, expenditure on various items in rural areas was to be 14.85 billion yuan, or roughly 20 yuan for each man, woman, and child in the countryside. Given a per capita total personal income of under 100 yuan, that 20 yuan was a considerable sum. Less than 2 billion yuan of that sum, however, appears to have been designated for relief.[19] Most of the rest of these funds were to be allocated to capital construction and to other production inputs. Still, if 2 billion yuan was in fact allocated to relief and was directed to the 100 million poorest people, that sum represents 20 yuan per capita on top of a per capita collective income of only 50 to 60 yuan.

Until more data become available, however, no statement can be made with confidence about how relief funds are distributed.

Little more is known about how government investment funds designated for rural areas are allocated. Certainly richer regions, such as those designated as "high and stable yield areas," have not been starved of funds. There has been some discussion over whether funds should be allocated to areas where they would have the biggest effect on production or whether distributive considerations should dominate, but there is no systematic study of this subject as yet. Some indirect evidence suggests, however, that the poorest provinces have not fared either particularly well or particularly badly in the allocation of research activity and of key agricultural inputs. Increases in grain yields are a measure of the effectiveness of research and of other key inputs, although they are much less reliable guides to the quantity of such inputs. As the data in Table A-5 indicate, there were large differences in the rates at which yields increased between 1957 and 1979, ranging from 6.3 to 153.9 percent. Some of the poorest provinces, notably Gansu and Guizhou, had the lowest rate of increase, but other of the poorest provinces, notably Henan and Shandong, had high rates of increase. Not surprisingly, there is some positive correlation between provincial per capita output in 1979 and the rate of yield increase between 1957 and 1979, but there is no such significant correlation for 1957.[20] In short, whatever caused these increases in yields, their effect was neither progressive nor regressive. Provinces that experienced substantial increases in yields rose relative to the others, and those in which yields stagnated fell, but the level of inequality overall changed little. The only input data currently available on a province-by-province basis are for certain measures of the level of mechanization. The more mechanized areas are generally the richer provinces and the suburban regions of the large cities.[21]

There is little evidence, therefore, that Chinese government policy toward agricultural investment has had a strong egalitarian thrust. Conceivably government policy has acted to offset the natural advantages and higher rates of investment of the richer communes and thus to prevent increasing inequality, but there is no hard evidence to support such speculation.

Could the government have done more to reduce inequalities within the rural sector? Certainly the level of welfare subventions could have been raised. In 1980 alone the cost to the budget of the combination of high farm purchase prices and urban sales prices for agricultural products was 15.94 billion yuan.[22] In economic terms it would have been feasible to raise urban sales prices to cover costs and to use the money to subsidize the rural poor rather than the much better-off urban residents. The poorest 200 million people in the rural areas would have received more than 70 yuan each. Whether a transfer of funds of this size would have been politically feasible, of course, is quite another matter.

Would a major reallocation of investment funds have reduced inequalities in rural production? No firm conclusion is possible, but there are grounds for skepticism. Guizhou and Gansu are poor not so much because no one has tried to do anything about their poverty, but because the barriers to increasing output in these provinces are formidable. Similarly, there is no easy way to bring water to the parched mountainous regions of Shaanxi, nor does it make much sense for industries in Shanghai to subcontract with the poor communes of Anhui. It is much more economical to subcontract with the nearby rich communes of suburban Shanghai and southern Jiangsu.

In short, other than through welfare subventions, there is no easy or quick way to reduce inequalities within the agricultural sector. There is no way, that is, as long as it is government policy to keep 800 million people in the rural areas trying to make a living on 100 million hectares of land divided up into sections of varying size and quality.

Income Differences between Rural and Urban Areas

The discussion to this point has ignored the migration of farmers out of the rural areas into the cities because Chinese government policy throughout the 1960s and 1970s successfully blocked such migration for all but a few. It is useful to look first at the effect of this policy on differences in income between rural and urban areas over time and then to explore briefly the implications of this policy for inequality in China more generally.

Between 1957 and 1977 the average wage of urban workers in state enterprises changed little. In fact, the basic eight-grade wage scale for blue-collar workers remained fixed throughout the two decades. At the same time, farm incomes per capita were rising, mainly as a result of increased purchase prices for farm products. These two trends—one stagnant, the other rising—would appear to indicate that differences between rural and urban incomes were narrowing. Appearances in this case, however, are deceiving.

The deception results from the fact that in comparing wage rates with per capita rural incomes, one series based on per worker income is being compared with another based on per capita income, including nonworking dependents. The correct procedure would be to compare either income per worker or income per family member in each case. Because the data used to make these calculations are flawed in several respects, the conclusions reached are rough and should be used with caution.

The results of these calculations are presented in Table 6-6. Incomes per worker in urban and rural areas did narrow from a ratio of 5.5:1 in 1957 to 3.5:1 in 1975, to only 2.9:1 in 1979. This narrowing occurred despite the fact that the ratio of value added per capita in the two sectors rose from 4:1 to 8:1. In effect, incomes in rural areas were rising in step with agricultural production, but urban workers were receiving a smaller and smaller share of the value added of industry.

For measuring family welfare, however, per capita, not per worker,

Table 6-6. *Measures of Disparities in Income and Productivity between Rural and Urban Areas*

	Value added per capita		State wage bill		Rural collective income	
Year	Agri-cultural sector	Non-agricultural sector	Per state worker	Per urban resident	Per laborer	Per rural resident
1949	55	120	n.a.	n.a.	n.a.	n.a.
1952	69	300	446	94.9	n.a.	n.a.
1957	79	455	636.5	156.8	114.7	40.5
1962	79	426	592	n.a.	n.a.	46.1
1965	106	615	652	231.1	139.4	52.3
1970	113	926	609	n.a.	n.a.	59.5
1975	126	1098	613	345.5	173.3	63.2
1977	123	1176	602	n.a.	n.a.	65.0
1978	132	1312	644	n.a.	n.a.	74.0
1979	161	1310	705	411.3	238.7	83.4
1981	191	1624	812	591.2	254.0	101.3

Note: Value added figures and wage bill and collective income figures are all in current prices.

n.a. Not available.

Sources: Ministry of Agriculture, *Zhongguo nongye nianjian, 1980*, pp. 41, 374; *Zhongguo jingji nianjian, 1981*, pp. VI-3, 7; *Zhongguo jingji nianjian, 1982*, p. VIII-3; and State Statistical Bureau, *Statistical Yearbook of China, 1981*, pp. 135, 199, 202, 434–36. There are slight discrepancies in the data within and between sources, but they are not large enough to materially affect these calculations.

Table 6-7. *Consumption per Capita in Urban and Rural Areas*

Year	Urban population (millions of persons)	Urban retail sales (millions of yuan)	Worker cost of living index (1979 = 100)	Urban retail sales per capita (1979 prices)	Nonfarm consumption per capita (1979 prices)	Farmer consumption per capita (1979 prices)	
						Adjusted[a]	Unadjusted
1952	71.63	11,380	78.4	202.8	189	115	92
1957	99.49	22,520	85.9	263.5	239	135	108
1965	101.70	32,590	94.3	339.8	258	134	107
1975	111.71	58,190	94.6	550.4	343	165	132
1979	128.62	76,770	100.0	596.9	406	190	152
1981	138.70	102,600	110.3	670.6	450	213	170

a. The in-kind share of rural consumption valued at farm purchase prices, assumed to be half of total rural consumption, was multiplied by 1.5 to make the figures comparable with urban retail prices for food (mainly grain). When more detailed retail price data are published, a more systematic calculation of the differences in food prices between urban and rural areas will be possible. It was assumed that retail prices in both areas were similar enough not to require adjustment.

Sources: Zhongguo jingji nianjian, 1981, pp. VI-3, 20, 23, 25; 1981 data are from, or derived from, *Zhongguo jingji nianjian, 1982,* pp. VIII-3, 23–26, 28. The data in the two yearbooks for the same categories are not identical, presumably due to minor revisions.

incomes are more meaningful, and there the gap between urban and rural incomes was widening from 3.9:1 in 1957 to 5.5:1 in 1975, with a slight reduction to 4.9:1 in 1979. The gap widened the most during the period of the most egalitarian rhetoric (1965–75) and actually declined slightly during a period when the government leadership seemed most disposed to accept increasing inequality (1977–79). Because these figures are in current prices and involved the assumption that state workers were also urban workers, it is useful to see if similar results are obtained with the data available on consumption per capita in real terms. These figures are presented in Table 6-7 and indicate urban-rural ratios in 1957, 1975, and 1979 of 1.9:1, 3.2:1, and 3.1:1, respectively. The rise from 1957 to 1975 is even sharper than with the income data, but the fall from 1975 to 1979 is no longer significant. Extending the period covered into the early 1980s does not appreciably alter these results. It is still too early to tell whether the responsibility system and the introduction of urban bonuses over the longer run will widen or narrow the rural-urban gap or will have no appreciable effect at all.

What is the explanation for this seeming paradox? The answer is surprisingly simple and is related to one form of the urban bias so common to the economic programs of many developing countries. Throughout the 1950s to the 1970s, the state poured most of its investment into large-scale industry located in cities or into infrastructure related to that industry. Employment in the state and urban collective sector, as a result, rose fourfold from 31.0 million in 1957 to 99.7 million in 1979. The urban population, in contrast, rose by less than 30 percent during this same period. Does this mean that most new state employees were located in the rural areas? Some, perhaps, but in general the answer to that question is clearly negative. Most new state employees lived in urban areas or in communes close enough to cities and towns so that they could commute to work on a daily or weekly basis.

State policies effectively prevented migration from rural to urban areas. In fact, because of the program of sending urban youth to the countryside, there was a substantial net reverse migration. Industry and related services in the cities, however, were growing at 9 percent a year, while the urban population was increasing at only 1 percent. Even with a rapid rise in the capital intensity of production, industry still needed more workers. The solution was to employ a higher proportion of urban residents, particularly women, since most men were already employed, and to draw on nearby communes for the remainder (mostly men in this latter case). There may also have been some migration of men from more distant places who came without their families. The result was that most urban families had more than one wage earner by the late 1970s, and most suburban communes had many residents who brought in substantial income but were not classified as commune members. Thus, while wage rates stagnated, family incomes in and around cities rose substantially, more than doubling between 1957 and the mid to late 1970s.

Did this rising disparity between urban and rural incomes have to occur? The answer is clearly not. Freer migration policies would have kept urban incomes from rising and, if the migrants had come from the poorer areas of rural China, would have made a significant dent in the poverty problems of those areas. There would have been a cost, of course. Either the state would have had to put much larger investments into urban housing and infrastructure, or it would have had to allow shack towns to proliferate around all of its cities, as has occurred in many other developing countries. As it was, the state put almost no investment into housing between 1967 and 1976, and since then has had to build apartments at a record pace simply to alleviate the extreme crowding that already existed despite the lack of new migrants.

Conclusion

This is not the place to explore the full implications of alternative urban development strategies for China. The subject is raised here only because it is fundamental to understanding the distribution of income within the rural sector and how that income compared with that of urban residents.

China was able to substantially narrow differences in income within rural areas in the 1950s. The ratio of 4:1 or 5:1 between the incomes of the top and bottom 10 percent compares favorably with the 8:1 ratio found in the Republic of Korea, a country that also experienced a genuine land reform.[23] The ratios in countries that have not undergone land reform are much wider.

But, as the data in this chapter indicate, differences within rural areas have narrowed little, if at all, since the 1950s, and the gap between urban and rural areas has actually widened. In the short run, China can alleviate the worst aspects of rural poverty through various welfare subsidies. Allowing the poorer areas to make more complete use of the household-based responsibility system may also help. Over the longer run, however, the only real solution is to allow farmers, particularly those in the poorest regions, to go to the cities. They may not have to go to Shanghai or Beijing, but they must go to cities somewhere. The alternative of trying to industrialize the Guizhou or northern Shaanxi countryside makes no economic sense. Nor will vast investments in agriculture ever make farmers in China well-off as long as each family has a half hectare or less to work with. Everywhere else in the world, the main method for removing rural poverty has been to turn most farmers into urban workers, and there is no reason to think that China has found an acceptable alternative.

Notes to Chapter 6

1. An important source for some of the analysis in this study is C. Robert Roll, "The Distribution of Rural Income in China: A Comparison of the 1930s and the 1950s," Ph.D. dissertation, Harvard University, Cambridge, Mass., 1974.

2. Recent studies using these data include E. B. Vermeer, "Income Differentials in Rural China," *China Quarterly*, vol. 89 (March 1982), pp. 1–33; and Keith Griffin and Ashwani Saith, *Growth and Equality in Rural China* (Singapore: ILO Asian Employment Programme, 1981). Another useful study based on Hong Kong refugee interviews is by William L. Parish, "Egalitarianism in Chinese Society," *Problems of Communism* (January–February, 1981), pp. 37–53.

3. Even at a growth rate of 2 percent per capita, a fairly high rate for agriculture, it would have taken thirty-three years to increase rural incomes by 90 percent. At the actual rate of 1.2 percent per capita (of gross value of agricultural output), a 90 percent increase would have taken fifty-four years (in constant prices).

4. There have been several good studies of the Chinese land reform experience. The best known is William Hinton, *Fanshen* (New York: Random House, 1966). A useful scholarly study of the process is by John Wong, *Land Reform in the People's Republic of China* (New York: Praeger, 1973).

5. Data supplied to the American Economics Delegation in 1979 indicated that the richest counties in Jiangsu had incomes of more than 220 yuan and the poorest, incomes of 50 to 60 yuan. For Shaanxi, the poorest areas had incomes under 50 yuan and the richest had incomes in the range of from 150 to 200 yuan.

6. These figures are from "Peasants' Income Goes Up," *Beijing Review* (June 21, 1982), p. 7. They also appear in State Statistical Bureau, *Statistical Yearbook of China, 1981* (Hong Kong: Economic Information Agency, 1982), p. 441.

7. The 1957 data are from *Tongji yanjiu* data office, "A Survey of the Distribution of Income and Benefits in 228 Agricultural Producer Cooperatives in 1957," *Tongji yanjiu* (August 23, 1958), p. 12. The 1965 figure is derived from S. J. Burki, *A Study of Chinese Communes, 1965* (Cambridge, Mass.: Harvard East Asian Monographs, 1969), p. 40.

8. The names of these poor counties are listed in People's Commune Management Office of the Ministry of Agriculture, "The Situation Nationwide with Respect to Poor Counties, 1977–1979," *Xinhua yuebao*, no. 2 (February, 1980), pp. 117–20.

9. We are indebted to D. Gale Johnson for first suggesting the use of 1957 figures for this purpose.

10. The average price of grain in 1979 was 12.86 yuan for fifty kilograms. Ministry of Agriculture, *Zhongguo nongye nianjian, 1980*, p. 381.

11. The full text of Li Xiannian's speech was not published, but this statement was reported in the part of the Hong Kong press with close ties to China.

12. The figure of 47 percent is an estimate from official data in Dwight H. Perkins, *Market Control and Planning in Communist China* (Cambridge, Mass.: Harvard University Press, 1966), p. 111.

13. Throughout this discussion of industrial and commercial and profits taxes it is assumed that the tax, although paid by enterprises, was passed on to the rural consumers in the form of higher prices. Formal analysis of the incidences of these taxes would modify this statement but would not affect the basic argument.

14. The precise rates can be found in various sources, including Li Chengrui, *Zhonghua renmin gongheguo nongye shui shrgao* (1962), p. 388 (of the Japanese translation).

15. These rates are given in *Zhonghua renmin gongheguo fagui huibian* (January–June, 1958), p. 263.

16. The 1970 figure is from *Peking Review* (November 9, 1973), p. 10. The 1978 figure is from a release of the New China News Agency of July 6, 1979 (in *FBIS, China*, July 10, 1979).

17. This figure is for 1977 and includes industrial and commercial taxes paid by rural enterprises as well as the agricultural tax. New China News Agency (February 9, 1979) (in *FBIS, China*, February 12, 1979).

18. These data were supplied to the American Economics Delegation (1979) by government officials in the three areas. The main work on the regional distribution of government revenues and expenditures is that of Nicholas Lardy, using data mainly for the 1950s; see "Centralization and Decentralization in China's Fiscal Management," *Chinese Quarterly* (March 1975), pp. 25–60 and *Economic Growth and Distribution in China* (New York: Cambridge University Press, 1978).

19. The Chinese finance minister's report does not give a relief figure, but does give a figure that includes rural capital construction, circulating capital, and relief funds (7.8 billion yuan) and separately gives the capital construction figure (5.46 billion yuan).

20. Taking the gross value output per capita in 1957 as the independent variable (x) and the percentage increase in yield from 1957 to 1979 as the dependent variable (y), produces the equation $y = 83.04 - 0.0824x$, with a correlation coefficient (r) of 0.114. Although a full estimation of this relation would require eliminating the simultaneous equation bias, it is clear that there is essentially no significant correlation between output per capita and yield increases for the eighteen provinces for which 1957 gross value data are available. There is a strong relation between the rate of increase in output and of yields between 1957 and 1979, but all that says is that yield increases led to increases in output.

21. A regression of gross value output per capita as the independent variable (x) and the percentage of land cultivated mechanically as the dependent variable (y) yields the following equation $y = -1.36 + 0.2084x$, with a correlation coefficient (r) of 0.81. These results suggest a very strong relation between output per capita and mechanization. Since mechanization also affects output, this particular estimate is subject to simultaneous equation bias. No likely bias is likely to alter the basic result, however, and no attempt is made here to develop a model to eliminate this bias.

22. This figure is from Yang Fangxun, "Persist in the Principle of 'Giving Simultaneous Consideration to the Profits of the State, the Collectives and the Individuals' and Stabilize the Prices of Agricultural Products," *Jingji yanjiu* (April 1982), p. 28.

23. The Korean data are more complete than those for China, which are for collective incomes only. Including private income in the Chinese figures might raise the ratio, but this is not certain. The Korean data are from S. H. Ban, P. Y. Moon, and D. H. Perkins, *Rural Development: Studies in the Modernization of the Republic of Korea, 1945–1975* (Cambridge, Mass.: Council on East Asian Studies, 1980), p. 307.

Chapter 7

~~~~~~

Health Care

CHINA HAS MADE GREAT PROGRESS in improving rural living conditions by emphasizing preventive health care and raising the level of nutrition. It is one of the few countries in which a measure of symbiosis is evident between traditional and modern medicine in the final quarter of the twentieth century. Not only is traditional medicine still widely accepted, it also benefits from strong government support. This is a testimony to the quality of the services provided, but it also reflects the tenacity of beliefs, which have been nurtured over several millennia and are inextricably woven into the mass culture.

Historical Background

The Nei Ching Su Wen (Yellow Emperor's Classic of Internal Medicine), the oldest medieval text in existence, was written before the emergence of the Shang dynasty and is more than 4,000 years old.[1] It was the first step in the development of medical thought and practice, which reached an apogee during the Song dynasty in the tenth and eleventh centuries. Thereafter the process of refinement slackened, although the volume of medical writing continued to swell until the nineteenth century, by which time a limit was reached in philosophy, technique, and empirical advance. At about that time western medicine, premised on very different physiological and methodological ideas, drew ahead and began to gain acceptance in China.[2]

Although traditional Chinese medicine lost popularity in the urban areas, especially after modern hospitals were built in the last third of the nineteenth century, it faced no real challenge in the countryside. Further, the efficiency of many herbal potions and of techniques such as acupuncture was never seriously questioned. Nor did the populace lose its faith in the principal maxims of the traditional medicine, such as the primacy of preventive measures over curative ones and the important link between proper nutrition and health.[3] The public health strategy of the Communist regime, aside from drawing liberally upon the traditional materia medica, has effectively used traditional notions regarding prevention and cleanliness. These were already in the air but had lacked a scientific basis and could not be translated into a countrywide program of action because the government did not yet have instruments to organize people.

The Chinese first became acquainted with western medicine through the Jesuit Fathers who came to the country in the seventeenth century and through the doctors employed by the East India Company. Missionary activity and the increased number of Europeans living in the port cities spread the benefits of western medicine. But the imperial administration made little effort to exploit the new medical technology until it was roused by the outbreak of plague in Manchuria during 1910.[4] The success of the Plague Prevention Bureau did not, however, inspire increased efforts to control other infectious diseases. The republican government, which toyed with several policies, including the creation of a public health board, centralized medical licensing, and control over medical education, was also unable to make much headway before being extinguished by the political turmoil of the warlord era.

The nationalists created a Department of Health Administration, but the government's resources and administrative capabilities were too meager to improve conditions in the rural areas. Even in the large cities, adequate, modern health facilities were available only to the better-off. The Peking Union Medical College (PUMC), founded in the 1920s with support from the Rockefeller Foundation, together with a handful of other medical schools produced a trickle of doctors trained in the latest medical techniques, but few of these men ever ventured outside the cities.[5] In any case, their numbers were so small—no more than 38,000 in 1949—that they could not possibly have improved health services for the bulk of the population. Thus, the few pilot projects designed to test variants of a public health system that could be introduced throughout the country came to nought, although they may have influenced measures taken after 1949.

Rural Epidemiology before 1949

With rural health care largely entrusted to midwives and traditional herbalists who had no cure for infectious diseases, and with the life in the countryside disrupted by war and food shortages, it is hardly surprising that the average peasants' existence was disease-ridden and short. Tuberculosis was by far the major cause of death, being responsible for 10 to 15 percent of all adult deaths, but other respiratory illnesses were also common.[6] An epidemiologic survey conducted in Ting Hsien during 1933 showed that tuberculosis was responsible for 400 deaths per 100,000, with other respiratory diseases responsible for 225 deaths.[7] Unsanitary living conditions, polluted water supplies, use of human feces for fertilizer, and shortages of cooking fuel made gastrointestinal diseases endemic. Most villagers suffered from intestinal parasites, hookworm being common in Sichuan and the areas south of the Yangtze. Widespread malnutrition during the 1930s and the 1940s increased the susceptibility of the farm population to gastric ailments and worsened the debility arising from parasitic infestation. Mortality from toxic dysentery was in excess of 20 percent. Schistosomiasis posed a significant health problem in the rice-growing areas extending from the Yangtze delta to Yunnan and including the coastal provinces. In Chekiang province, 55 percent of male cultivators and 12 percent of the women were afflicted by schistosoma japanicum, and half of the deaths in that area were linked with the disease. The visitations of smallpox and diphtheria were feared throughout the country, whereas syphilis (the fourth most common diagnosis for new patients visiting hospitals) was more often encountered in the cities. Each year thousands were killed by malaria, which was a serious concern in parts of Manchuria and whose incidence rose south of the Yangtze, reaching hyperendemic proportions in the hilly southern parts of the country. Kala-azar raged in the plains lying between the Yangtze and the Yellow Rivers, and relapsing fever and typhus were common in the northern provinces.[8]

In short, the epidemiologic picture, dominated by infectious diseases, was typical of a backward, rural society devoid of a public health infrastructure. There were 80,000 hospital beds available in 1949, one-quarter of which were in the rural areas where nine-tenths of the populace resided, giving a ratio of less than 1:24,000.[9] Predictably, the crude death rate was high, exceeding 27 per 1,000 in the 1930s, with the farm population having a life expectancy at birth of twenty to twenty-five years. Infant mortality for the whole population was 156 per 1,000, but it may have been closer to 200 per 1,000 among the farm populace, with neonatal tetanus being the principal killer. Approximately a third of all children died before the age of five. Maternal mortality was almost 1.5 percent, in spite of the "reproductive efficiency" of Chinese women, possibly because of nutritional deficiencies and the treatment received at the hands of the local midwives.[10]

Thus, health conditions in rural China on the eve of the Communist takeover were rather dismal and not very different from those encountered until quite recently in the poorest Asian and African countries. Traditional medicine offered some partial remedies against certain bronchial conditions, malaria, schistosomiasis, hypertension, and a few kinds of gastric disorders, but it could not cure the potent infectious diseases such as tuberculosis, smallpox, and syphilis. The problem was compounded by the squalor that prevailed in the villages. Without access to clean water or soap; with people crowded together in poorly ventilated, smokey dwellings with earthen floors and thatched roofs; and without a scrupulous concern for the safe disposal of fecal waste or any understanding of the etiology of parasitic diseases, there was no easy solution to health problems even if modern vaccines and antibiotics had been available. For instance, the spread of tuberculosis could be halted if the contamination of the air within homes was averted through treatment of the infected. But first, those suffering from tuberculosis had to be identified and a way found to provide them with powerful antimicrobial drugs (such as isoniazid and streptomycin) and to create a system of surveillance to follow their progress and avoid a relapse. Drugs alone could not eradicate intestinal diseases, which were easily spread by contaminated fingers. A change in the people's living habits was required. The ubiquitous intestinal parasites could be controlled only if village sanitation was drastically improved and, in the case of schistosomiasis, if an attempt was made to eliminate the vector. Finally, antibiotics could not promise much relief unless the nutritional status of the populace was also raised to stiffen resistance to pathogenic organisms and unless the rural inhabitants learned the causes of infectious disease and the modern methods for safeguarding health. To improve rural living conditions, an effective procedure for organizing public health activities had to be devised.

Strategies for Disease Control

As discussed in Chapter 5, the Communists brought to the task of rural development an uncompromising ideology centered on mass mobilization and considerable experience in organizing villagers. In the early 1950s, as it attempted to develop a workable system of centralized government, the regime sought focuses of political support. Land redistribution and the subsequent division of rural society into cooperatives was one ideologically impeccable way to arouse popular support and, at the same time, to draw the people into administratively manageable structures. With land, the Party was grasping the very axis of rural society. It tried to dismantle the kinship networks, which had long articulated social relations, to sweep aside class enemies. But a marked improvement in the peasants' living standards would accelerate the process of political dominion. A rural health program to combat infectious diseases offered just such an opportunity. A modest expenditure of material resources could yield very large returns, if, that is, the masses could be properly motivated by the Party. In effect, a major health campaign could complement the efforts under way to redistribute land, to expand administrative capabilities, and to raise the level of literacy. The Party stood to gain political capital by reducing human suffering. By orchestrating mass campaigns with a profound bearing on rural living habits, it could penetrate to the very core of the society, adding another layer to the complex infrastructure of surveillance, which the state was attempting to put in place.

Campaigns against Infectious Diseases

A series of public health campaigns aimed at specific diseases were started in the early 1950s, using the "mass line" approach, which attempted through exhortation, Party, and peer pressure to involve people directly in activities related to health. At mass meetings, politically adept "health activists" or medical personnel trusted by the people explained the problem and outlined a solution in general terms. Each village then established a special team to direct its health work and was periodically visited by the health activists who coordinated operations within the district. In many instances, activists went from house to house to discuss health problems and associated preventive measures.[11] Environmental sanitation, because it called for a virtual revolution in living habits, presented special difficulties.

To elicit the needed support, a "patriotic health campaign" was waged from 1952 through 1958, which sought, very successfully it turned out, to provoke public action by raising the possibility of bacteriological warfare. To motivate the people, "confessions" extracted from captured American pilots were linked with a well-known attempt by the Japanese to deploy bacteriological weapons during 1938–39. As Worth

puts it, "These messages contained very powerful tools for the propagation [and] acceptance of the germ theory of disease and were probably
. . . responsible for the general acceptance of the new antiparasitic
methods of handling nightsoil."[12]

Mass vaccination campaigns by mobile health teams were highly
effective in virtually eradicating smallpox and in taking the first steps
toward controlling tuberculosis. To reduce the incidence of gastrointestinal diseases and the plague, the entire nation was mobilized against the
"four pests" (mosquitoes, flies, rats, and sparrows) using whatever
means were at hand. Although a few flies survived, most were not so
lucky. Today, a quarter of a century later, the number of flies, even in
the countryside, remains remarkably small. Syphilis, more of a problem in the cities, was curbed by weeding out prostitution. But the
extensive screening program to track down cases also played a crucial
role. Infant mortality was lowered by retraining many of the traditional
midwives and by creating a corps of social workers skilled in child care.
Schistosomiasis, malaria, kala-azar, and filiariasis proved more resistant, but significant progress was made in curing the infected and
alerting people to the causes of these diseases.

The control of helminthic infections called for initiatives in several
areas: designing dry latrines, providing containers for feces collection,
prohibiting the emptying of excrement into the river; penning animals
in separate enclosures; composting; and mixing urine and feces to
destroy schistosome eggs. In provinces where schistosomiasis was rife,
thousands of workers turned out to kill snails by hand, by using poisons
such as calcium cyanide, by building dikes, and by filling drainage
ditches. Villagers were even induced to mount snail patrols on the
waterways. Side by side with the assault on snails, public health units in
the provinces sent out paramedics to administer a three-day regimen of
antimonial drugs.[13]

There is little doubt that the government's venture into the domain of
public health was singularly successful, even though some of the claims
made in the 1960s were exaggerated. Diseases, which for centuries had
rendered survival an arduous obstacle course, were all of a sudden in
retreat. In a very real and palpable sense, the welfare of the ordinary
peasant was improved, and this change was unambiguously associated
with the efforts of the administration. Ostensibly the campaigns sought
to improve individual welfare, but political overtones were always
present. Cadres never tired of explaining how improvements in health
strengthened the nation. Political dividends aside, the government

gained a critical foothold in a part of village life that had been thought to be private. The campaigns of the 1950s legitimized the state's right to supervise sanitary activities in the countryside and to involve itself with what the peasant fed himself and his family and how he reared his children. Layer after layer of privacy, which had shielded peasants from the gaze of the state, was peeled away. And although the immediate significance of the beachhead established was rather small, it grew in importance during the 1970s when family planning moved to the center of the government's attention.

Transition from Infectious to Chronic Diseases

The crude death rate declined to 17 per 1,000 in 1952 and to 11 per 1,000 by 1956. Infant mortality also declined to about 110 per 1,000 in the rural parts of the country, a striking improvement over the rate prevailing less than a decade earlier.[14] The hold of smallpox, cholera, and other gastrointestinal infections on rural epidemiology was broken. Syphilis faded from the cities, and for the first time respiratory and helminthic diseases were decisively challenged. It took much longer to bring the latter diseases under control, however, and even today their elimination remains a distant prospect. Some 10 million people were still suffering from schistosomiasis in 1956, and, even though new nonantimonial drugs and stringent waste disposal procedures continue to whittle away at the numbers, some 2.5 million cases were reported in 1981.[15]

Malaria has also turned out to be an extremely resilient disease, a fact that is being rediscovered in many parts of the world today. However, the number of cases reported annually has declined steadily, from perhaps 30 million before the liberation to a few million currently. The incidence of leprosy, which claimed more than half a million victims in 1949, had been cut to half that number by 1982.[16] Reducing the prevalence of tuberculosis has been an uphill task, and it remains common among poor team members. In the first place, prevention through BCG (bacillus Calmette-Guerin, an attenuated strain of tubercle bacilli) inoculation is certainly not foolproof. Second, the cure entails a carefully supervised treatment extending over several months. Third, the incubation period of the bacteria is forty years, and the reservoir of mycobacterium tuberculosis in China was very large. Progress has been slow but steady, with the incidence falling to about half the level prevailing in 1949. More than 6.5 million people are reported to have active tuberculosis, the mortality rate in 1979 was 13.7 per 100,000, and the average age of those succumbing to the disease had risen from twenty-nine to sixty-two years.[17]

On the eve of the Great Leap, China's rural health drive had crossed an important threshold. The strategy of disease control, with its emphasis on prevention, had proved to be highly effective. No longer was the average peasant perennially threatened by an array of deadly ailments. Modern medicine had rescued him from such thralldom. But it was not just drugs that bought reprieve. Improvements in nutrition also played a vital role. As described in earlier chapters, food production rose appreciably in the first half of the 1950s, and, even when allowance is made for grain transfer to the cities, supplies were relatively abundant in the countryside. Further, the formation of cooperatives, which distributed income in favor of the poorest, had dramatically altered the consumption standards of peasants. Not only was more food available, it was also divided more equally among the population.

Development of a Public Health Infrastructure

But as one set of problems was being solved by reducing the severity of endemic infectious diseases, the focus shifted to a new and less tractable set. Although mass campaigns had been adequate to organize the peasants to cope with a restricted range of diseases whose etiology was well understood, they were scarcely suited to provide routine health care in the future. For that, a public health infrastructure, which would monitor infectious diseases while being responsive to everyday needs, was necessary. It had to be designed to benefit the largest number without straining the resources of the community or making extraordinary demands on the government's purse. Finally it had to consider the strong undercurrent of feeling in the Party that the distribution of medical resources was biased against the rural sector, that the provision of medical care was in the grip of health professionals who had to be displaced by ideologically committed generalists, and that the rich heritage of traditional medicine, condemned as worthless by modern doctors, could still be used with suitable encouragement from the state.[18]

Initiatives during the Great Leap

During the Great Leap years the contours of the rural health infrastructure began to emerge side by side with the establishment of communes. To reverse the urban bias of medicine and the new trend favoring the practice of curative, hospital-based medicine, influential Party members threw their weight behind the accelerated development of rural health services.

None of the major issues in health care had been resolved by the time the Party brought the Great Leap to an end. But the commune structure was firmly in place and provided the basis for a decentralized health network. This system evolved gradually during the following two decades, and its basic structural features can be outlined.

What was eventually to grow into a three-tier system of linked institutions began with the founding of commune health centers during 1958–60. They were financed largely through commune and county budgets and offered simple, curative services virtually free of charge. Fiscal difficulties encountered in the early 1960s caused many of these centers to be closed. As the economy recovered from famine and institutional dislocation, however, medical facilities at the commune level were rehabilitated, and schemes were devised to share costs between commune members and the county authorities. Routine medical problems were treated by the commune centers, whereas the more complex ones, requiring sophisticated facilities, were referred to better-equipped county hospitals. By 1965, every county had at least one hospital of about 120 beds, which was able to handle cases needing specialized attention.[19]

Developments during the Cultural Revolution

Mao's June 26 directive, which signaled the start of the Cultural Revolution, also opened a new phase in the development of rural health services. Four noteworthy changes were introduced. First, another tier was added to the health infrastructure in the form of a brigade health station. Second, commune clinics were upgraded into full-fledged hospitals, staffed with several doctors, nurses, and other health workers, and provided with the basic equipment. Third, the number of paramedics, called barefoot doctors and modeled on the Russian feldshers, was greatly expanded.[20] With three months of training, which enabled them to identify the most common ailments and equipped them with a rudimentary knowledge of a few medications, these paramedics became the conduit for disseminating routine health services to the rural populace. They staffed the brigade health centers, along with a midwife or two, and provided on-the-spot care for production teams affluent enough to afford their own medical personnel.[21]

A fourth change of considerable significance was the elevation in the status of traditional medicine, which had survived as a living force for a decade and a half while the Party debated its future and doctors condemned it as ineffectual. The official recognition of traditional medicine had much to do with Mao's own convictions, convictions which he shared with most of the rural inhabitants for whom such medicine continued to be of value, although they fully recognized the strengths of modern drugs and surgery in particular cases. With more than half a million practitioners, many of them scattered across the larger rural villages, the stock of traditional medical knowledge was too precious a resource to be abandoned. Support for indigenous medicine also drew upon fiscal exigencies. Although the government was committed to providing the peasantry with better health services, it could not raise the funds to modernize, beyond a point, the public health network in the countryside. Traditional medicine provided a partial answer. It was still respected, practitioners were fairly numerous, it offered effective cures for a variety of disorders, and herbs were cheap to produce. Communes could produce their own supplies, whereas it was financially impossible for them to purchase adequate quantities of many modern drugs.

Thus, in the late 1960s and early 1970s a system of public health, which in many ways seemed ideally suited to the needs of a capital-poor, predominantly agrarian economy, began to take shape in rural China. Between 70 and 80 percent of the communes offered cooperative medical care to their members. In line with the relative economics of preventive—as opposed to curative—treatment and the country's age-old medical traditions, the stress was on prevention. Health services were labor intensive, and traditional techniques were skillfully combined with modern ones to extract the largest gross medical product out of the available resources and skills.

Barefoot doctors aided by sanitarians (usually drawn from a production team) and midwives were the primary source of health education, assistance, and medication. The barefoot doctors (approximately three in each brigade) were supervised by trained physicians based in commune hospitals. These facilities served as nodal points in the rural health network, handling all cases that brigade stations could not cope with and, in turn, referring patients needing sophisticated therapy to county hospitals. By the mid-1970s, this system embraced much of the rural sector. Of course, the quality of services varied greatly depending on a commune's resources, and the ratio of barefoot doctors to the populace ranged from 1:1,000 in Henan to 1:340 in Kiangsi (the ratio of public health workers nationwide was 1:285), but unlike any time in the past, most farmers were able to obtain services at moderate cost, thanks in part to the government's willingness to allocate 60 percent of the health budget to the rural sector, as compared with 20 percent before 1965.

On the average, cooperative medical insurance cost the individual 7.5 yuan a year for a family of five. The fee was calculated from the communes' expenditures during the previous years and varied considerably depending on the incidence of serious illnesses and the use made of herbal as against modern medicine (which could account for up to 80 percent of total expenses). Hence insurance payments could range from 0.35 to 6 yuan. In addition, the team contributed between 0.1 and 1 yuan per member to the commune's health fund. For every visit to the brigade health station there was a registration fee of 0.05 to 0.1 yuan to discourage indiscriminate use of medical services, and the patient paid a small amount for the medicines he was given. Those referred to county hospitals had up to half of their costs reimbursed by the commune. However, the modest fee levied on even major operations, in the region of 10 yuan, placed sophisticated treatment within the reach of the great mass of rural inhabitants.[22]

Support from the government took several forms. Training of doctors, the expenditure on county and higher level hospitals, and the free provision of vaccines and contraceptives were some of the ways in which fiscal resources reached the peasant. But the state, on occasion, would donate equipment for the commune clinics and periodically eased the strain on local budgets by cutting the prices of drugs. The government's financial responsibilities for the barefoot doctors ended once they had completed their courses, either at urban hospitals or in commune health clinics, which had arranged for mobile teams of doctors to offer training sessions. Thereafter, the paramedics, who totaled a million in the late 1960s and whose numbers peaked at 1.8 million in 1976, were paid in work points and were expected to put in 100 to 150 days of farm work.

Legacies of the Cultural Revolution

The Cultural Revolution marked the high tide of the leftist vision in health. During this often tumultuous period, which came to a close soon after Mao's death in 1976, strenuous efforts were made to establish a socialist form of health care in the countryside. Some of the more extreme measures have since been reversed, but other initiatives have taken root and are likely to remain a part of the rural health system well into the future. The reliance on paramedics is likely to continue so long as the curative approach does not come to dominate medical thinking. In recent years, the number of barefoot doctors has been reduced by about 23 percent to 1.4 million in 1981, and concern is being expressed that their skills are not adequate for the task they are expected to perform.[23] But they remain the most cost-effective channel for delivering health services, and, if nothing else, fiscal constraints will help keep them in existence. On the training of doctors, the position taken during the Cultural Revolution has been abandoned, experts are firmly in the saddle, and the one-sided emphasis on quantity at the expense of quality is felt to have been a mistake. The curricula of medical schools, which was revised and sharply truncated in the early 1970s, is again as ortho-dox and demanding as it used to be. Further, the policy of dispersing doctors through the countryside is no longer in force. This measure, which was part of a general effort to break what Mao and others considered as being the elitist spirit of urban cadres and intellectuals, enjoyed limited success in bringing better medical care to the peasants, as doctors were often forced to do physical labor unrelated to medicine. With leftist ideological concerns in abeyance and the medical establish-ment in full control of the Ministry of Health, most of the 129,000 students in China's 113 medical schools can expect to be employed in the urban areas or, at worst, in the county hospitals.

The attempt to marry traditional with modern medicine seems to have borne fruit. By encouraging research on herbs and by introducing traditional practices into the country's hospitals, the Cultural Revolu-tion rescued what in the 1950s appeared to be a dying craft, gave it a new respectability, and won it a measure of acceptance by even modern practitioners. The anesthetic properties of acupuncture, certainly the most bizarre of medical techniques, is now thought to be linked with the body's secretion of opiates called enkephalins, which can raise the pain threshold, and the procedure is used widely in Chinese hospitals.[24] Moreover, the traditional materia medica has yielded a rich lode of drugs, many of which have been able to pass stringent clinical tests designed to prove their effectiveness. Not only has the herbalist earned a secure niche, but also most, if not all, hospitals maintain a staff of traditional doctors, whose skills are used to treat several diseases for which modern medicine does not offer a clearly superior cure. The government now maintains twenty-four institutes for traditional medi-cine, enrolling 20,000 students.[25]

The share of health expenditure allocated to rural areas, the increase in the number of hospital beds per 1,000 of the rural populace (from 0.2

to 0.3 in 1955 to 1.1 in 1978), the progress made in reducing infant mortality (down to about 50 per 1,000 in the late 1970s), and the rise in life expectancy all indicate that the urban bias of medicine was eroded during the Cultural Revolution. Whether the gains will be retained if the drift toward hospital-based, curative medicine continues to gather momentum is discussed in more detail later. Last, the use of health services as means of social control has become more apparent. The Cultural Revolution witnessed a deepening bureaucratic penetration of rural families. As people grew accustomed to the surveillance, the record keeping, the inspections, the selective provision of knowledge on appropriate habits, and the visits by medical personnel to question, to observe, and to reassure, their ability to resist national policies communicated through the organizations to which they had become tied grew weaker. When, in the early 1970s, the state began to urge a reduction in family size, peasants, worried about the effect of fewer children on their incomes and security during old age, tried to ignore the directives. But the government has persisted, and the many-faceted network of control, more than two decades in the making, has become less and less easy to circumvent.

Rural Epidemiology in the 1980s

Rather surprisingly, despite the far-reaching monitoring capabilities of the health bureaucracy, epidemiologic data on China remain spotty to this day. Very large-scale screening campaigns are slowly closing this gap, but for the moment only somewhat episodic information is available. Such data show that the disease profile in China is becoming very similar to that of the advanced industrial economies. Infectious (usually acute) diseases, particularly tuberculosis and other respiratory ailments, have been largely displaced by noninfectious (generally chronic) diseases as the principal causes of mortality. Economywide statistics for 1979 indicate that one-third of all deaths resulted from heart attacks, cerebral vessel disease, and cancer, in that order, a situation similar to that in East Asian countries such as the Republic of Korea and even the United States.[26] This change is clearly reflected in the fact that life expectancy—now almost sixty-nine years—has risen by an average of 1.5 years for each calendar year since 1949. It is a record of sustained improvement that is hard to match, since the standard for developing countries is less than a third of this rate. To a considerable extent, the increase in life expectancy is also the outcome of a sharp drop in infant mortality, which is around 50 per 1,000 for the nation as a whole, down from 200 per 1,000 in the mid-1950s. Although a lower birth rate has undoubtedly made it possible for each child to receive more care, the protection being provided against several infectious diseases may have been more significant in lowering the odds against survival. The war against diphtheria, pertussis, measles, and poliomyelitis has been waged since the early 1960s, and reports suggest that public health campaigns have been broadened further since then, with 60 million persons having been inoculated every year since 1977 against infantile paralysis, measles, whooping cough, diphtheria, and tetanus.[27]

The increasing incidence of chronic diseases has coincided with a growing interest in epidemiology. As a consequence much information is being gathered through extensive surveys conducted around the country by specially trained paramedics and supervised by specialists. An investigation of medical records in the cities of Xian, Wuhan, Nanjing, Beijing, Kunming, Tianjin, and Hangzhou in 1976 found that the incidence of stroke was 48 per 100,000, which is higher than in North America, while 21 to 42 per 100,000 suffered from acute myocardial infarction, a rate that is less than the average for North America.[28] Possibly the most disquieting aspect of vascular problems in China is the frequency of chronic valvular heart disease of rheumatic origin, which is caused both by the three-day, broad-spectrum antibiotic treatment for streptococcal infections and by the use of drugs for combating parasitical infestation during the periodic health campaigns. Another finding that has aroused concern is the growing incidence of hypertension. During the mid-1970s it was believed that some 20 million to 30 million people were affected, more in the north than in the southern parts of the country. But the condition has spread very quickly. In cities such as Beijing and Shanghai the rates are as high as in the United States, with 10 percent of the population at risk, although the incidence in the rural areas was in the region of 2 to 3 percent.

Cancer causes an estimated 11 percent of all deaths in China, for a national total of 700,000 in 1979. During the past five years, 600,000 health workers have screened 800 million people to map the concentrations of cancer throughout the country and to identify the most common forms of the disease.[29] Unlike the United States, where lung cancer is dominant, stomach, esophageal, liver, and nasopharyngeal cancers are the most common in China. Cancer of the stomach and the esophagus correlates with high levels of nitrites, nitrates, and nitrosamines in water and food, with depressed levels of such trace elements as molybdenum, as well as the contamination of food by candida and aspergillus.

Nasopharyngeal cancer is thought to be linked with the amount of nickel in rice and water.

Of late, lung cancer is also emerging as a serious health hazard, and its spread is being closely associated with the increase in smoking and the growing use of soft coal in North China for heating. Shanghai, which reported lung cancer mortality of 30 per 100,000 in 1963–65, had reached a level of 55 per 100,000 in 1980.[30]

Present and Future Strategies for Health Care

In reviewing the epidemiological statistics two questions come to mind. First, how well equipped is the country, in terms of medical facilities, to deal with the problems of chronic diseases? Second, what should be the nature of health strategy in the future? That is, for the rural populace, what are the relative merits of preventive as against curative medicine, how should preventive medicine be pursued, and how would the public health system help to implement such a strategy? The discussion earlier in this chapter on the structure and financing of rural health care provides a clue to its effectiveness. Other clues can be drawn from an appraisal of medical inputs, although information specifically relating to the rural sector tends to be sparse.

Medical Facilities

Data on the number of hospital beds, medical personnel, and trained doctors are presented in Tables 7-1, 7-2, and 7-3. In terms of numbers, the expansion of the Chinese medical system is not unprecedented, but is substantial nevertheless. Although population about doubled during the past thirty years, the number of hospital beds increased more than twentyfold, and the number of doctors with western-style training rose sevenfold. There are no completely reliable measures of the quality of these inputs, but impressionistic evidence supports the view that on balance quality per unit of input has risen gradually since the early 1950s. The system might have regressed somewhat during the Cultural Revolution, when training was poor or nonexistent and qualified doctors were cut off from the latest international advances in medicine. The quality of training in the premier research institutions and teaching hospitals might also be lower than it was in the 1950s. Against this decline at the pinnacle of the system must be put the improved quality of rural health workers, many of whom were an outright menace to

Table 7-1. *Number of Western-style Physicians*

Year	Physicians (thousands)	Ratio of doctor to population	Year	Physicians (thousands)	Ratio of doctor to population
1950	41	1:13,500	1978	359	1:2,680
1957	74	1: 8,740	1980	447	1:2,210
1965	189	1: 3,840	1982	557	1:1,820

Sources: 1950 and 1957, State Statistical Bureau, *Ten Great Years* (1960); 1965, estimated by Leo Orleans and Chu-Yuan Cheng; and 1978–82, provided by the Chinese Ministry of Public Health.

Table 7-2. *Number of Medical Personnel*
(thousands of persons)

Year	Western medicine		Doctors of Chinese medicine	Nurses	Total[a]
	Senior doctors	Junior doctors			
1950	41	53	286	38	555
1952	52	67	306	61	690
1957	74	136	337	128	1,039
1965	189	253	321	235	1,532
1978	359	423	251	407	2,464
1980	447	444	262	466	2,798
1982	557	436	303	564	3,143

a. Includes "other medical personnel" not listed in table but excludes part-time health workers (barefoot doctors).

Sources: State Statistical Bureau, *Statistical Yearbook of China, 1981* (Hong Kong: Economic Information Agency, 1982), p. 477; and State Statistical Bureau, *Zhongguo tongji zhaiyao* (Beijing: China Statistical Publishers, 1983), p. 92.

Table 7-3. *Number of Hospitals and Hospital Beds*

Year	Hospitals	Hospital beds (thousands)		Ratio of hospital beds to population	
		Total	In rural areas	Nationwide	In rural areas
1949	2,600	80	20	1:6,667	1:24,201
1957	4,179	295	74	1:2,174	1: 7,392
1965	42,711	766	308	1: 943	1: 1,932
1978	64,421	1,856	1,140	1: 515	1: 693
1980	65,450	1,982	1,214	1: 495	1: 655
1982	66,149	2,054	1,221	1: 493	1: 658

Source: State Statistical Bureau, *Zhongguo tongji zhaiyao, 1983*, pp. 13 and 92.

health in the early 1950s; the greater availability of good medicines at low cost; the accumulated experience of doctors trained in the 1950s and 1960s; and, finally, the great increase in the share of the population served by the system. In 1955, large parts of the countryside had no access to hospital services, but by 1978 there were few, if any, areas in such a predicament. County and commune hospitals had roughly 800,000 beds and an unknown but sizable number of doctors. As Tables 7-4 and 7-5 indicate, differences in health care remain between provinces, and the quality of medical services in cities such as Shanghai is greatly superior to what is available in the commune, but such differences do not detract from the magnitude of the achievement.

Preventive versus Curative Medicine

Looking ahead, the government has two options: it can slowly expand capital- and skill-intensive, hospital-based services, which can ameliorate but not cure the chronic diseases now gaining ground, or it can retain the preventive orientation of rural health care while changing the mix of skills provided to the paramedics and the services offered by the county hospitals in response to the disease profile. The medical establishment seems to prefer the first option. And the equipment being installed in urban hospitals and the medical research being encouraged both indicate that there is considerable pressure on the Ministry of Health to move toward a very conventional, capital-intensive system of health care in which the doctor is the linchpin. But experience with chronic diseases, the sheer cost-effectiveness of preventive medicine

Table 7-4. *Comparison of Medical Personnel and Hospital Beds in the Entire Country and in Shanghai, 1978*

Item	Medical personnel	Senior western doctors	Hospital beds
Country			
Total	2,460,000	350,000	1,850,000
Per 1,000 persons	2.57	0.37	1.93
Shanghai			
Total	85,000	13,000	57,000
Per 1,000 persons	7.74	1.18	5.19

Sources: Country data are from State Statistical Bureau, "Communique on Fulfillment of China's 1978 National Economic Plan," June 27, 1979. Shanghai data are from a briefing on Shanghai given to the American Science Policy delegation in July 1979. It is assumed that the Shanghai figure for western doctors included only "senior" doctors.

given the size of the population, the shortage of budgetary resources, and the abundance of paramedics all serve to underline the superiority of the second option.

The diseases of affluence and long life spans, most of which are chronic ailments, remain beyond the reach of curative measures

Table 7-5. *Health Care Personnel and Hospital Beds, 1979*

Area	Health care personnel per 1,000 persons	Hospital beds per 1,000 persons
Provinces		
Anhui	2.13	1.52
Fujian	2.29	1.84
Gansu	2.48	1.77
Guangdong	2.77	1.83
Guizhou	2.22	1.46
Hebei	2.33	1.70
Heilongjiang	3.99	2.90
Henan	1.79	1.48
Hubei	3.20	2.35
Hunan	2.40	2.21
Jiangsu	2.47	1.93
Jiangxi	2.29	2.09
Jilin	3.75	2.73
Liaoning	4.17	3.13
Qinghai	3.74	2.87
Shaanxi	2.70	1.90
Shandong	2.22	1.60
Shanxi	3.35	2.72
Sichuan	2.37	1.80
Yunnan	2.18	1.87
Zhejiang	2.24	1.58
Autonomous regions		
Guangxi	1.81	1.31
Nei Monggol	3.54	2.51
Ningxia Hui	3.12	1.95
Xizang	3.61	2.26
Xingjiang Uygur	4.28	3.37
Municipalities		
Beijing	8.28	3.08
Shanghai	7.84	4.22
Tianjin	6.22	2.42
Country total	2.37	1.99

Source: Ministry of Health, Statistics and Finance Bureau, *China Encyclopedia, 1980* (Beijing, 1980), p. 560.

throughout the world. Diseases such as schizophrenia, most cancers, multiple sclerosis, nephritis, diabetes mellitus, hypertension, and diverticular disease have not been curbed in spite of the enormous funds that have been lavished on research in the West. Similarly, coronary thrombosis and stroke cannot yet be much affected by any technology available. An example of this is the experience with medical care in the United States, which is surely the epitome of capital-intensive treatment. Between 1960 and 1975 expenditure in health rose 314 percent, yet the average life span increased by just 15 percent. Moreover, compelling evidence shows that the most significant chronic diseases are caused by improper diet, excessive drinking, smoking, drug abuse, pollution, and the lack of exercise. In addition, epidemiologists estimate that 70 to 90 percent of all human cancers may derive from exposure to chemical carcinogens in the environment.[31]

It is not clear thus far whether the Chinese are prepared to redirect their public health machinery against the principal causes of hypertension and cancer or to discourage changes in eating habits that are precursors of certain metabolic disorders well known in the West. If the initial attempts to curb cancer and hypertension are any guide to the direction of official thinking, prevention is being translated into early detection, with thousands being tested for signs of these diseases. For example, in the mountainous regions bordering on Honan, Shensi, and Shansi, where esophageal cancer is common, paramedics use a tube with a net-covered balloon to detect carcinomas. The tube is lowered down the patient's throat, the balloon is inflated, and then it is slowly drawn out, carrying mucosal cells with it. These are later examined under a microscope for signs of cancer. A blood test for elevated levels of alpha-fetoprotein is used to screen against liver cancer, and barefoot doctors are being trained to scrutinize sinus areas with mirrors for signs of nasopharyngeal cancer.[32]

On a limited basis screening combined with surgery or chemotherapy is quite feasible, but on a nationwide scale such a campaign would be prohibitively expensive. It is possible that cost considerations may ultimately induce health authorities to redirect their energies, concentrating instead on nutrition, environmental causes of disease, and living habits.

Rural Nutrition

As stated earlier, Chinese medical tradition has always associated good health with a properly balanced diet. This is amply borne out by modern research. Malnutrition can impair the immune systems by producing an atrophy of the thymus and the lymph tissues, depressing albumin output, and interfering with the generation of antibodies.

Frequent famines largely eliminated the food taboos often found in other cultures and induced the Chinese to search wild plant sources for edible items. Thus the range of food consumed is very wide and offers some protection against diseases caused by deficiencies in the diet. There are a few other noteworthy health-related characteristics of traditional Chinese eating habits. Water is generally boiled before it is drunk, an extremely important precaution in the rural areas, where only a small percentage of the peasants have access to clean water. This tradition is linked with tea drinking, which became widespread during the Song dynasty. A great emphasis on fresh vegetables and meat is another feature of Chinese eating habits, as is the aversion to raw foods. The reliance on stir frying with high heat preserves vitamins apart from conserving fuel and cooking oil. A peasant diet, which traditionally has contained a preponderance of grain, vegetables, and tubers and only small quantities of meat and fat, has minimized the intake of cholesterol and sugar, while providing large amounts of complex carbohydrates and roughage. Modern medicine has discovered that such a diet can offer useful protection against cardiovascular and metabolic diseases. Throughout the ages, Chinese peasants have consumed very limited quantities of dairy foods and have depended on grain, legumes, and soybeans for virtually all their protein, calcium, and vitamins. These habits are rooted in the fear that relying on dairy foods would force closer trading relations with the nomads, who threatened China's integrity for several millennia.[33]

In short, a first glance at the diet of an average Chinese peasant does not suggest that there is much room for improvement according to the current state of medical knowledge. The caloric intake is not excessive, and hence obesity is nonexistent. There is an excessive reliance on grain (average consumption of unprocessed foodgrain in 1981 was 256 kilos per commune member), but that is not injurious to the health so long as the necessary calories and nutrients are consumed.[34] White sugar and refined flour, which are steadily infiltrating the diets of Chinese in Singapore and Hong Kong, are not much in evidence. And there is more than enough dietary fiber from vegetables as well as grain.

A closer inspection of the peasant diet, however, is less reassuring. The problem has several dimensions. Dividing the food supply by the number of mouths gives a figure of 2,500 kilocalories per capita for 1981.[35] This amount is probably adequate when stature and climate are

considered. But the distribution of foodstuffs remains somewhat uneven, so that peasants from the poorer provinces in the north- and
southwestern areas fall below the threshold of sufficiency.[36] In particular, the diets of the poorest peasants are deficient in soy products and
leguminous grains, which in the absence of milk and meat are the main
sources of calcium, iron, and high-quality proteins, as well as being rich
in the amino acids lysine and methionine that are not in grains. Villagers
in the hilly regions of northern China, whose diet consists almost
exclusively of coarse-milled grain, beans, cabbage, and sweet potatoes,
frequently suffer from deficiencies of vitamins A and C. A more general
problem is that the vegetables traditionally eaten in northern China,
such as cucumbers, gourds, pumpkins, melons, and Chinese cabbage,
have rather low nutritional value. In the winter, when dried cabbage is
the only vitamin supplement, the nutritional status of poorer peasants
can be quite precarious and may explain the limited resistance to
bronchial infections. The expansion of private plots (see Chapter 5), has
raised the supply of pork (the country had 294 million hogs in 1981) and,
with it, the per capita consumption of pork. The urban average rose
from 3 kilos in 1959 to 11 kilos in 1979. Rural consumption of pork has
also increased to around 7.5 kilos, usually at the time of festivals, but
there has been only a modest change in the consumption of other meat,
eggs, or fish.[37]

   Thus, rural health could be improved by greater efforts to supply
vegetables, soya products, and vitamin supplements to areas that experience shortages at certain times of the year. A more effective distribution of such products would also dislodge certain injurious constit-
uents of the Chinese diet. Shortages have over the ages introduced an
enormous variety of preserved foods into the Chinese diet. Chang
remarks that "the Chinese preserve their food in many more ways and in
greater quantities than most other peoples. Food is preserved by smoking, salting, sugaring, steeping, pickling, drying, soaking in many kinds
of soy sauces and so forth, and the whole range of foodstuffs is involved—grains, meat, fruit, eggs, vegetables and everything else."[38]
These methods of preservation appreciably elevate salt consumption,
which is often correlated with hypertension and stroke. But, in addition, they introduce into the diet large amounts of nitrosamines, which
are suspected to cause cancers of the stomach and esophagus.

   When a large percentage of the rural population is living on the
margin of adequacy and many people are still undernourished, the use
of public funds to expand sophisticated hospital facilities would not
seem to be cost-effective. Since close to a quarter of all deaths are still

connected with infectious diseases, the rural population in particular would derive far more welfare if health officials could improve the quality of the diet. Aside from nutrition, two other areas in which further progress would yield significant health dividends are village sanitation and environmental pollution.

Village Sanitation and Environmental Pollution

Village sanitation revolves around the disposal of fecal waste and the supply of clean water.[39] The first problem has received considerable attention, and there is little doubt that composting methods have advanced and that the use of dry latrines has spread to many, if not most, villages. But the elimination habits of young children remain fairly casual, and another dose of health education may be needed to change parental attitudes.

The problem of a clean water supply, however, has not been dealt with as successfully. No more than a third of all villagers have safe water, from either deep wells or other sources. Without adequate supplies of clean water it is impossible to cap the efforts at bettering sanitation, but there is little evidence from official publications that improving the water supply figures prominently in rural health programs. The spread of modern farming techniques and industrialization has increased water contamination, and, for the villagers, water now carries not only the infectious diseases that were the scourge of yesteryear, but also an entirely new range of chemicals that have been implicated in causing cancers, birth defects, and a host of other diseases. The problem has now become one of environmental pollution.

The salience of cancer in modern epidemiology and periodic outbreaks of diseases related to the presence of PCBS (polychlorinated biphenyls), mercury (the Minamoto incident), and other chemicals in the water and the air are forcing public health authorities in the industrial countries to rethink their strategy. So far, most of these diseases are incurable, although in many instances expensive treatment can prolong life temporarily. Although a cure remains elusive, scientists suspect that many cancers, for example, may be caused by industrial chemicals and pesticides in the environment. The organic chemicals believed to possess a high tumorogenic potency are mostly hydrocarbon derivatives, with short chains and benzene rings, rarely found in living matter. Since they are much smaller than either viruses or bacteria, they can slip past the body's defenses without triggering an enzymatic or antibody response, which could break them down and render them harmless.

Being lipophylic, they accumulate in adipose tissue and the body retains them for long periods, causing a buildup of substances, which has a general toxic effect, interferes with the immunologic system, and can cause cancers.[40]

The air pollution in China's large cities has been frequently noted, but it is now becoming known that the waterways downstream from the cities are seriously contaminated. Smil observes that the waters of the Le Jiang in the vicinity of Guilin have been badly polluted by phenols, arsenic, chlorides, and cyanide, and, as a result, most of the cormorants used for fishing have died. Release of untreated wastes into the Chang River near Xian has killed most aquatic life in the lower reaches of the river, and many of the tributaries are choked with garbage.[41] Suburban industrial sites release PCBS, chlorinated phenols, organic solvents, benzene, and heavy metals, which are not removed by filtration, adsorption and the action of soil microorganisms. They seep into the underground aquifers from which peasants in the surrounding areas draw their water.[42]

Industrial pollution is compounded by the increasing use of organochlorine pesticides and the accumulation of nitrates from artificial fertilizers in the water. Nitrates, when ingested, are converted into highly carcinogenic nitrosamines by bacteria in the stomach.

Contamination of the rural environment by industrial chemicals does not, of course, approach the levels reached in more developed countries, but the deterioration is quite evident. Since cancer is already one of the principal causes of mortality, and its treatment is likely to remain costly in the foreseeable future, water and waste treatment facilities, which could be directly instrumental in preventing disease, may turn out to be a far more beneficial investment in rural health than an increase in the number of county hospitals.

Organizational Instruments to Control Chronic Diseases

One of the themes running through this book has been the regime's effectiveness in using organization to garner political support, develop farming, and raise the living conditions of the peasants. The ability to exert control over rural inhabitants was crucial when it came to redistributing land, collectivizing agriculture, constructing irrigation works, spreading new farming technology, and restructuring the institutions that regulated a myriad of social and economic relations. Organizational skill also lay behind the success of the measures taken to stamp out infectious diseases and prevent their reappearance. In fact, the actions taken during the 1950s vindicated the biases of traditional medicine and the beliefs of the leftist elements in the Party. For those who felt that change, whether in the sphere of health or in other areas, required a full involvement of the masses and an arousal of local initiative, the rural health campaigns revealed how much energy there was to be tapped in the farming communities. Once those infectious diseases readily susceptible to vaccines and antibiotics were under control, however, the campaigns eventually reached the limits of their utility.

Further progress in disease control and health maintenance activities required an infrastructure of clinics and hospitals manned by a competent staff. This did not mean that preventive medicine no longer had a role, but that, first, preventive measures had to become more systematic and, second, that a balance between preventive and curative procedures had to be struck. As rural health moved into the orbit of commune clinics and county hospitals and as epidemiologic conditions tilted in the direction of chronic diseases, the pull of curative treatment, in which modern medicine has an immense investment, grew more compelling. In turn, it generated a pressure for capital-intensive hospital facilities, located inevitably in urban centers. By increasing the role of hospital-based care, this approach reduced the flow of public health investment to the rural sector. It also drew attention away from the policies toward nutrition and rural living conditions that helped to strengthen resistance to disease.

During the Cultural Revolution, rural health concerns were brought to the surface by the force of proletarian politics. By breaking the power of the medical establishment, leavening the scientific elitism of modern medicine with some of the wisdom of traditional health care, and hammering away at the centrality of preventive policies, the Maoists sought to ensure that medicine did not draw away from the lives of rural inhabitants. The move had strong political overtones as well, since it tried to elicit political approval while enabling the state to develop new procedures to regulate rural society when the official bureaucracy was under attack. Essentially, the government desired a system of indirect controls through village committees, work groups, and local regulatory bodies, which preserved the appearance and even some of the reality of local initiative, but within a larger structure of supervision managed by official agencies, together with the Party.

At this stage it is uncertain to what extent the government intends to disengage from the rural health policies of the early 1970s. The shift toward remuneration through individual and household contracting does, however, appear to be undermining the barefoot doctor system.

Wages of paramedics have not kept pace with farm incomes, and commune members are often reluctant to provide the needed financial support for paramedic services now that the funds for them are collected directly from individuals instead of being drawn from collective income. It is improbable, though, that fiscal if not ideological and political concerns will permit even a partial abandonment of the preventive approach and a heavy reliance on individualistic, hospital-based, and doctor-centered health services. Far too much is at stake. Not only could past gains be eroded, but the care of larger and larger numbers of people suffering from chronic diseases would be unbearably expensive. Above all, preventive medicine, by virtue of its interventionist ethos, has already forged the organizational means to change entrenched living habits and even to regulate such critical decisions as the size of the family, an asset that a state committed to "four modernizations" might be loath to surrender. A brief account of the family planning program illustrates the efficacy of the organizational instruments used by the rural health authorities.

Family Planning

Major efforts to lower fertility and limit population growth in the 1950s ran up against a wall of resistance from literal-minded Marxists who tagged all proponents of family planning as "neo-Malthusians." Ma Yinchu, the most prominent individual to suggest that rapid population growth was not desirable, was purged from his post as president of Peking University and was not rehabilitated until 1979.

Efforts to promote family planning began again in the early 1960s, but the political vulnerability of the program meant that efforts had to be couched in terms of improving the health of mothers by such methods as better spacing of children. These were only faint echoes of the notion that a smaller number of children would be a good idea, and these echoes were drowned out by Cultural Revolution rhetoric in the late 1960s that extolled the virtues of a large population and labor force. Still, despite the rhetoric, family planning became an integral part of the expanding rural health system. Health workers and doctors were trained in the various methods from abortion to pills, and they in turn educated the rural population. The state, in the meantime, was developing and producing inexpensive contraceptives and making them available nationwide.[43]

The effects of this and the rising age of marriage began to be felt in the 1970s, when total fertility declined to 4 from an average of 5.68 in the previous decade. By 1980 it had fallen to 2.24. With the crude national birth rate down to 18 per 1,000, population growth had slowed to 1.2 percent in 1979, despite the increasing percentage of women of child-bearing age.[44] By then, the public health apparatus had developed a system to regulate family size based on provision of free contraceptives through brigade health stations, family planning clinics, and roving barefoot doctors; had assigned female cadres from individual production units to indoctrinate local women, through frequent face-to-face meetings, on the personal benefits and national imperatives of having fewer children; and had established commune committees on planned birth to provide an organizational axis for such work. These actions were reinforced by campaigns against early marriages and also for marriage by free choice, which had not taken hold in the rural areas despite the fact that the Marriage Law had been in existence for almost two decades.[45] Finally, by offering to provide at least minimal assistance for old people with no sons, the communes tried to dilute the security incentive for having large families.

Toward the close of the 1970s any remaining political barriers against reducing population growth had disappeared. Furthermore, moral pressures and education had been supplemented by material incentives and disincentives. In many parts of the country, a family promising to have only one child now receives five yuan per month until the child reaches the age of fourteen and may be given additional plots of land for private use. A family that has three children will have to pay more for the grain to feed that third child, and, unlike the first two, will not receive an extra allocation of private land. There is also different treatment in access to higher education. It is not certain whether future progress will be slowed by the turn toward farming by contract, which puts a premium on large families. Still, control through rural organizations will be crucial in making incentives work and averting a return to higher population growth rates.[46]

Conclusion

China's experience in bringing health care to the rural areas seems to support the case for preventive health care carried out by a highly motivated organization, which ceaselessly elicits the active participation of the peasantry. In China's case such organized effort was closely linked to the institutional structure that was developed in the late 1950s. The commune greatly facilitated the mobilization of labor that was so crucial to campaigns against the four pests and smallpox, for example. And the communes were well suited as a vehicle to support rural clinics, to select and support local people for special training in health care, and, more recently, to facilitate the mass screening surveys, which are beginning to place rural epidemiology on a solid empirical footing.

Notes to Chapter 7

1. I. Veith, trans., *The Yellow Emperor's Classic of Internal Medicine* (Berkeley: University of California Press, 1972).

2. See H. Agren, "Patterns of Tradition and Modernization in Contemporary Chinese Medicine," in A. Kleinman and others, eds., *Medicine in Chinese Cultures* (Washington, D.C.: National Institutes of Health, 1975), pp. 40–41; and J. Needham, *Clerks and Craftsmen in China and the West* (Cambridge: Cambridge University Press, 1970), pp. 406–07.

3. Traditional attitudes toward preventive medicine, personal hygiene and diet are discussed in Needham, *Clerks and Craftsmen in China and the West*, pp. 343–54 and 365–67.

4. R. C. Croizier, *Traditional Medicine in Modern China* (Cambridge, Mass.: Harvard University Press, 1968), pp. 45–46.

5. On the founding of the PUMC and its role in Chinese medicine, see R. Sidel and V. W. Sidel, *The Health of China* (Boston: Beacon Press, 1982), pp. 24–25; P. Buck, *American Science and Modern China* (Cambridge: Cambridge University Press, 1980), pp. 47–51. As to the estimate of the number of western-trained doctors, opinions vary. Sidel and Sidel mention a figure of 40,000 (p. 27), while Agren ("Patterns of Tradition and Modernization in Contemporary Chinese Medicine," p. 42), quotes a number of just 12,000.

6. See R. M. Worth, "The Impact of New Health Programs on Disease Control and Illness Patterns in China," in Kleinman and others, eds., *Medicine in Chinese Cultures*, p. 478; J. L. Scherer, ed., *China: Facts and Figures Annual*, vol. 4 (Gulf Breeze, Fla.: Academic International Press, 1981), p. 324.

7. Referred to in H. King, "Selected Epidemiologic Aspects of Major Diseases and Causes of Death among Chinese in the U.S. and Asia," in Kleinman and others, eds., *Medicine in Chinese Cultures*, p. 488.

8. This information has been culled from several sources: E. Grey Dimond, "Medical Education and Care in the PRC," *Journal of the American Medical Association*, vol. 218, no. 10 (1971), pp. 1552–57; Huang Kun-Yen, "Infectious and Parasitic Diseases," in J. R. Quinn, ed., *Medicine and Public Health in the PRC* (Washington, D.C.: Department of Health, Education, and Welfare, 1973); World Health Organization, "Report on a Technical Visit to the PRC," Western Pacific Advisory Committee on Medical Research, Regional Office for Western's Pacific (July 1979); and Worth, "The Impact of New Health Programs," p. 480–81.

9. Sidel and Sidel, *The Health of China*, pp. 31, 48.

10. The estimate for the crude death rate was drawn from a study by Barclay and others; see J. Banister and S. H. Preston, "Mortality in China," *Population and Development Review*, vol. 7 (March 1981), p. 107. On child mortality, see R. M. Worth, "Health in Rural China: From Village to Commune," *American Journal of Hygiene*, vol. 77 (May 1963), pp. 228–39: King, "Selected Epidemiologic Aspects of Major Diseases and Causes of Death," p. 509, is the source for the information on maternal mortality.

11. See Worth, "Health in Rural China," p. 480.

12. Ibid., p. 481.

13. The control of schistosomiasis has received much attention: See R. L. Andreano, "The Recent History of Parasitic Disease in China: The Case of Schistosomiasis, Some Public Health and Economic Aspects," *International Journal of Health Services*, vol. 6, no. 1 (1976), pp.53–61; and Huang, "Infectious and Parasitic Diseases," note 8.

14. W. L. Parish and M. K. Whyte, *Village and Family in Contemporary China* (Chicago: University of Chicago Press, 1978), p. 96; and State Statistical Bureau, *Statistical Yearbook of China, 1981* (Hong Kong: Economic Information Agency, 1982), p. 89.

15. See Scherer, *China: Facts and Figures Annual*, p. 324.

16. "Leprosy Declines in China but Remains Feared," *New York Times* (May 31, 1983), p. C-2.

17. Scherer, *China: Facts and Figures Annual*, p. 324.

18. Much has been written on the survival of traditional medicine in the 1950s and its efflorescence in the late 1960s and 1970s. See for instance, Crozier, *Traditional Medicine in Modern China*, pp. 45–46; P. Wilenski, *The Delivery of Health Services in the PRC* (Ottawa: International Development Research Center, 1976); D. Mechanic and A. Kleinman, *The Organization, Delivery, and Financing of Rural Health Care in the PRC*, Center pub. 10–70 (Madison, Wis., Center for Medical Sociology and Health Services, 1978); B. Hook, ed., *The Cambridge Encyclopedia of China* (Cambridge: Cambridge University Press, 1982), pp. 139–50; R. Garfield and J. Warren Salmon, "Struggles over Health Care in the PRC," *Journal of Contemporary Asia*, vol. 11, no. 1 (1981), pp. 91–103. On the role of traditional healing practices the recent books by A. Kleinman and Margaret Lock are useful guides: A. Kleinman, *Patients and Healers in the Context of Culture* (Berkeley: University of California Press, 1980); and M. M. Lock, *East Asian Medicine in Urban Japan* (Berkeley: University of California Press, 1980).

19. Sidel and Sidel, *The Health of China*. See V. W. Sidel, "Health Services in the PRC," in J. Z. Bowers and E. F. Purcell, eds., *Medicine and Society in China* (New York: J. Macy Foundation, 1974); Mechanic and Kleinman, *The Organization, Delivery, and Financing of Rural Health Care*, note 17; and Hu Teh-wei, *An Economic Analysis of the Cooperative Medical Services in the PRC*, NIH no. 75–672 (Washington, D.C.: Department of Health, Education, and Welfare, 1973).

20. The function of feldshers in the Soviet medical system is described in H. M. Leichter, *A Comparative Approach to Policy Analysis: Health Care Policy in Four Nations* (Cambridge: Cambridge University Press, 1979), pp. 222–25. Barefoot doctors attracted as much attention outside China as they did within it. The literature is quite voluminous, although not consistently interesting, much less enlightening. But see Sidel and Sidel, *The Health of China*, note 5, chap. 3; and E. M. Rogers, "Barefoot Doctors," in *Rural Health in the PRC*, NIH no. 81–424 (Washington, D.C.: Department of Health and Human Services, November 1980).

21. See Hu, *An Economic Analysis of the Cooperative Medical Services*, p. 243.

22. See Chen Pi-Chao, *Population and Health Policy in the PRC*, Occasional Monograph Series (Washington, D.C.: Smithsonian Institution, 1976), no. 9, esp. chap. 3; Hu, *An Economic Analysis of the Cooperative Medical Services*, p. 243; Parish and Whyte, *Village and Family in Contemporary China*, p. 88; and B. Michael Frolic, *Mao's People* (Cambridge, Mass.: Harvard University Press, 1980), p. 221. Additional information on the financing of health care in rural areas can be found in World Health Organization, *Primary Health Care: The Chinese Experience* (Geneva, 1983), pp. 57–71; and D. Mechanic and A. Kleinman, "Financing of Medical Care in Rural Health in the PRC," report of a visit by the Rural Health Systems Delegation, June 1978, NIH no. 81–2124, U.S. Department of Health and Human Services, Washington, D.C., November 1980, pp. 17–22.

23. State Statistical Bureau, *Statistical Yearbook of China, 1981*, p. 479.

24. The history of acupuncture is described in Lu Gwei-Djen and J. Needham, *Celestial Lancets: A History and Rationale of Acupuncture and Moxa* (Cambridge: Cambridge University Press, 1981); a more accessible source is J. Needham, *Science in Traditional China* (Cambridge, Mass.: Harvard University Press, 1981), ch. 4; the link with enkephalins has been reported in a

number of scientific publications; see for instance, L. Wingerson, "Painkilling Needles Make the Body Soothe Itself," *New Scientist* (November 27, 1980), p. 370; and J. Langome, "Acupuncture," *Discovery* (August 1984), pp. 70–73.

25. S. S. Nunn, "Research Institutes in the PRC," *U.S. China Business Review*, vol. 3 (March–April 1976), pp. 39–50. For additional details on herbal medicines, see American Herbal Pharmacology Delegation, *Herbal Pharmacology in the PRC* (Washington, D.C.: National Academy of Sciences, 1975).

26. See N. Goldman, "Far Eastern Patterns of Mortality," *Population Studies*, vol. 34, no. 1 (March 1980), pp. 5–17; H. C. Trowell and D. P. Burkitt, eds., *Western Diseases: Their Emergence and Prevention* (Cambridge, Mass.: Harvard University Press, 1981), especially chaps. 20, 21; and "Circulatory Ills Leading Cause of Death," *Korea Newsreview* (October 8, 1983), p. 23. Vascular disease was the cause of 300 out of every 1,000 deaths in Korea during 1981. Cancer was third, at 143 per 1,000.

27. Information on infant mortality is drawn from Banister and Preston, "Mortality in China," note 10. Chinese sources indicate that it may be only 20 to 30 per 1,000. See World Health Organization, *Primary Health Care: The Chinese Experience*, p. 22; and Scherer, *China: Facts and Figures Annual*, p. 321.

28. Mechanic and Kleinman, *The Organization, Delivery, and Financing of Rural Health Care*, note 17; World Health Organization, "Report on a Technical Visit," note 8; Cheng Tsun, and others, "Medical Education and Practice in the PRC," *Annals of Internal Medicine*, vol. 83 (1975), p. 717, and "Hypertension in China," *Science News*, vol. 118 (November 29, 1980), p. 344.

29. H. S. Kaplan and P. J. Tsuchitani, eds., *Cancer in China* (New York: Alan R. Liss, 1978); J. A. Miller and G. McQuerter, "The Great Struggle against Carcinoma," *Science News*, vol. 113, no. 8 (1978), pp. 124–25.

30. "Chinese Report Surge of Some Cancer Types among Local Groups," *New York Times* (September 24, 1979); "Studies by Chinese Finds Much Stomach Cancer," *New York Times* (April 1, 1980).

31. J. Cairns, "The Cancer Problem," *Scientific American* (November 1975), pp. 64–78; and R. G. Harvey, "Polycyclic Hydrocarbons and Cancer," *American Scientist* (July–August 1982), pp. 386–91.

32. See note 29.

33. K. C. Chang, ed., *Food in Chinese Culture* (New Haven, Conn.: Yale University Press, 1977), pp. 358, 361. The shortage of arable land and the greater efficiency of growing soybeans as against raising herds of cattle also influenced the supply of animal foods. See J. Goody, *Cooking, Cuisine, and Class* (Cambridge: Cambridge University Press, 1982), p. 107; and R. Tannahill, *Food in History* (New York: Stein and Day, 1973), p. 139.

34. State Statistical Bureau, *Statistical Yearbook of China, 1981*, p. 444.

35. A. Piazza, *Trends in Food and Nutrient Availability in China, 1950–81*, World Bank Staff Working Paper, no. 607 (Washington, D.C.: World Bank, September 1983), p. 76.

36. Ibid., p. 41; E. L. Rada, "Food Policy in China," *Asian Survey*, vol. 23 (April 1983), p. 531. Rada notes that, although China's food situation has been improving, the population remains precariously close to the edge of massive malnutrition and widespread hunger; see also the data in E. Croll, *The Family Rice Bowl* (London: Zed Press, 1983), pp. 138–41.

37. On these matters see R. O. Whyte, *Rural Nutrition in China* (London: Oxford University Press, 1972), especially pp. 26–28; D. Bonavia, *The Chinese* (New York: Lippincott and Crowell, 1980), p. 26; and Scherer, ed., *China: Facts and Figures Annual*, p. 331.

38. Chang, ed., *Food in Chinese Culture*, p. 9.

39. See "Cleaning Up Third World Diseases," *Economist* (September 10, 1983), pp. 92–93. A very detailed discussion of excreta management and parasitic diseases is contained in Richard G. Feachem, David J. Bradley, Hemda Garelick, and D. Duncan Mara, *Sanitation and Disease: Health Aspects of Excreta and Wastewater Management*, World Bank Studies in Water Supply and Sanitation, no. 3 (Chichester: John Wiley and Sons, 1983).

40. "Pesticides: The Human Body Burden," *Science News* (September 24, 1983), p. 199.

41. V. Smil, "Environmental Degradation in China," *Asian Survey*, vol. 20 (August 1980), p. 781. Smil has described the environmental problems in greater detail in *The Bad Earth* (Armonk, N.Y.: M. E. Sharpe, 1984), chaps. 3 and 4. The authorities' awareness of the problem was expressed in a speech by Wan Li, "Wan Li Discusses the Role of Ecological Economics," *Renmin Ribao* (April 6, 1984) (in *FBIS, China*, April 18, 1984, pp. K7–K13). See also, Marjorie Sun, "China Faces Environmental Challenge," *Science*, vol. 221 (September 23, 1983), pp. 1271–72.

42. Case histories of groundwater contamination have identified the following as the principal culprits: metals, organics, insecticides, chlorides, and nitrates, ranked in descending order. See V. I. Pye and R. Patrick, "Ground Water Contamination in the U.S.," *Science* (August 19, 1983), p. 715.

43. P. Andors, "The Four Modernizations and Chinese Policy on Women," *Bulletin of Concerned Asian Scholars*, vol. 13, no. 2, part 1 (1981), pp. 47–50.

44. "Nationwide Fertility Survey Conducted," *Beijing, Xinhua* (March 28, 1983) (in *FBIS, China*, April 1, 1983, p. K21). The age of marriage for rural women rose from 19.2 years in 1950–63, to 21 years in 1964–72, and to 22.8 years in 1973–74. See H. Yuan Tien, "Age at Marriage in the PRC," *China Quarterly*, no. 93 (March 1983), p. 94; and State Statistical Bureau, *Statistical Yearbook of China, 1981*, p. 89.

45. The Marriage Law of 1980 set the minimum age of marriage for men at 22 years and for women at 20 years. Tien, "Age of Marriage in the PRC," p. 98.

46. The draconian measures being taken to restrict family size have been widely commented upon. The official line is presented in the following: *Renmin Ribao* (February 5, 1982) (in *FBIS, China*, February 16, 1982, pp. K11–K14). See also, S. W. Mosher, "Birth Control: A View from a Chinese Village," *Asian Survey*, vol. 22 (April 1982), pp. 356–68; J. S. Aird, "Population Studies and Population Policy in China," *Population and Development Review*, vol. 8 (June 1982), pp. 267–97; J. M. Maloney, "Recent Developments in China's Population Planning," *Pacific Affairs* (Spring 1981), pp. 100–15; A. Saith, "Economic Incentives for the One Child Family in Rural China," *China Quarterly*, no. 87 (September 1981), pp. 493–500; and N. Keyfitz, "The Population of China," *Scientific American* (February 1984), pp. 38–47.

Chapter 8

~~~~~~

Education

THROUGHOUT HISTORY governments have searched for instruments to promote national integration, but have had only limited success. It is very difficult and demanding to instill certain desired values, inculcate a respect for institutions that can bind a nation together, generate a commitment to the social order, and impart a sense of discipline. Overt indoctrination alone is ineffective. But it can be very potent when combined with a prolonged social conditioning through a system of national education.

Although such a system has only recently been installed in China, education has for centuries been harnessed to social and political ends. Recent research has also underlined the economic benefits of education. There is, for instance, a close link between education and the readiness to entertain new ideas and innovate.[1] Schooling can improve a producer's ability to allocate his resources efficiently over the range of opportunities that are revealed by information on prices, markets, and technologies.[2] And aside from engendering specific skills, education also prepares the individual for organized activity of a kind ever more important in industrial societies.

Traditional Education

In some respects China is uniquely suited to use education as a tool for development, whether economic or political. A reverence for education is very deeply rooted in the culture. In imperial times, proper schooling was the key to prestige, wealth, and power, by way of government service.[3] Two of Confucius' greatest innovations, which remained a part of the culture for two and a half millennia, were to create the role of a private teacher and to accept students from all backgrounds.[4] Education was available to anyone with ability and dedication, if not the means to see him through long years of hermetic study. Even the poor were encouraged to acquire the rudiments of literacy by virtue of their contact with a highly bureaucratic state and their desire to avoid being cheated by merchants and tax collectors. Lineage organization, whose influence permeated all social interaction, was itself pegged to written genealogies.

A variety of institutions catered to the demand for schooling. Village schools, supported by local clans or through charitable donations, provided elementary education. Their efforts were supplemented by private teachers, drawn from the ranks of lower-level literati and those who had failed to measure up to civil service examinations. In the cities, government-owned schools and privately maintained academies offered opportunities for students who had set their sights higher.[5] There were many levels of literacy, starting with the peasant and the urban laborer whose comprehension did not extend beyond the few hundred characters needed to read work contracts, documents concerned with the division of property, or the cheap works of fiction, which were both popular and widely available. At the other end of the spectrum were the scholars who had devoted at least twenty years to mastering the classics, gaining command over 10,000 or more of the 50,000 ideographs encompassed by the written language and assimilating the complex stylistic conventions that governed all written communications between the literati.[6]

Centuries of veneration and the stimulus to literacy given by the qualifications needed for entering government service—long the most honored and desirable of occupations—led to a steady increase in the ranks of the educated. It has been estimated that by the late nineteenth century between 30 and 45 percent of the male population could read and write, although no more than 15 percent could claim much acquaintance with the classics.[7] This was a period of great ferment in China. Exposure to western culture and technology had starkly revealed China's backwardness, and, at the same time, military victories by both the western nations and Japan had wounded the national pride. Urban intellectuals, in particular, were deeply frustrated because they were most keenly aware of the potential inherent in China's vast economic and cultural resources and the tantalizing possibilities that western technology placed within the nation's reach. They attempted to devise a process of modernization that would infuse a new dynamism into Chinese society and displace traditional methods of thinking and acting with new scientific knowledge. To achieve this, they focused attention on education that nourished youths and prepared them for a role in society.

It was inevitable that all those who saw China treading the western path to modernity, would be disappointed by the Confucian axis of traditional learning. Confucianism, with its profoundly moral concerns, its emphasis on the proper but static ordering of human relations, and its belief that such relations orchestrated both public and private morality, seemed wholly unequal to the task of providing China with the array of skills needed for development. Nevertheless, many reformers of that era continued to believe that the values buttressed by Confucian teachings were worth salvaging, if only to maintain cultural unity, cohesiveness, and a sense of national purpose. But even they had to concede that traditional education, for all its discipline and erudition, could not compete with western-style education when it came to producing students able to master modern technologies.

The Beginnings of Modern Education

Exposure to western schooling practices began through the missionary schools founded in the third quarter of the nineteenth century, and, after 1872, a few students were allowed to seek education abroad. However, the reform of education was slow in gathering momentum.[8]

The Manchu court founded the Peking University in 1898. In 1905, the civil service examinations, which for generations had molded and selected the men governing China, had given practical value to education, had determined the curriculum, and had defined how a student approached his text, were abolished.[9] Western science and non-Confucian subject matter were also introduced into the school curriculum. The Japanese influence was dominant between 1908 and 1922, after which the American model won favor, no doubt through the efforts and influence of Chinese students who had studied in the United States. The U.S. system, based on six years of primary schooling followed by three years each of junior and senior school, was duly introduced in the cities, supplementing, although not altogether displacing, traditional schools. In the rural areas the traditional schools remained, by and large, the only source of education and received support from the lineage networks dominated by landlords. Thus, from around the turn of the century a dualistic education system began to emerge, comprised of modern, state-controlled schools concentrated mainly in the cities and rural schools that remained loyal to the traditional texts and the method of rote learning. The government, in effect, lost its grip on rural education, and the efforts of men, such as Liang Shu-ming, who tried to raise the level of teaching in the rural schools, were not very successful. Their attempts failed because modern primary schools were difficult to maintain outside of the cities and because the supply of teachers and wealthy patrons was meager.[10] The respect that traditional texts continued to enjoy in rural society was another hurdle that reformers faced. Moral training, with its promise of social harmony, was important to the peasantry. Peasants felt that scientific knowledge threatened to disrupt their social existence, and they were chary of accommodating it, especially when they were unable to understand how the alien concepts being taught in modern schools might enable them to improve their material conditions.

The disorder that ensued during the warlord era acted as a further brake on progress. Many of the chieftains who rose to power feared and despised intellectuals and were loath to expand education. Thus revenues from land, title deeds, business and sales taxes, as well as the likin which had been used to finance rural education, were frequently diverted elsewhere.[11] The Japanese invasion and the disruption caused by the conflict between Nationalist and Communist armies further eroded rural finances, and, although some schools were established in the Communist-occupied areas, rural education tended to languish. Teacher training standards were not developed nor did the schools move toward a fixed curriculum. Above all, the rural schools retained their classical tenor.

There appears to have been little change in the level of literacy during the first half of the twentieth century. Surveys conducted by J. L. Buck in the 1930s showed that about half of the male population of southern China was literate to varying degrees. The average for the remainder of the country was 35 to 40 percent. By comparison only 2 to 3 percent of females over the age of seven had received any education, and perhaps half that number could be classified as literate.[12] At the time of the Communist takeover in 1949, anywhere between 20 and 40 percent of the population could be described as being literate, depending upon the criteria used. Most of those who could read and write were concentrated in the cities, but rural literacy was fairly high compared with countries at an equivalent level of development. Although virtually all of the 5,000 secondary schools and the 205 universities and colleges were located in the cities, a significant percentage of the 347,000 modern primary schools were in rural areas. In addition, there was the vast network of traditional schools, which, if they did not introduce their pupils to modern learning, at least acquainted them with the classics, the complex mode of writing, and the routine of a modern school system.[13] Thus, a large proportion of the rural male populace had received some exposure to the formal routines and disciplines intrinsic to modern education. The notion of self-improvement through learning had already been implanted by the cultural tradition. And even the brief spell of schooling had helped quicken the desire for achievement, sharpened a national consciousness, and increased an openness to new ideas and techniques.

For all its drawbacks, the educational heritage of imperial times did provide a firm basis for the initiatives taken by the Communist regime to bring modern schooling to the rural sector. This has been partially obscured by the apparent clash between the Communist world view and the ethos of the society they were attempting to dislodge. The Communists appeared to shun tradition because it was retrogressive and to repudiate inherited institutions because they were vehicles for class domination. But this appearance of turning away, of having rejected both the China of the Qing dynasty and the feudal-capitalist hybrid that had begun to take shape in the first half of the twentieth century, was deliberately contrived. Ideology was not just an intellectual device to assist the elect in navigating and interpreting, it was also a way to mask continuities by emphasizing the sense of upheaval and mental break with the past. For the Communist Party to succeed in capturing the imagination of the people as well as gaining their political backing, a compelling sketch of how the future could unfold under socialism was a necessary ingredient of the ideology being promoted. But the ideology also had to engineer a measure of disengagement from the past, its institutions, alliances, commitments, and modes of thought. Without some such rejection there could be no guarantee of enduring political fidelity and a wholehearted pursuit of modernization along socialist lines. It would also be impossible to clear the ground, more or less completely, of "class enemies."

Thus, from one angle, Communist ideology gave the impression that an extended chapter in China's history had been irrevocably closed.

Furthermore, the systematic way in which the Party weeded out the gentry and suppressed long-established social practices suggested that their mode of governing and the social structures they intended to erect to regulate the lives of the people were hermetically independent from the past and free of the many accumulated flaws that had brought down traditional China. But to an extent this was only a ruse. Much was carried over and skillfully reworked so that it could be bent to new purposes. Heeding the advice of social thinkers such as Liang Chi-chao and Liang Shu-ming, who felt that Chinese tradition could provide grist for reformers and modernizers, the Communists leveled the social structures that had shored up the gentry's power while exploiting the relays and the wiring that had animated these institutions. To put it differently, under the cover of ideology, the regime knew the importance of resting new institutions and practices on the people's deep-seated beliefs regarding the management of the society. The centralized and bureaucratic system that the new regime created, the ethic of service to the nation that it preached, and its often reiterated emphasis on collective responsibility were not the least unfamiliar to the average villager. Only the vigor with which political maxims were translated into practices and the extent to which the Party permeated the life of even distant villages was unusual.

For centuries, education allied with Confucianism had enabled the state to gain a measure of control over the minds of the peasants. Under the Communists, moral conditioning in the schools was reaffirmed with equal fervor, except that commitments to family, kin, and clan were replaced by moral obligations to the masses, the Party, and the state. In a sense, the moral world of the peasant became coextensive with the universe of politics. Similarly, the method of learning by rote was largely retained even though the curriculum was emptied of the classics and standardized for the country as a whole. Finally, in spite of efforts at centralization, the financing of primary schooling remained the responsibility of the local communities.

These continuities should not in any way deflect attention from the major change introduced by the government, however. The objectives of mass education and universal literacy fundamentally altered the scope of schooling in China. The complete substitution of a modern curriculum for the traditional texts not only rendered obsolete the traditional learning against which a legion of reformers had struggled with limited success, but also altered radically the outlook of most of the young and at least some of the older generations.

Swings in Education Strategy

Policies on rural education have been deployed at three levels during the past three decades: basic literacy; primary, secondary, and vocational education; and the training for science and research. Education policy oscillated with the changing fortunes of powerful factions within the upper reaches of the Party. From the very beginning, the education strategy has been subject to conflicting goals and constrained by inadequate financing. After the Communist regime came to power, priority was given to wresting control over modern as well as traditional schools. This meant dislodging private groups and foreign missionaries in the cities and the influence of clans and notables in the villages. The process began with the establishment of a Ministry of Education in October 1949 and was completed by 1954 when the teaching of English was suspended. By then the new regime was fully in control, and economic concerns had to a degree again superseded political ones.

At least through 1957, education was seen as principally serving economic objectives. The emphasis lay on improving the quality of schooling and providing it to the largest number through a centralized system, with the central government shouldering most of the outlay. As the system evolved, however, many in the Party came to feel that the moral and political content of education was becoming diluted and that the demand for skills to support China's development was injecting a pronounced urban bias, making education elitist, and also raising the cost to the central government.

With the Great Leap the orientation of schooling shifted toward the political. There was an enormous, and ultimately futile, effort to increase the education services offered to the peasants by introducing a range of informal schooling programs and by making rural education less structured and more relevant to farming activities. During this time the government also reversed the drift toward fiscal centralization by shifting some of the costs of education back to the provinces and the communes.[14]

When the Great Leap collapsed and the regime took stock of the economic costs that had been incurred, there was a gradual return to an emphasis on quality and a reining in of the exuberant programs to expand primary and secondary enrollment. The time students were supposed to spend on political study and productive labor had greatly increased during 1958–60, and these requirements were cut back. But some of the spare-time education schemes as well as the part-time schools, which had mushroomed in the late 1950s, were retained after the mood of the Party swung toward the moderate. Financial exigencies also ensured that the minban schools, largely supported by local funds, were left in the control of the communes.[15] What might, for lack of a better term, be called economic objectives remained paramount until 1965, even though ideological considerations had begun to loom ever larger after 1963, as Mao's influence again started to be felt in the Party circles.

Once the Cultural Revolution was unleashed in 1966, the pendulum again swung back toward an education policy saturated with political and ideological aims. Class struggle, never very far from the classroom door, now erupted with full force inside the school, and beliefs regarding the function as well as the mechanics of education, which had germinated in the early 1940s during the Party's "Yenan Period," were translated, with some difficulty, into practice. Elitism, supported by "key schools" and the tracking system, was one of the earliest victims.[16] Education of peasants once again was a priority. Manual labor became an important part of every student's life. Many senior Party cadres had long considered it as indispensable for molding correct attitudes, bridging the gap between urban and rural sensibilities, and facilitating an identification with the masses. In addition, much more time was devoted to political topics, to discussions of Maoist and Leninist thought, and to the search for the insidious contradictions forever lurking beneath the surface of society. From 1966 up to the death of Mao ten years later, education policy combined the Maoist conviction in the malleability of man with the Confucian view, accepted by the Communists, that schooling can serve as an avenue to human perfectibility. The Maoists started from the assumption that the peasant was a "blank sheet of paper" who could be inculcated with values supporting the official image of the social structure and thus be forged into an irresistible tool of development. Human will was seen as the prime force in economic development, and the schools were entrusted with the task of focusing the energy of the youth.

But the attempt to transform the style and content of education, instead of raising its effectiveness, caused serious disruption by encumbering schools with more innovations than they could absorb. Since many of these new practices went against the grain of entrenched pedagogical methods and were accompanied by far-reaching changes in teaching staff and the curricula, higher level education sailed very close to chaos during that tumultuous decade. Primary schools did not escape unscathed, but they were affected much less. Because of this and because of the consideration given to the interests of peasants, rural education came through the 1966–76 period with relatively few scars. In fact, it could be said that the gap between urban and rural schooling narrowed, with enrollments rising and peasant children gaining greater access to secondary schools and colleges. However, the increased enrollment was counterbalanced by a decline in the quality of education as a consequence of changes in teaching material, the greater intrusion of physical labor in the schooling schedule, and the replacement of politically unreliable teachers with individuals whose only redeeming quality was ideological rectitude.[17]

The damage was far more visible at the other end of the educational scale. The closing of universities and some research institutes between 1966 and 1970 and the highly politicized environment in tertiary institutions through the first half of the 1970s, reduced the supply of skilled agricultural technicians and scientists and lowered the standards of both education and research.

Very soon after the death of Mao and the arrest of the Gang of Four, the regime recalibrated its goals, making economic modernization the principal concern. The ramifications of this for education were immediate. One of the first changes was to severely curb the intrusion of politics into schooling. Informal teaching methods and manual labor were scaled down, and open book exams fell from favor. Strict classroom discipline, the two-track system, and key schools were all slowly brought back, as the concern for quality edged out the earlier preoccupation with numbers. For the agricultural sector, the emphasis placed on expanding vocational schools and colleges to train technicians and researchers was the most significant step. An increased supply of skills should enhance farm productivity and improve the crop mix. But the meritocratic orientation of the school system, which has become very noticeable in the past few years, limits the ability of students from a rural background to enter the better secondary and tertiary institutions. A form of discrimination, which Party ideologues objected to in the early 1960s and which the Cultural Revolution tried unsuccessfully to eradicate, may be seeping back.

Throughout the movements in education policy since 1949, the regime has held firm to the belief, deeply rooted in Chinese culture, that by instilling the appropriate values, schools can help create a cohesive and politically supportive public. But opinions have differed on how effectively moral fervor and profound ideological commitments that are only modestly supported by scientific skills can cope with the problems of development. And the content, the direction, and the quality of Chinese education has depended on whether those in command of the Party were being guided primarily by practical economic concerns or swayed by the call of ideological purity.

Four questions remain: how adequately has the system of education coped with the needs of rural development; how has the system been administered, and what is the nature of its efficiency; in which direction is it headed; and how appropriate is the current approach within the socioeconomic context?

With information on China becoming plentiful, the contours of the education system have emerged quite clearly, but much of the available evidence deals with education for the country as a whole, and the details of rural education are often lost in the aggregates. Hence it is difficult to treat comprehensively the question of adequacy. The best that can be done is to give an idea of the size of stocks and flows, starting with the just-literate, working upward through the ranks of those who have received or are currently receiving some form of schooling, and ending with those who enjoy the benefits of a college education.

Literacy Campaigns

As stated above, possibly four-fifths of the population could be classified as illiterate in the late 1940s, and one of the goals of the Communist regime was to whittle away at this enormous overhang.[18] The campaign was slow in gathering momentum because of a shortage of teachers and textbooks, but the nature of written Chinese also posed unique difficulties. Memorizing a large number of characters is an arduous enterprise, and forgetting is all too easy. The complexity of the characters, which average eleven strokes, and the lack of a phonetic correspondence only compound the problem. But although this was something which had been of concern to the Communists during their spell in Yenan, no shortcut offered itself.[19] Romanization and the shift to a phonetic alphabet meant surrendering the mutual intelligibility that ideographic writing made possible in a country of 1,800 languages and dialects. Simplification by reducing the number of strokes (an expedient that was introduced in 1956) entailed the loss of the important combinatory property of the signific and the phonetic, sometimes even overlooking the root of the character.[20]

Functional literacy called for a knowledge of some 3,000 to 3,500 characters and took an average of five years of study—an impossibly long time to a regime in a hurry for results. The criterion for literacy was instead set at 1,500 characters for peasants and 2,000 characters for urban workers, and in the winter of 1949–50 a concerted effort was made to enroll peasants in winter schools and to teach them a few hundred characters during the slack season from November to March. Enrollment was 1.8 million in 1950 and rose to 35 million two years later, but it quickly became apparent to the authorities that four months of painful memorization was forgotten by the following winter because the peasants had little opportunity to practice their embryonic skills and often could not gain access to printed material. By 1955–56, the winter schools had been replaced by informal schools that were open all year round. Although some new teachers were trained to staff these facilities, much of the instruction was provided by 1.4 million primary school teachers. To solve the shortage of reading material, model textbooks were especially prepared for the campaign and were distributed to the classes.[21]

By 1957 it was claimed that 22 million adults, an unknown fraction of whom were peasants, had achieved literacy through spare-time study. With the start of the Great Leap, the literacy drive picked up enormously as cadres were pressured to meet unrealistic targets. A year later, adult illiteracy for the country as a whole had supposedly been cut to just 30 to 40 percent, a truly phenomenal achievement. As it later emerged, cadres quickly learned that accurate reporting of results was politically unwise and occasionally dangerous. Thus, gross exaggeration became the rule. Of the thousands who were forced to attend courses on reading and writing, most lapsed back into illiteracy once the campaign had subsided.

Efforts to spread literacy did not, of course, come to an end, but for several years were tempered by a sober appreciation of the costs involved and the limited effectiveness of mass campaigns lasting just a few months. The Cultural Revolution then once again stoked sentiments for informal education and spare-time study for the illiterate. Many different programs were tried between 1968 and 1976, and, even though the claims made often exceeded actual progress, little by little, illiteracy among the adult population appears to have been rolled back. A report presented by the vice minister of education in 1979 claimed that 127 million peasants had been taught to read and write since 1949. About 70 percent of the young adults in the rural sector were literate. But the report also stated that more than 120 million youths between the ages of fifteen and twenty-five, most of whom were probably living in rural areas, could not be classified as functionally literate because of the quality of education they received during the Cultural Revolution years. In the winter of 1978 yet another campaign was launched to combat illiteracy among youths as well as members of the older generation remaining outside the pale.[22] Some 6 million people attended spare-time literacy courses in 1981, and the effort to spread literacy is now being taken up by the radio and TV networks, both of which offer basic and advanced courses in selected subjects such as language and mathematics.[23]

To have pushed literacy from around 20 percent to almost 70 percent in thirty years is a considerable feat—something that few countries in a comparable income class can rival. However, on the assumption that most of the people who are classified as literate can comprehend no more than 1,500 characters, it is questionable whether the cause of rural development has been greatly advanced. A knowledge of a thousand or more characters enables an individual to read newspapers and popular magazines, thus allowing the government to communicate its objectives, expectations, and views more effectively. Political support becomes a little easier to mobilize, and the regime has an additional channel through which to influence the way people think. But so modest an understanding of the written language does not really enable a peasant to obtain more than a very limited understanding of a farm manual or a guide on how to repair a tractor or any of the myriad publications through which scientific knowledge is transmitted. And it is such knowledge that today is the prime mover of agricultural development. No one can deny that literacy is a laudable goal, but the purpose of spreading it is to increase the range of usable knowledge. The numbers emanating from China are impressive, but what they signify is less apparent. The standards by which literacy is judged are low, and the complexity of written Chinese raises the odds against retaining the facility to read and write without practice. If so, how many peasants who satisfy the government's criteria for literacy can derive practical use from the skill they have acquired? Properly constructed sample surveys could answer this question, but such investigations have apparently not yet been conducted. Meanwhile, the campaigns to raise literacy continue.

Primary and Secondary Education

Only a quarter of the children in the relevant age group, about 24 million in all, attended primary schools in 1949. Less than a million and a quarter (3 percent of the age group) were enrolled in secondary schools.[24] Most of the students receiving secondary schooling and a sizable number of those attending modern primary schools were drawn from the urban areas. The vast majority of rural children went to traditional schools. In areas that had been liberated by the Communists, they also had the choice of attending minban schools, originally conceived in the 1930s and 1940s to provide a formal education, untainted by either traditional or elitist notions of schooling and under conditions of extreme financial stringency.

Determined to break the grip of traditional habits of thought and to gain sole mastery over the system of education, the regime energetically tried to abolish the traditional curriculum and establish a network of modern schools. The strong desire to keep "bourgeois" western culture at a distance combined with the sense of ideological identification with the Soviet Union induced Chinese educators to imitate the Russian school system. The process of transplanting Soviet pedagogy began in 1952, starting with the translation of Russian textbooks by the Chinese Academy of Sciences and other institutions. By 1956, some 1,400 titles had been translated, of which 14 percent were on agriculture, and the books had been absorbed into the curriculum.[25] The duration of schooling remained unchanged, with six years in primary school followed by three each in junior middle and senior middle schools. Although this rule was applied throughout the country, only some 10 percent of rural primary schools were able to provide more than five years of training in the early 1950s. As the supply of teachers grew and more funds became available from the government, the norm was increased to six years. From 1952 to 1958, the policy toward education remained highly centralized and, in fact, the government took over most of the minban schools, which had been established through a pooling of local resources.

Nationwide statistics on the number of schools, total enrollment, and the enrollment ratios in 1958 indicate that some 86 million children, 67 percent of the relevant age group, were studying in some 770,000 primary schools. At the same time, about 29,000 regular secondary schools accommodated 8.5 million youngsters, an enrollment ratio of 17 percent.[26] The difference between rural and urban enrollment rates was probably quite small for primary education, but this may not have been the case at the secondary level. Perhaps no more than 10 percent of the rural population in the secondary school age group was enrolled because the schools were few in number and located in large towns or cities, because many students had poor academic training, and because many such schools were only for boarders and thus quite expensive.

Innovations during the Great Leap

The creation of the communes in 1958, which closely coincided with the start of the Greap Leap, spawned a number of innovations. Encouraged by the government, the communes established more than 800,000 spare-time middle and primary schools and experimented with an "open door" policy to integrate schooling with other rural activities. More important, the minban system was revived, thus transferring many of the responsibilities for primary schools back to the communes. Agricultural middle schools set up and run by the communes were a third innovation. They admitted students who had completed primary school, operated from November to April so as not to interfere with farming operations, and, in addition to a general education, imparted some training on pest control, water conservancy, plant botany, and animal husbandry.

The main problem with the Great Leap was that too much was attempted in a very brief span of time. Many of the schemes were soon found to be unsustainable. Grandiose education plans for expanding literacy as well as the enrollment of primary, secondary, and vocational schools ran aground, and many new schools housed in empty public buildings, shrines, and caves and run by voluntary labor were closed down. However, both the minban system and the agricultural middle schools were retained during the retrenchment after the Great Leap. The minbans made fiscal sense at a time when the government was short of finances. Fees in such schools were quite high, ranging between 12 and 20 yuan a year (for two terms), as they had to cover teacher salaries. Agricultural middle schools survived because they served a useful purpose. Peasants felt that the knowledge diffused through these schools was of value, and, as communes gained in experience, the agriculture schools were made more effective. Small and well-dispersed facilities suited the village folk, as they were easier to reach and could be more flexible in dividing the students' time between school and farm work. It was also found that teaching only a few subjects was advantageous, hence the curriculum was narrowed to language, political studies, mathematics, and the fundamentals of agriculture.

Efforts to consolidate the school system in the early 1960s reduced the number of primary schools to 682,000 and slowed the growth of enrollment. By the mid-1960s, about 70 percent of all primary-school-age children were receiving education; 16 percent in the secondary age group. But the emergence during this period of key schools and the multiple track system at the primary and secondary levels made it difficult for children from rural backgrounds and relatively inferior schools to gain access to the better secondary institutions and the nation's universities.

Changes during the Cultural Revolution

All schools were closed from 1966 to 1968 because of the Cultural Revolution, and tertiary institutions did not reopen until 1970. The resumption of schooling was followed by far-reaching changes. To start with, there was a marked shift in the length of schooling. Until 1965, six years in elementary school followed by three years each in junior and senior middle schools had been the norm, but to stretch out existing facilities and provide more children with at least a minimum education, primary school was reduced to five years and middle school to four (two each at the junior and senior levels). Most schools switched to the new schedule, but it was not universally adopted. Some schools in Guangdong, and possibly in other provinces as well, retained the six-year middle school. Others cut back primary schooling to five years but then required children to go through two years of junior school, thereby lengthening the period of education.[27]

The second major reform was in the content of schooling. Mao believed that the curriculum was ideologically rather anemic and did not politically motivate the students. Further, a grave weakness of the middle school curriculum was that it trained students for the next stage of education. Most of the population, however, could not proceed to college and were quite naturally dissatisfied with their circumstances, reluctant to find work in the countryside, and unequipped to put their learning to any good use without further training. Therefore, Mao proposed a drastic overhaul, starting with the course material. Most textbooks were withdrawn and rewritten, a truly Herculean task, so as to incorporate the revolutionary point of view. A strong emphasis was placed on the relevance and practical applicability of what was being taught. Abstract theorizing was deliberately downplayed, and the centrality of rural life and the need to build a strong agricultural economy were strongly emphasized.

Many teachers were purged, and those remaining had to accept a much less authoritarian approach in conducting their classes. They were now required to engage the students in debate and to indulge in self-criticism. The object was to nudge education away from rote memorization and to induce students to form their own views rather than slavishly to accept what they were told. Students were encouraged to question the teachers' views and to discuss the content of their courses with the staff, and villagers were invited to recommend what should be taught in the schools and to advise on the contents of the new textbooks. To integrate schooling with the existence of workers and peasants, individuals from such backgrounds were hired to teach in schools and were instructed to emphasize political education and give the students a graphic account of the exploitation that had prevailed in bourgeois-feudal times. Closely linked with the above was the so-called open door policy, which made factories and farms extensions of the school and called upon all students to work between four weeks (for primary) and eight weeks (for senior and middle) during each school year. The stress on manual work was partly motivated by the desire to level aspirations, to suppress elitist illusions, and to reverse the incipient alienation from peasant life.[28]

There were three other facets to the education strategy that was followed during the Cultural Revolution. First, the regime tried to end discrimination against those from a peasant background. The instruments of discrimination were entrance examinations, the curricula, and the attitudes of teachers. Thus, entrance examinations were largely abolished, and exams were generally de-emphasized, with students being allowed to consult books and each other. No one was failed. Most textbooks were rewritten, and, as stated above, teachers were either "rectified" or replaced by new recruits with the "right" frame of mind. In addition, school administrators were pressured into giving primacy to the political credentials of applicants and accepting students from groups that had been discriminated against in the past. As a result of these measures, the urban bias of schools was eroded to a degree.[29]

A second facet of the education strategy during 1966–76 was the abolition of key schools and the two-track system of the early 1960s, ostensibly because they promoted elitism and segregated students, to the detriment of rural candidates. A third facet, which harkened back to the policies adopted in 1958–59, was a move to transfer more of the fiscal responsibilities to the communities operating the schools. Almost all rural primary schools were required to obtain financial and administrative support from the brigade, although the government continued to pay the salaries of elementary school teachers in some of the poorer areas of the country. Middle schools came under the purview of either the county or the provincial government or the central government, but the Ministry of Education took care of stipends given to teachers.

The fate of vocational education provided by agricultural middle schools and other spare-time institutions is unclear. One of the charges leveled against the Gang of Four is that they closed down vocational schools "under the pretext of criticizing the . . . bourgeois double stream system."[30] But the literature from that period makes many references to training, such as that provided through schools, many of which set up their own workshops and emphasized the practical aspects of education, and through informal training programs run by the thousands of scientists, engineers, and researchers who were dispersed through the countryside. To quote one observer,

> Literally millions of peasants have been trained for specific technical tasks, including identifying and monitoring diseases, devising integrated control measures, noting differences in cultivars, etc. Peasant organizations proliferated as a result of the Cultural Revolution . . . Academics from the institutes, colleges and universities were sent down to the communes to help solve the farmers' problems . . . basic contact points were set up . . . Small experimental stations established and field extension work organized. Research personnel were expected to devote [from one-third to two-thirds of their time] squatting at the points.[31]

Recent announcements imply that a severe shortage of skills prevails in the agriculture sector because of the damage done to vocational and tertiary institutions during 1966–76, something which escaped the eyes of the numerous trained observers from the West who visited China in the first half of the 1970s. The many trip accounts do not, of course, add up to a refutation of the current claims, and the actual state of vocational training during 1968–76 can only be illuminated if the government releases additional data.

Developments in the 1970s

The Cultural Revolution seriously disrupted schooling during 1966–68, but thereafter primary and secondary enrollments steadily expanded. In 1976 for instance, it was announced that 95 percent of all children in the appropriate age group were attending rural primary schools. In fact, several provinces had achieved that level in 1974.[32] But the figures released in 1980 tell a somewhat different story. In 1979 more than 150 million youngsters were studying in some 924,000 primary schools. They comprised about 93 percent of the relevant age group for the entire country (see Table 8-1). Approximately 90 percent of the children in rural areas were attending primary schools, with possibly a higher percentage in more prosperous provinces such as

Table 8-1. *Student Enrollments*
(thousands of persons)

Year	Colleges	Secondary schools	Primary schools
1949	220	2,300	45,000
1952	330	5,500	88,000
1957	680	11,000	99,400
1962	1,230	12,400	102,900
1965	930	19,700	160,200
1978	890	69,300	152,600
1979	1,050	62,100	151,000
1980	1,160	57,800	148,900
1981	1,280	50,300	143,900

Source: State Statistical Bureau, *Statistical Yearbook of China, 1981* (Hong Kong: Economic Information Agency, 1982).

Guangdong. On an average, each of the country's 52,000 communes had fifteen primary schools. About half of all middle-school-age children (60 million) were enrolled, although the enrollment rate in rural areas was below 50 percent.[33]

Strenuous efforts have been made to upgrade the quality of the education, which the government claims had deteriorated gravely in the early 1970s. New textbooks modeled on western publications have been introduced; examinations have once again regained their earlier standing; strict discipline and the authority of teachers are being restored, although progress in the rural areas has been slow, with reports of students beating and insulting teachers and damaging school property; the two-track system and key schools have reappeared; both political study and physical labor have been downgraded, especially the latter; and a move is under way to slowly reinstate six years of primary schooling (currently most rural schools provide five) and three years of senior secondary schooling (now two years). One feature that has not changed is that the brigade continues to pay the salaries of minban elementary school teachers.

As mentioned earlier, the schools are again seen as handmaidens to modernization. They are expected to create the expertise China so desperately needs to realize its ambitions. Given this objective, the political, ideological, and practical orientation that characterized the schooling strategy some years ago is being replaced by one that is biased toward the academic. Being from a peasant or worker family is no longer as important for gaining admission into secondary and tertiary institutions, but the heavy reliance on examination scores during 1978–80 has also been broadened to include consideration of political attitude, along with performance in secondary school and athletics. Furthermore, the school program assigns specifically to political education only a small fraction of the thirty to thirty-four hours spent weekly in school. Children in primary school spend between a half and a third of their study time on language, around a fourth on mathematics, and the balance on science, art, and physical education. In middle school, the work load, which once included several hours of physical or practical activities and a sizable dose of practical education, now is rather evenly divided between Chinese, math, a foreign language (usually English), physics, and chemistry. History, geography, and civics absorb about two hours each every week.[34]

Although the change in focus might well enhance the supply of needed skills, it is not entirely beneficial to the agriculture sector, as it places rural students at a disadvantage in competing for a place, in the better middle schools and then in colleges. The general schools are geared to prepare students for the next level of schooling, although not many of the children in rural primary schools can expect to enter a rural middle school and eventually find their way into a university. To minimize the inevitable frustrations, rural secondary education may take on a marked vocational coloration. Increasing the number of technical and part-time vocational schools would enable most of those who complete primary education to acquire usable skills but would not generate high expectations regarding their future academic career. Some change in education policy might be desirable. Rural students are showing very little interest in their studies, since the chances of a seat in a university and eventually employment in the city are very slim. Since even a job in the commune administration is difficult to find, most school graduates have no option but to return to their villages.

Although vocational training may be the direction rural secondary education could take, as yet the numbers enrolled in vocational programs are fairly small. From a national total of 0.7 million vocational school students in 1982, about one-third were in technical agricultural schools or in senior secondary schools offering courses in agriculture.[35] Part of the problem is the shortage of teachers, but more serious is the lack of interest among students, who do not see vocational schooling as a ticket to a job outside the farming sector. Many youngsters pay little attention to what is taught in these schools because they feel that such skills will be acquired in due course once they are back on the farm. Those who choose to study agriculture have scores that are below average. The situation may change as the program gathers momentum, however. More than 3,000 general secondary schools (junior as well as senior) were offering some agriculture courses in the general curriculum as of 1980, and a further 300 secondary schools, enrolling close to 100,000 students, were converted to agricultural technical schools in 1981. During the next few years, one-third of all secondary schools in the rural areas are scheduled to be converted into agricultural schools.[36]

Financial Aspects

There is no way to accurately estimate the budgetary outlay on rural education. Available data only indicate the expenditures made by the central government. During the early 1950s, 7 percent of the state budget was earmarked for education. Expenditure per student, which included the capital costs of schools as well as operating expenses, came to a modest 12 yuan a year in 1952–55 and 8 yuan (4 U.S. dollars) in 1956. By the late 1950s, education was absorbing 10 percent of state funds. Its share dropped to 9 percent in 1960, but thereafter information is hard to find. The state budget for 1979 allocated 10.8 percent of total expenditures for culture, education, health, and science, with education receiving between 6 and 6.5 percent. The allocation rose to 13 percent in 1980 and by another 1 percent in 1981, but per capita expenditures decreased because the student body and teaching staff expanded.[37] These funds cover the salaries of teachers on the government payroll and defray a part of the capital costs of schools. But, especially in the rural areas, they are supplemented by a significant volume of local resources, which support both the operating and the capital costs of the schools. It is estimated that total expenditure per student for primary education was 20 U.S. dollars, while for secondary level schooling, it was close to 50 U.S. dollars.[38] In all, the percentage of GNP spent on education in the late 1970s was probably less than 3 percent.

Compared with the median outlay on education in developing countries—about 3.9 percent of GNP—China's allotment is appreciably less, but from the perspective of the peasant family, the cost of sending children through primary and middle schools is fairly high and is one of the reasons many children drop out of elementary schools after three to four years or do not continue on to junior middle schools after graduation. Tuition fees in rural primary schools range from 5 to 7 yuan for each term. Books, which are priced at around 30 fen, and meals add another 2 to 3 yuan for a total of nearly 10 yuan, about 2 to 3 percent of an average peasant family income. The cost of junior-level schooling is in the region of 10 to 12 yuan, while annual tuition in upper middle schools averages 14 yuan. The cost of books and supplies for senior high students is 15 to 17 yuan, while dormitory fees add another 12 to 20 yuan, for a total of about 40 yuan.[39]

Quality and Efficiency

The quality and efficiency of Chinese schooling has varied over the years, although less at the primary level than in secondary schools and colleges, but until recently the evidence available was highly impressionistic. Now, with the release of reliable data on class size and certain other indicators, a clearer picture of schooling, if only at the elementary level, has begun to emerge. More than 90 percent of rural children enter primary school, the 7 to 10 percent who do not being mostly girls. Few of these children have had any preschool training, and many enter late so that in some years enrollment in primary schools has exceeded the age group. Until recently, grade promotion was fairly automatic, and the repetition rate was no more than 2 to 3 percent. The dropout rate is heavy, however, with about 40 percent of the students being unable to complete five (or six) years of education, the minimum required to attain an effective standard of literacy.[40] Of those graduating, only 30 percent reached a fifth grade academic standard.

Primary school teachers numbered 5.2 million (not including part-time teachers) in 1978; 3 million of these were minban teachers supported by the communes, and the remainder were on the government's payroll (see Table 8-2). Less than half had received any training.[41] With

Table 8-2. *Students per Teacher, by Level of School*

Year	Tertiary institutions		Secondary schools		Primary schools	
	Number of teachers (ten thousands)	Students per teacher	Number of teachers (ten thousands)	Students per teacher	Number of teachers (ten thousands)	Students per teacher
1949	1.6	7.3	8.3	15.3	83.6	29.2
1952	2.7	7.1	13.0	24.2	143.5	35.6
1957	7.0	6.3	29.3	24.2	188.4	34.1
1965	13.8	4.9	70.9	20.2	385.7	30.1
1978	20.6	4.2	328.1	20.2	522.6	28.0
1979	23.7	4.3	319.1	18.9	533.2	27.2
1980	24.7	4.6	317.2	17.9	549.9	26.6
1981	25.0	5.1	300.9	16.7	558.0	25.7

Source: State Statistical Bureau, *Statistical Yearbook of China, 1981.*

a class size of fifty and teaching staff of 1.22 per class, the teacher–student ratio was 1:41, a relatively high figure in view of the instructors' limited training, but not unmanageable given the relatively disciplined behavior of young Chinese students.[42] Since many of the urban youths sent out to the country have drifted back to the cities, finding primary school teachers is even more of a problem than in the past. Young men are not attracted to teaching because the pay is low and it is thought to be a woman's job. Hence, teacher training schools can only entice girls from poor families to enroll by eliminating tuition fees.

Most rural elementary schools are housed in ramshackle, poorly lit, and unheated buildings with very rudimentary furniture. But the supply of textbooks, often a serious constraint in developing countries, is adequate. Learning is accomplished through traditional rote memorization, despite the efforts made during the Cultural Revolution to develop a mode of teaching that nurtured a child's curiosity and creative abilities. In part, the traditional method has persisted because of a tenaciously held view that memorizing moral verities promotes ethical behavior. But, in addition, a good writing style in Chinese is more formulaic than in many other languages and is acquired by memorizing accepted writing patterns. On the surface, such an approach allied with an inflexible authoritarianism says little for the quality of schooling, but the experience of the Republic of Korea, Japan, and the Soviet Union, together with recent investigation in the West, suggests that learning by rote may be a more efficient way of training young minds than the discovery method.

Everything considered, the state of Chinese primary education may not be particularly healthy. Aside from the large classes and the reliance on memorization, on which opinions differ, other factors—the miserable facilities, insufficient teacher training, high dropout rate, and the recent admission that 120 million youngsters who had received their schooling in the 1970s, were not functionally literate—suggest that there is much room for improvement at the primary level, and very probably at the secondary level as well.[43]

As observed above, knowledge of the state of secondary schooling remains limited to a few aggregates. Enrollment in junior school comprises 75 percent of the age cohort, although it may be lower in the rural areas, with perhaps 40 to 50 percent of primary school graduates entering the next level. About 29 percent of the relevant age group were in senior middle schools toward the close of the 1970s.[44] The problems noted in primary schools are evident at higher levels as well. A report on the Peking Municipality indicated that less than 30 percent of the junior middle school students in the 1981 graduation class were up to the graduation level. Of those promoted to senior school, only a little over a third had scored higher than 60 percent on six subjects.[45] For the nation as a whole, only 50 percent of junior school students moved to the next level. Those with little chance of attending a university are anxious to leave school as soon as possible, since job allocation is often not closely linked to school records. In Changzhou city (Jiangsu province) only 27 percent of the junior school graduates went on to senior high in 1980. The lack of motivation in rural areas is probably much greater.

Tertiary Education and Skilled Manpower

Information on changes in the supply of technical skills in the agriculture sector since 1949 is extremely sparse. Agricultural research and teaching institutions suffered from the Cultural Revolution, and many were closed from 1966 to 1970. A slow start was made in the early 1970s, but these institutions have recovered their stride only recently. Since 1949, agricultural colleges have graduated 290,000 students, but less than half of them are still doing agricultural work.[46] Thus, the current stock of trained manpower in the rural sector is probably about 130,000, with each commune having on average one technical person. This situation is felt to be far below the country's requirements, and it has focused a good deal of attention on tertiary-level training facilities.

In 1981, there were sixty-five colleges of agriculture and forestry, and nine of them had "key" status.[47] Total enrollment, which has shown a rising trend, was 92,000 (approximately 7 percent of the number of tertiary students in the country), and most students were expected to complete their studies in three to four years, with some programs extending to five or six years. Nearly 14,000 students graduated with agricultural degrees in 1978, 10,000 in 1979, and 8,800 in 1981, but, with enrollments climbing, the agriculture schools should be graduating 15,000 or more students a year in the near future. Although this constitutes a substantial improvement over the trickle produced less than a decade ago, it is still not enough. Currently, the ratio of technical personnel to the rural labor force is less than 1:1,000 compared with 2:1,000 in Mexico and 16:1,000 in the United States.

Current Problems and Future Concerns

During the Cultural Revolution, Maoists believed that Chinese students were being given education that deadened revolutionary consciousness and was unrelated to the needs of the country. The children of peasants and workers were inadequately provided for because both the location of schools and the content of courses made it difficult for them to compete successfully for a place in middle level and higher institutions. Even elementary education was out of reach of the poorest peasants because the cost of sending a child to school was not insignificant, and classes often conflicted with farm activities. The Maoists believed that in a country where close to 85 percent of the population lived in the rural areas and the regime espoused a proletarian ideology, it was essential to raise the proportion of students in middle schools and colleges from worker or peasant households, as long as the price was not excessive in terms of cost and lowered quality.

As is now well known, reform measures that could be considered reasonable were in practice pushed far beyond the limits of prudence. There is no doubt that higher education was seriously affected by the long closure of universities (1966–70), changes in curricula, and so forth. The Cultural Revolution may have cost China, if not a generation of scientists and skilled technicians, at least a significantly reduced supply of highly skilled manpower for several years. Elementary schools weathered the storms without much strain, but in middle schools and institutions of higher learning, radical fervor was not always under the leash of sober pragmatism, discipline broke down, and classrooms dissolved into chaos. With the teachers' authority seriously compromised and in the absence of any well-thought-out procedures to replace the earlier method of rote learning, the schools were hard put to control the students and maintain acceptable standards of quality. The withdrawal of most textbooks was also damaging. Although attempts were made to produce new material that measured up to ideological expectations, such efforts were both insufficient and uncoordinated. For a time, schooling had to be carried on without the pedagogical support of textbooks, and when new ones began to appear their quality left much to be desired. To make higher education available to students from the rural areas, class background and political commitment were allowed to dominate entrance requirements. And to ensure that students who would have to spend most of their lives in the countryside did not develop too much of a taste for urban, white-collar occupations, great importance was given to manual work and unceasing indoctrination. The effects on academic performance of changing entrance requirements, downgrading the role of exams, emphasizing manual work, and enlarging the dose of practical indoctrination were predictably disastrous.

More students from the rural sector were able to enter secondary and tertiary institutions, but that may have been the sole achievement of the reforms. Otherwise, they worsened some of the existing problems and created a host of new ones. This would not be especially daunting were it not that the pursuit of the Four Modernizations since 1977 is putting considerable stress on a system whose health remains rather fragile. Thus, the system of education is faced with a hierarchy of problems related to inadequate resources, many of them inherited from the past; pressures generated by the resurgence of scholastic elitism, urban bias, and rising unemployment among middle school graduates; and uncertainty about moral values, as well as cynicism and frustration resulting from shifts in political mood and the policy toward education.

Consequences of Inadequate Resources

There is little doubt that China has been able to make considerable headway in rural education at a moderate cost. But the results of a low investment in education are very visible all the way from primary schools to the country's most distinguished universities. Rural schools are often in deplorable shape, their facilities are primitive, and the students are packed together in tiny classrooms. The insufficiency of equipment and facilities is even more noticeable in the middle schools and the agricultural colleges, and it gravely hampers training in scientific fields. To make matters worse, the quality of the teaching staff is poor, and their motivation to impart a decent education is not helped at all by low salaries. None of these problems can be solved overnight, but if there is to be some melioration over the medium term, budgetary commitments to education will have to increase. Salaries of teachers who are employed by the Ministry of Education, which range from 42 to 120 yuan a month, were raised by 10 percent in 1981, and rural commune school teachers who are not on the payroll of the state will have their annual subsidy from the government increased by 50 yuan.[48]

Raising the government subsidy is only a partial solution to the problem created by the switch from remuneration through work points to household contracting (see Chapter 5). Until very recently, teachers received work points equal to those of an average commune worker plus an allowance. And while they still receive a stipend from the state, much of their earnings are now derived from farming a plot of land assigned to them. With agricultural production as their principal source of livelihood, teaching inevitably has a lower priority. A new method needs to be devised to adequately compensate teachers hired by the commune. At the same time, expenditures on infrastructure and teacher training facilities will have to be increased if the quality of education is to be improved.

Elite Schools and Mass Frustration

Manpower planning and the emphasis on technical skills came back into favor with the Four Modernizations, even though it had yielded indifferent results in the 1950s and had led to a considerable misallocation of resources.[49] With the better teachers and facilities being concentrated in the key schools and the ablest students being funneled to these institutions by the multitrack system, pupils in other schools, particularly those in the rural areas, are liable to be at a disadvantage. First, neither their parents nor their environment can provide the intellectual stimulus or the cultural support that would raise the standard of their academic achievement. Second, the key schools, by absorbing a disproportionate volume of the resources, are impoverishing other institutions still further. And third, with few students from non-key secondary schools having much prospect of entering a university "study appears pointless."[50] Compounding the disillusionment of rural youths is the increasing inability of school graduates to find jobs in the cities, a fact which greatly dilutes one of the attractions of education and dulls the hope of economic and social betterment through schooling. Thus, the return of elitism, an anathema to the Maoists and partially suppressed during 1968–76, confronts China with a problem with which many developing countries have struggled ineffectually for some time. In Unger's words, "without enough modern sector jobs or school places to go around, the great majority of students will spend years drilling for examinations most of them will never pass, and be trained in rote skills having little relation to their later lives. In the process of their schooling, they will learn to view the most common occupations of their society with disdain, and then, as 'failures,' they will be consigned to those very occupations."[51] Little wonder that hopelessness is being overlaid by the cynicism and frustration that recent observers have found so prevalent.[52]

The strategy for rural education emerging in the wake of the Four Modernizations was attempted once before in the mid-1960s. It involves detaching most of rural schools from the education ladder oriented toward the urban university, since the countryside is the "weak link" in the system; reorienting the expectations and attitudes of the rural students; and providing trained manpower for the villages.[53] The policy can succeed if rural youths—and the Chinese populace in general—are animated by a new vision and a sense of hope arising from the opportunities that a dynamic and expanding agricultural economy could provide.

The Direction of Rural Education

As discussed earlier in this chapter, a strategy of education can be inspired by moral or political as well as economic objectives. In 1949, political concerns were clearly dominant, and there existed a long tradition of furthering political ends through moral training. The state of farming technology also tempered the urgency of economic claims. Chinese agriculture remained locked in the traditional mold, but over the centuries continued experimentation within virtually fixed parameters of scientific knowledge had enabled cultivators to reach a fairly high level of productivity by using traditional inputs and their deep familiarity with the environment. So long as the technology remained more or less unchanged and traditional practices prevailed, education could contribute little to enhance productivity. Hence, even though rural literacy was low, few children were receiving modern elementary schooling, and the supply of modern farming skills was extremely meager, the economic argument for expanding education was completely overshadowed by the political. In fact, the policies followed in the 1950s served both political and economic ends. The number of colleges and other tertiary institutions to train technicians and agricultural scientists were increased, and primary education made millions of Chinese youngsters potentially receptive to new farming techniques.

When modern biological and mechanical innovations were introduced in the early 1960s, the agriculture sector was ready to transcend the boundaries of traditional methods and to advance the production frontier. The continuing spread of basic education and literacy ensured that the technology would be readily adopted, but it was necessary to assimilate and adapt new production methods for Chinese conditions and to make them available to the peasants. The scientists and skilled technicians needed to do this were not entirely ready in the 1960s, but a good part of the infrastructure for increasing their numbers was in place.

At this juncture, a decisive shift in education policy toward economic goals was desirable from the limited perspective of rural production. But the Cultural Revolution reversed the swing of the pendulum, and development based on skills was displaced by development based on an ideologically conditioned mass effort. Now, less than a decade after the death of Mao and the entombment of many of his policies, the regime is increasingly preoccupied with economic concerns. There is no doubt that agriculture is short of certain types of skills and that an increase in the number of researchers and technicians should accelerate the movement from intermediate technologies to more advanced ones. Hence, it does seem reasonable to downplay ideological factors, lighten the curriculum of its political content, and convert the system into an efficient albeit elitist producer of skills.

However, the economic goals might be more easily realized if the political enthusiasm of Chinese youth could be stimulated. Maddox writes,

> Maoist propaganda told young people [in the 1960s] that ultimate meaning in life came from their willingness to sacrifice themselves in service of the people. To serve the people meant to make a positive contribution to the Chinese revolution. It meant making full use of one's individual talents to push China along the revolutionary road defined by Maoist ideology . . . In the . . . 1960s significant numbers of the . . . youths were still able to believe this Maoist rhetoric . . . But the Cultural Revolution shattered this fragile basis for idealism. Mao launched the Cultural Revolution in the name of the highest ideals yet it quickly degenerated into arbitrary violence and mindless terror.[54]

In a very similar vein Butterfield observes that

> The Communist Party was founded on idealism and willingness to sacrifice. It was the Communists' belief in their cause which enabled the older generation to accept privation and tight political controls during the revolution and up to the 1960s. But in the Cultural Revolution something snapped. The Communists lost popular confidence, a critical ingredient to ruling such a vast country . . . like the mandate of heaven, the traditional principle that gave legitimacy to China's emperors. Today, if China is to meet its goal of becoming a modern industrial power it needs productive workers and creative scientists not semieducated malcontents and frustrated cynics.[55]

Unless a moral consensus is restored, the nature of political obligation could easily be obscured, with the government becoming merely an institutional device employed by the Party to impose a bureaucratized unity on the society. Not only would this be unhealthy socially, it would undermine the economic initiatives being taken—initiatives whose success demands some of the motivation and the spirit of self-sacrifice that was so abundant in the 1950s and 1960s.

Education policy must be responsive to economic opportunities, but it also must consider the societal context and the tensions created by the political process. The Cultural Revolution rendered brittle values that had been systematically implanted for almost two decades. But it also gave rise to certain expectations among the rural populace. For ten years, those from worker and peasant backgrounds were repeatedly told that the education system had discriminated against them and that they were, at last, to be given a privileged access to secondary and college education. From the late 1960s through the mid-1970s, the proportion of pupils from the countryside did in fact increase. Now, with the entrance to higher level institutions being stringently controlled by examinations, the chances of increased discrimination have again reappeared.[56] And vocational education, of which so much is being made, may not be an acceptable substitute, since it carries the stigma of a second-class educational status and promises only the life of a barefoot doctor, a commune accountant, an extension agent, or a farm mechanic.[57]

China needs to add to its stock agricultural scientists and technicians and to improve the quality of rural primary education. These measures could, at relatively low cost, accelerate the pace of agricultural modernization. But above and beyond that, the regime may need to stabilize expectations among students in rural areas by modifying the political and ethical dimensions of the curriculum. There are signs that political study is beginning to receive attention once again, but the hierarchical system that is emerging, as Stanley Rosen points out, "does not seem conducive to the successful transmission of rural values."[58] An acceleration of the industrial growth rate during the next decade, which would appreciably enlarge the demand for labor and provide an outlet for the underemployed in the rural areas, will ease the problem in the long run, but for the medium term other remedies may need to be considered.

Notes to Chapter 8

1. See A. Inkeles and D. H. Smith, *Becoming Modern* (Cambridge, Mass.: Harvard University Press, 1974), chap. 9, p. 143; and F. Machlup, *Education and Economic Growth* (New York: New York University Press, 1975), pp. 7–8.

2. This view is supported by a good deal of empirical research. T. W. Schultz, *Economic Crises in World Agriculture* (Ann Arbor, Mich.: University of Michigan Press, 1965); T. W.

Schultz, "The Value of the Ability to Deal with Disequilibria," *Journal of Economic Literature*, vol. 13 (March 1975), pp. 827–46; F. Welch, "Education in Production," *Journal of Political Economy*, vol. 78, no. 1 (January/February 1970), pp. 46–47; D. P. Chaudhri, *Education, Innovations, and Agricultural Development* (London: Croom and Helm, 1979); Dean T. Jamison and Lawrence J. Lau, *Farmer Education and Farm Efficiency* (Baltimore, Md.: Johns Hopkins University Press, 1982).

3. See E. S. Rawski, *Education and Popular Literacy in Ching China* (Ann Arbor, Mich.: University of Michigan Press, 1979); F. W. Mote, *Intellectual Foundations of China* (New York: Knopf, 1971); and Chang Chung-li, *The Chinese Gentry* (Seattle, Wash.: University of Washington Press, 1955).

4. Mote, *Intellectual Foundations of China*, pp. 37--39; and R. Dawson, *Confucius* (New York: Hill and Wang, 1981), pp. 17–19.

5. Rawski, *Education and Popular Literacy*, pp. 34–39; on the role of private academics from late Ming times, see F. W. Wakeman, "The Price of Autonomy: Intellectuals in Ming and Ching Politics," *Daedalus*, vol. 101 (Spring 1972), pp. 43–45.

6. Rawski, *Education and Popular Literacy*, note 3, pp. 1–4.

7. Mote, working back from Ho Ping-ti's estimate of 600,000 sheng-yuan (elementary degree holders) in the mid-nineteenth century, suggests that there must have been 20 million to 30 million people qualified at the level of high literacy. F. W. Mote, "China's Past in the Study of China Today—Some Comments on the Recent Work of R. Solomon," *Journal of Asian Studies*, vol. 32 (November 1972), pp. 107–20; Ho Ping-ti, *The Ladder of Success in Imperial China* (New York: Columbia University Press, 1962).

8. For a discussion of educational reforms during 1890–1911, see S. Borthwick, *Education and Social Change in China: The Beginnings of a Modern Era* (Stanford, Calif.: Hoover Institution Press, 1983).

9. The importance of the exams and the manner in which they were conducted is described by I. Miyazaki, *China's Examination Hell* (New Haven, Conn.: Yale University Press, 1981); and Borthwick, *Education and Social Change in China*, pp. 4–6.

10. See for instance, G. S. Allito, *The Last Confucian* (Berkeley: University of California Press, 1979); and D. D. Buck, "Cities and Education in Modern China," *Comparative Education*, vol. 11 (March 1975), pp. 74–75.

11. Yip Ka-che, "Warlordism and Educational Finances, 1916–27," in J. A. Fogel and W. T. Rowe, *Perspectives on a Changing China* (Boulder, Colo.: Westview Press, 1979), pp. 185 and 189. The likin was a tax first levied in 1853 on grain passing through the grand canal, but after 1862 it grew into a tax on goods in transit and was adopted by all provinces. A. Feuerwerker, "Economic Trends in the Late China Empire, 1870–1911," in J. K. Fairbank and Kwang-Ching Liu, *The Cambridge History of China*, vol. 11, part 2 (Cambridge: Cambridge University Press, 1980), pp. 61–62.

12. J. L. Buck, *Land Utilization in China* (Nanking: Nanking University Press, 1937), p. 373. Rawski, *Education and Popular Literacy*, pp. 140, 241, estimates that if 45 percent of men, comprising 52 percent of the population in the late nineteenth century, were literate and 2 to 10 percent of the women, then between 24 and 28 percent of the population could be so classified.

13. This is a point underlined by Dore in his study of the Tokugawa period. R. P. Dore, *Education in Tokugawa Japan* (Berkeley: University of California Press, 1965), p. 211.

14. J. Unger, *Education under Mao* (New York: Columbia University Press, 1982), chap. 3; J. I. Lofstedt, *Chinese Educational Policy* (Stockholm: Almqvist and Wiksell International, 1980), chap. 6, pp. 96–97; R. N. Montaperto, "Introduction: China's Schools in Flux," *Chinese Education*, vol. 11, no. 4 (Winter 1978–79), pp. 6–12.

15. Min-ban gung-zhu (people-managed, government-assisted) schools were financed by local villages, towns, and counties and usually offered a truncated curriculum.

16. Special schools for the brightest students. These schools offered better facilities, a superior teaching staff, and lower student-teacher ratios.

17. The "innovations" introduced during 1966–76 are described by Unger, *Education under Mao*, note 14, chaps. 6–9. See also S. Pepper, "Education and Revolution: The Chinese Model Revisited," *Asian Survey*, vol. 18, no. 9 (1978), pp. 852–74; S. Shirk, "Educational Reform and Political Backlash: Recent Changes in Chinese Educational Policy," *Comparative Educational Review*, vol. 23, no. 2 (June 1979), pp. 185–91; and D. I. Chambers, "The 1975–76 Debate over Higher Education Policy in the PRC," *Comparative Education*, vol. 13, no. 1 (March 1977), pp. 3–14.

18. *Area Handbook for the PRC* (Washington, D.C.: Government Printing Office, 1972) estimates the level of illiteracy as being 80 percent (p. 209). See also L. Orleans, *Professional Manpower and Education in Communist China* (Washington, D.C.: National Science Foundation, 1961), p. 49.

19. From January 1937 to March 1947, Yenan, a city in the north of Shaanxi, was the seat of the Central Committee of the Communist Party and the capital of the Communist-controlled parts of China. B. Hook, ed., *The Cambridge Encyclopedia of China* (Cambridge: Cambridge University Press, 1982), p. 267.

20. E. J. Gibson and H. Levin, *The Psychology of Reading* (Cambridge, Mass.: M.I.T. Press, 1975), pp. 162, 523. On the debate revolving around the reform of writing see also J. De Francis, "Mao Tse-tung and Writing Reform," in J. A. Fogel and W. T. Rowe, eds., *Perspectives on a Changing China* (Boulder, Colo.: Westview Press, 1979).

21. Lofstedt, *Chinese Educational Policy*, pp. 75–76, 89–90.

22. *Xinhua, Beijing* (December 12, 1979) (in *FBIS, China*, December 14, 1979, pp. L-2–L-3); and Loftstedt, *Chinese Educational Policy*, p. 152.

23. Ten million peasants were being educated in more than 400,000 schools of all kinds in 1981. State Statistical Bureau, *Statistical Yearbook of China, 1981* (Hong Kong: Economic Information and Agency, 1982), p. 461.

24. Ibid., p. 451.

25. See Orleans, *Professional Manpower and Education*, pp. 13–14; R. F. Price, *Education in Communist China* (New York: Praeger, 1970), pp. 102–03; and Lofstedt, *Chinese Educational Policy*, p. 62. In many schools, what has been described as a "three copy" method of teaching prevailed, with the teacher first copying Soviet teaching materials, then reproducing them on the blackboard so that they could be copied by the students. R. MacFarquhar, *The Hundred Flowers* (London: Stevens, 1960), p. 97.

26. J. Prybyla, *The Chinese Economy* (Columbia: University of South Carolina Press, 1979), p. 212.

27. W. L. Parish and M. K. Whyte, *Village and Family in Contemporary China* (Chicago: University of Chicago Press, 1978), p. 79.

28. See M. Zachariah, " 'Massliners' vs. 'Capitalist Roaders' in China's Education Ring: Round Four to Capitalist Roaders," *Comparative Education Review*, vol. 23, no. 1 (February 1979), p. 102. R. F. Price, "Community and School and Education in the PRC," *Comparative Education*, vol. 12, no. 2 (June 1976), pp. 168–69. On the rustication movement, which transferred some 15 million youths to the countryside, see Unger, *Education under Mao*, note 14, chap. 8; and T. P. Bernstein, *Up to the Mountains and Down to the Villages* (New Haven, Conn.: Yale University Press, 1977), especially p. 212.

29. How far the urban bias was reduced during the Cultural Revolution remains a matter of controversy. Political cadres were often able to use their influence to have their children admitted, and the system of classifying students was elastic enough to allow those from urban families to retain their access to educational institutions. See Shirk, "Educational Reform and Political Backlash," pp. 190–91; and S. Pepper, "Education and Revolution," p. 883.

30. *Beijing Ribao* (October 14, 1979), p. 1 (in *FBIS, China,* October 25, 1979, p. R2).

31. J. R. Harlan, "Plant Breeding and Genetics," in L. A. Orleans, ed., *Science in Contemporary China* (Stanford, Calif.: Stanford University Press, 1980), pp. 298–99.

32. J. Sigurdson, "Technology and Science: Some Issues in China's Modernization," in "Chinese Economy Post-Mao," papers for the Joint Economic Committee, vol. I, Washington, D. C., November 9, 1978, p. 505; Parish and Whyte, *Village and Family in Contemporary China,* p. 371; and J. Gardner and W. Idema, "China's Educational Revolution," in S. R. Schram, ed., *Authority, Participation, and Cultural Change in China* (Cambridge: Cambridge University Press, 1975), p. 226.

33. State Statistical Bureau, *Statistical Yearbook of China, 1981,* p. 451. Middle school enrollment declined to 50 million in 1981, and many schools were closed to husband resources and improve the quality of education in lower-level institutions and technical schools. S. Pepper, "China's Schools Turning an Old Leaf," *Asian Wall Street Journal Weekly* (September 21, 1981), p. 11; P. Mauger, "Changing Policy and Practice in Chinese Rural Education," *China Quarterly,* no. 93 (March 1983), p. 139; and "Restructuring Middle Education Is a Major Task," *Peking Daily* (October 14, 1979) (in *FE/6256/BII/4,* October 27, 1979).

34. Information obtained by Dwight Perkins during a visit to China in 1982.

35. State Statistical Bureau, *Statistical Yearbook of China, 1981,* p. 452; "Quarterly Chronicle and Documentation (April–June 1983)," *China Quarterly,* no. 95 (September 1983), p. 588. For information on Guangdong, Guangxi, and Yunnan, see Mauger, "Changing Policy and Practice in Chinese Rural Education," pp. 140–41.

36. There were 2,655 agricultural and vocational schools in 1981 with an enrollment of nearly a half million students. *Beijing, Xinhua* (October 27, 1982) (in *FBIS, China,* October 28, 1982, p. K2). Bastid refers to the current trend, which is to convert most (up to 60 percent) ordinary senior middle schools into vocational schools or to introduce vocational training into the curriculum, possibly in the early 1990s. M. Bastid, "Chinese Educational Policies in the 1980s and Economic Development," *China Quarterly,* no. 98 (June 1984), p. 195.

37. See Orleans, *Professional Manpower and Education,* p. 15; Lofstedt, *Chinese Educational Policy,* p. 171; and Bastid, "Chinese Educational Policies in the 1980s," p. 200.

38. Lofstedt, *Chinese Educational Policy,* p. 150, quotes the figure of 20 yuan per primary school pupil and 100 yuan for those in secondary schools. Information in the text was obtained during a visit to China.

39. Parish and Whyte, *Village and Family in Contemporary China,* p. 80; Prybyla, *The Chinese Economy,* p. 220; Lofstedt, *Chinese Educational Policy,* p. 172; and S. Pepper, "Education and Revolution," p. 853.

40. Only 60.5 percent of the primary school students in Guangdong complete the five-year course. This may be about the average for the country as a whole. See Mauger, "Changing Policy and Practice in Chinese Rural Education," p. 139; and Bastid, "Chinese Educational Policies in the 1980s," p. 194.

41. The poor quality of the teaching staff is referred to in Mauger, "Changing Policy and Practice in Chinese Rural Education," pp. 139 and 144–46. He quotes an official of the Guangxi Education Bureau, who noted that "only one-third of primary school teachers are competent" (p. 139). The deputy director of education in Yunnan stated that "of our teaching staff, only 20 percent are up to standard, 40 percent teach with difficulty, and the other 40 percent are basically incompetent" (p. 145). The problem is equally serious in Guangdong, where the standard of 30 percent of primary school teachers is below that of normal school graduates (p. 144).

42. Lofstedt, *Chinese Educational Policy,* pp. 149–50. The average for the country in primary schools was 1:28 in 1978 and 1:26 in 1981. State Statistical Bureau, *Statistical Yearbook of China, 1981,* p. 454.

43. New China News Agency (NCNA), April 20, 1980, BBC, May 23, 1980; *China Daily*, *Beijing* (November 14, 1982), p. 4 (in *FBIS, China*, November 16, 1982, pp. K14–15); and *Renmin Ribao, Beijing* (November 17, 1981), p. 3 (in *FBIS, China*, November 2๋, 1981, p. K7).

44. Statistics on Population Quality and Education, *Shanghai World Economy Guide* (October 18, 1981); BBC, FE/6894/BII/10 (December 1, 1981); and World Bank, *China: Socialist Economic Development*, vol. 3 (Washington, D.C., 1983), p. 150.

45. *Renmin Ribao, Beijing*, "On Improving Secondary Education" (November 12, 1981), p. 3 (in *FBIS, China*, November 18, 1981, p. K4).

46. *Renmin Ribao, Beijing*, "Wan Li's Speech of November 5" (December 23, 1982), pp. 1, 2, and 4 (in *FBIS, China*, January 4, 1983, p. K5).

47. There were fifty-five agricultural colleges and ten forestry colleges in 1981. State Statistical Bureau, *Statistical Yearbook of China, 1981*, p. 455.

48. *China Daily, Beijing*, "State to Increase Pay of Twelve Million Teachers" (November 22, 1981), p. 1 (in *FBIS, China*, November 23, 1981, p. K11).

49. C. Howe, *China's Economy* (New York: Basic Books, 1978), p. 28.

50. *Renmin Ribao, Beijing* (November 12, 1981), p. 3; and Bastid, "Chinese Educational Policies in the 1980s," p. 194. This is a problem encountered in many other socialist nations; see W. D. Connor, "Education and National Development in the European Socialist States: A Model for the Third World," *Comparative Studies in History and Society*, vol. 17 (1975), p. 335.

51. J. Unger, "Bending the School Ladder: The Failure of Chinese Educational Reform in the 1960s," *Comparative Educational Review*, vol. 24, no. 2, Part I (June 1980), p. 221.

52. F. Butterfield, *China: Alive in the Bitter Sea* (New York: Times Books, 1982), p. 201; and M. K. Whyte and W. L. Parish, *Urban Life in Contemporary China* (Chicago: University of Chicago Press, 1984), p. 61.

53. Unger, "Bending the School Ladder," p. 226.

54. P. G. Maddox, "Value Change in China," *Problems of Communism*, vol. 30 (November–December 1981), p. 75.

55. Butterfield, *China: Alive in the Bitter Sea*, p. 226.

56. C. Montgomery Broaded, "Higher Education Policy Changes and Stratification in China," *China Quarterly*, no. 93 (March 1983), pp. 136–37.

57. There have been reports of declining enrollment in rural schools. See "Rural School Enrollment Decline Reported," *Beijing Domestic Service* (November 16, 1982) (in *FBIS, China*, November 17, 1982, pp. K9–K10); and S. Rosen, "Chinese Education in Transition," *Current History*, vol. 82, no. 485 (September 1983), p. 257.

58. S. Rosen, "Obstacles to Educational Reform in China," *Modern China*, vol. 8 (January 1982), p. 34.

Chapter 9

~~~~~~

Lessons from Experience

FOR MORE THAN THREE DECADES, rural development has been a central concern in the People's Republic of China. Throughout much of this period the strategy followed has emphasized rural self-reliance. The central government supplied essential inputs to agriculture, such as chemical fertilizer, through the urban industries that it controlled, but for the most part Chinese farmers were expected to solve their economic and social problems with their own resources. The costs of health and education were covered out of commune and family funds, and inputs for production were to be increased by mobilizing the rural sector's own labor force and later by building small-scale factories in the countryside to produce cement and fertilizer.

Self-reliant or community-based development efforts have character-ized rural programs in many developing countries. Often a country has little choice but to pursue such a strategy. The central government has few resources with which to help, and urban and industrial develop-ment is at too early a stage to contribute much. But in China the choice of a self-reliant strategy was deliberate. The government budget di-rectly controlled nearly a third of national product, and industrializa-tion proceeded rapidly throughout the three decades, but these re-sources were directed mainly toward the machinery and steel sectors, not agriculture.

In other industrializing nations agriculture does not necessarily re-ceive a large share of the government budget, but poor farm families often escape poverty by moving to the cities and a factory job. In fact, the most common method of eliminating rural poverty is to transfer most of the farm population to the urban sector. But in China the option of rural to urban migration was deliberately eschewed.

The world is strewn with self-reliant, community-based rural development efforts that failed. Traditional rural societies are not fertile ground for such programs, and governments are either unable or unwilling to reorganize rural society to make self-help a reality. A few pilot projects prosper while there is special funding and dynamic leadership, but disappear when these scarce resources are removed. Not so in China. Self-reliant rural development has been the dominant mode of operation nationwide since the early 1950s. If sustained, large-scale community effort were the measure of performance, China's rural development program would be an unqualified success.

Reorganization of Rural Society

The reorganization of rural society that made China's program possible was the result of a continuous effort spanning many decades by the Chinese Communist Party. The leadership may not have been willing to commit economic resources to transforming rural society, but it was willing to commit political ones. The Party had come to power because it was able to restructure rural society in ways that benefited the majority economically and proved effective militarily against the Japanese and the Guomindang. In the 1950s these skills were put to the task of consolidating Party control in the countryside. As with most reforms in rural organization, therefore, the primary motive was political, but the changes that resulted had profound economic implications. Landlords were replaced by collective units where income was determined by effort expended, not ownership of property. Confucian values of obedience, which had helped traditional rural leadership to block change, were harnessed by the Party to promote change.

In addition to leadership by committed Party cadres, the key feature of the cooperatives and communes was that they provided individuals with the incentive to participate in various kinds of self-help efforts, from dam construction to sanitation. They participated in the belief that they would receive direct material benefits.

During the 1950s and much of the 1960s and early 1970s collectivization made it possible to mobilize rural labor on a scale that was historically unprecedented inside or outside of China. Hundreds of millions of people moved billions of tons of dirt and rock, and killed flies and sparrows in uncountable numbers. But did the results match the effort expended? Was Chinese society transformed beyond recognition? The answer is that profound changes occurred, but many characteristics of the past persisted. Health improved dramatically, but incomes rose significantly only among the poorest quarter of the population. Farm output increased, but no faster than in many other developing countries that invested much less effort.

Public Health

The most dramatic changes, not surprisingly, were in the areas that lent themselves best to collective effort. Public health is the clearest example. There are lessons for the rest of the world in the way China converted a nation in which life expectancy was less than forty years and infant mortality rates were more than 200 per 1,000 into one with a life expectancy of sixty-eight years nationwide (and fifty-nine years or more in even the poorest province) and an infant mortality rate of 12 in the cities and less than 60 in the countryside.

Having an effective rural political organization enabled China to implement preventive health measures. Motivating that political organization to act required central leadership concerned with the condition of the rural poor. But except for the highly skilled medical technicians needed to plan the program, the human and material resources needed to carry out prevention (and curative) work were already available in the countryside.

The most important preventive measures involved raising the nutrition level of the rural poor; improving sanitation, particularly in relation to rural water supplies; and organizing a variety of nationwide campaigns to inoculate children against diseases such as measles, pertussis, and diphtheria and to eradicate disease carriers, such as the snails responsible for schistosomiasis. Nutrition improved because income was redistributed during land reform and because communes, through their welfare funds, guaranteed minimum levels of consumption to all regardless of income. Sanitary water supplies and the attack on schistosomiasis were possible because the commune system was able to mobilize labor to move latrines and to bury the snails in old irrigation canals while digging new ones.

The commune organization also proved to be an effective vehicle for creating a curative system that reached into the poorest villages. A few individuals in a commune or brigade could be sent out for health training and return as paramedics (barefoot doctors) a few months later. Their income during training and on their return was provided by the people collectively through the commune. In principle, individual family farms could also have provided such support, but voluntary support on an individual basis is difficult to maintain.

These paramedics have also been an essential part of China's family planning effort, which apparently succeeded in lowering crude birth rates from 38.1 per 1,000 in 1965 to 17.9 per 1,000 in 1979. In addition, the rural health insurance system based on the commune provides much of the funding required to support commune and, to some degree, even county hospitals that handle the more serious diseases and injuries. In short, China has achieved remarkable advances in rural health through its ability to mobilize labor and funds from the rural areas nationwide for both preventive and curative activities. This ability to mobilize was a direct result of the commune form of organization and of the political strength and support of the Chinese Communist Party in rural areas.

Education

Rural education also benefited from the reorganization of Chinese agriculture on a collective basis and from the Party leadership that underlay that reorganization. As with health workers and commune hospitals, teachers were hired and schools built with commune funds, and mass campaigns were carried out to eradicate illiteracy. Illiteracy was not eradicated, but it was greatly reduced. By the early 1980s universal primary education was nearly a reality, and universal lower middle school education is a realistic target for the late 1980s.

A strategy based on mass campaigns and led by the Party also had serious drawbacks that were more apparent in the area of education than in that of health care. The tendency to pursue ideas that were not fully formulated to their logical extreme in health sometimes led to excessive use of traditional medicines and the misuse of highly trained personnel, but it did not produce long-lasting damage to the rural health system. In the field of education, however, the damage was much greater, although rural primary education clearly suffered much less than did the higher levels, particularly the universities. Still, even in the rural areas, discipline broke down and the quality of teaching fell as politics dominated the classroom. All societies use schools to promote accepted values, but in China, the effort to promote revolutionary values, at least during the Cultural Revolution, was at the expense of training in basic skills.

Agricultural Production

Although the commune organization and self-reliant development strategy proved to be an effective vehicle for providing the people of rural China with certain basic needs, such as health care and education, the more important test in the eyes of the Chinese leadership was whether the commune organization would greatly increase agricultural production. The results there have been mixed.

As indicated above, the commune was a very effective vehicle for mobilizing rural surplus labor. The North China Plain was made level. Irrigation ponds and ditches were built everywhere. And yet after all of this expenditure of effort, the irrigated acreage had expanded only modestly, and most of that expansion resulted from factors other than the public works carried out by surplus labor. Much of north China still suffers from a lack of water, and farm incomes that had grown in the early 1950s fell sharply in the late 1950s and then recovered, but did not increase in the mid-1960s very rapidly.

From the mid-1960s on, agricultural production has grown at a respectable 4 percent and more per year, but mobilized rural labor can claim comparatively little credit for this increase. Analysis of the sources of agricultural growth in China does not provide conclusive proof, but does suggest that increased inputs of chemical fertilizer and improved plant varieties—"the biological package"—accounted for half or more of this growth. And the increased labor that contributed to growth was the peak-season labor enhanced by the increasing use of machinery and electricity rather than the mobilized, off-season surplus labor.

Furthermore, the more rural China was reorganized to facilitate mobilization of mass labor, the greater were the problems related to management and individual incentives. The logic of large-scale labor mobilization called for ever larger organizational units in the country-side, culminating in 1958 in a basic accounting unit of 5,000 families. The diversity and complexity of Chinese farming techniques, however, necessitated a small unit, even where technically competent leadership was available. The smaller unit also reduced the amount of supervision required because individuals saw a clearer connection between the work they did and the income they received. Because of these problems of management and incentives, a production team of thirty families was made the basic accounting unit in the early 1960s, and the household responsibility system was fostered and private activities were expanded in the early 1980s.

The commune structure was also seen as a vehicle to introduce new technology into the countryside, and this initially secondary role had become the primary economic justification by the 1980s. As with health workers and teachers, a collective unit could support one or more of its members while they became specialists in some new technique. In addition, a commune, unlike an individual, had enough land to set some aside for experimental purposes. In that and other ways the risks could be shared.

Distribution of Income and Welfare

Up to this point, the contributions and drawbacks of China's rural development strategy have been discussed in terms of the effect of that strategy on the national aggregates of production and welfare. But what was the effect of this approach on the distribution of income and welfare? Again, where a problem could be solved by reorganization, limited data indicate that the commune was able to reduce inequality. Thus, although there are marked differences in health care and education in rural China, those differences have been greatly reduced over time; for example, even the people in the poorest provinces have quite long life expectancies.

But just as organization could not solve production problems, it also could not significantly redistribute income. The land reform of the late 1940s and early 1950s had the greatest effect on equality. Collectivization thereafter has had little measurable success in reducing inequality further. After eliminating the landlords, the remaining sources of inequality were the regional differences in the amount and quality of land owned plus the proximity of that land to large urban centers. Collectivization could reduce inequalities within villages, but had little effect on differences between villages. Allocating modern inputs in favor of the poorer rural areas might have reduced inequality, but this strategy was not pursued because it conflicted with the goal of accelerating the agricultural growth of the entire country.

A potential solution to the problems of the poorest rural areas would be to allow the people in those areas to migrate to the cities. But this solution would involve implicitly the abandonment of one element of the self-reliant strategy. It would imply that industrialization and urbanization will eliminate rural poverty, not the efforts of farmers themselves. Historically, however, this has been the only largely successful solution to rural poverty, but it is a solution the Chinese are reluctant to try, given their current stage of development and the condition of their urban infrastructure after two decades of neglect.

A Look to the Future

Where does Chinese rural development go from here? To achieve agricultural productivity gains in the immediate future, the Chinese leadership is counting on the incentive effects of the responsibility system plus increased inputs. Carried to its logical extreme, the responsibility system could lead to the complete abandonment of collectivized agriculture and the return to a system of individual family farms. But are China's leaders likely to let things go so far?

From the point of view of the Chinese Communist Party, the main danger of a family farming system in a country that is still predominantly rural is a loss of control. Could the party keep a firm grip on the countryside if its rural cadres had little direct influence over agricultural production?

The main gain from the responsibility system, as agricultural performance in the early 1980s has demonstrated, is a marked improvement in farmer incentives and a resulting spurt in output. But will this accelerated growth continue or would it come to a halt if some forms of collectivized agriculture were restored? The main problem is subsidiary output, which always seems to atrophy when collectivized, and certain cash crops may not do as well either. Grain output, on the other hand, may do almost as well under collectivized as under household-based agriculture. Furthermore, there are costs attached to a household-based system at least as it has been implemented in the early 1980s. The rural health system, which has done so much for the quality of life in the countryside, has clearly been hurt.

In essence, however, the argument comes down to one between politics and economics. How much control is the leadership willing to give up in exchange for how much of a rise in productivity? This will be a topic of debate for some time, with the outcome likely to be a compromise between the two goals.

Whatever the outcome of this debate, it is clear after three decades of experience that a strategy of self-reliant community development based on collectivized agriculture cannot itself solve China's problem of agricultural production or income distribution. China's 100 million hectares of arable land, parts of which are semi-arid, are simply not potentially productive enough for China ever to achieve high rural incomes through agriculture alone. In fact, it is questionable whether domestic agricultural production can meet the food needs of the Chinese people during the next several decades, or whether the nation will have to spend increasing amounts of scarce foreign exchange on food imports. Nor can collectivization solve the special problems of China's poorest regions.

China's agricultural future, therefore, does not appear to be markedly different from that of other nations that have achieved sustained economic development, particularly those in East Asia. Agricultural research and the increasing use of modern inputs will keep production growing, and rising income will keep the demand for food growing even with, or a bit faster than, supply. The problem of the gap between urban and rural incomes and of the poverty of large parts of rural China will be solved only by moving these people into urban employment with higher productivity.

Although China has not found an alternative path to higher agricultural production and advanced country levels of national income, it has found a way to ameliorate some of the costs of the transition when so many of the people in the rural areas are and must remain poor. Preventive health measures are inexpensive and they work, and the income of absentee landlords, if redistributed to the poorest 20 percent, can greatly reduce abject poverty.

Appendix A

~~~~~~

Provincial Data

PROVINCIAL DATA until very lately had to be collected one by one from newspapers and broadcasts from China. The recent publication of several yearbooks and statistical handbooks in China has reduced, but has not completely eliminated, the need to search widely for relevant provincial data. The data in this appendix come from both kinds of sources. These data are the basis for the discussion of regional differences in yield and agricultural growth rates between provinces in Chapter 3.

Table A-1. *Growth Rates of Population and Grain Output, by Province*

Province	Population growth rate (percent a year) (1)	Grain output growth rate (percent a year) (2)	Ratio (2) ÷ (1) (3)
Northeast			
Heilongjiang	3.44	2.9	0.84
Jilin	2.55	3.5	1.37
Liaoning	1.62	2.7	1.67
Northwest			
Xinjiang	3.64	3.0	0.82
Gansu	1.78	0.4	0.22
Qinghai	2.75	1.1	0.40
Ningxia	3.23	n.a.	n.a.
Shaanxi	1.99	3.3	1.66
North			
Beijing	3.58	n.a.	n.a.
Tianjin	} 1.22	n.a.	n.a.
Hebei		2.6	2.13
Nei Monggol	3.18	2.5	0.79
Shanxi	1.96	n.a.	n.a.
Shandong	1.33	3.3	2.48
Henan	1.79	1.0	0.56
East/Central			
Shanghai	2.27	} 4.0	} 2.92
Jiangsu	1.20		
Anhui	1.64	1.2	0.73
Zhejiang	1.86	3.4	1.83
Jiangxi	2.54	2.8	1.10
Hubei	1.88	2.4	1.28
Hunan	1.68	3.1	1.85
Southeast			
Fujian	2.44	2.6	1.07
Guangdong	1.85	1.6	0.86
Guangxi	2.68	3.6	1.34
Southwest			
Sichuan	1.39	1.5	1.08
Yunnan	2.28	1.1	0.48
Guizhou	2.21	0.6	0.27
Xizang	1.67	n.a.	n.a.
National	1.87	2.45	1.31

n.a. Not available.

Sources: Percentages were derived from data in Tables A-2 and A-3.

Table A-2. *Population Data, by Province*
(thousands of persons)

Province	1957, total population	1979 Total population	1979 Commune population	1979 Agricultural labor force
Northeast				
Heilongjiang	14,860	31,690	18,540	5,107
Jilin	12,550	21,840	14,776	3,202
Liaoning	24,090	34,410	22,289	6,155
Northwest				
Xinjiang	5,640	12,550	6,986	3,566
Gansu	12,800	18,950	16,146	5,516
Qinghai	2,050	3,720	2,675	1,053
Ningxia	1,810	3,640	843	971
Shaanxi	18,130	28,070	23,953	8,387
North				
Beijing	4,010	8,700	3,746	1,567
Tianjin	n.a.	7,400	3,601	1,458
Hebei	44,720	51,060	45,090	17,018
Nei Monggol	9,200	18,510	13,123	4,449
Shanxi	15,960	24,480	20,323	6,775
Shandong	54,030	72,280	65,375	25,099
Henan	48,670	71,870	65,427	23,868
East/Central				
Shanghai	6,900	11,310	4,283	2,742
Jiangsu	45,230	58,940	50,318	21,339
Anhui	33,560	48,040	42,553	16,014
Zhejiang	25,280	37,920	33,145	14,226
Jiangxi	18,610	32,290	27,949	9,513
Hubei	30,790	46,350	39,143	15,108
Hunan	36,220	52,260	46,158	19,219
Southeast				
Fujian	14,650	24,880	21,285	7,259
Guangdong	37,960	56,800	47,515	19,712
Guangxi	19,390	34,700	30,794	12,570
Southwest				
Sichuan	72,160	97,740	86,218	35,458
Yunnan	19,100	31,340	27,658	11,424
Guizhou	16,890	27,320	24,043	8,794
Xizang	1,270	1,830	1,513	812
National	646,530	970,920	807,387	308,381

n.a. Not available.

Sources: The 1957 figures are from State Statistical Bureau, *Ten Great Years* (1960), p. 11. The 1979 figures are from or derived from Ministry of Agriculture, *Zhongguo nongye nianjian, 1980*, pp. 6, 132–33.

Table A-3. *Grain Output, by Province*

Province	Production (thousands of tons)[a]		Growth rate, 1957 to 1979 (percent)
	1957	1979	
Northeast			
Heilongjiang	7,840	14,625	2.9
Jilin	4,280	9,030	3.5
Liaoning	6,705	11,940	2.7
Northwest			
Xinjiang	2,034	3,935	3.0
Gansu	4,250	4,615	0.4
Qinghai	640	820	1.1
Ningxia	n.a.	1,060	n.a.
Shaanxi	4,500	9,095	3.3
North			
Beijing	n.a.	1,730	n.a.
Tianjin	n.a.	1,385	n.a.
Hebei	10,100	17,795	2.6
Nei Monggol	2,957	5,100	2.5
Shanxi	n.a.	8,005	n.a.
Shandong	12,100	24,720	3.3
Henan	17,300	21,345	1.0
East/Central			
Shanghai	} 11,780	2,590	} 4.0
Jiangsu		25,140	
Anhui	12,370	16,095	1.2
Zhejiang	7,793	16,115	3.4
Jiangxi	6,987	12,965	2.8
Hubei	10,966	18,495	2.4
Hunan	11,244	22,185	3.1
Southeast			
Fujian	4,377	7,625	2.6
Guangdong	12,200	17,380	1.6
Guangxi	5,400	11,730	3.6
Southwest			
Sichuan	23,248	32,010	1.5
Yunnan	6,250	7,930	1.1
Guizhou	5,475	6,230	0.6
Xizang	n.a.	425	n.a.
National	195,050	332,115	2.45

Note: Unhusked grain including soybeans.

n.a. Not available.

a. In addition to soybeans, the figures include potatoes at one-fourth actual weight in 1957 and at one-fifth actual weight in 1979. Since potatoes make up less than 10 percent of total grain output, the error introduced by this change in conversion ratio is not great.

Sources: The 1957 data are from N. R. Chen, *Chinese Economic Statistics* (Chicago: Aldine, 1972), pp. 338–63. The 1979 data are from Ministry of Agriculture, *Zhongguo nongye nianjian, 1980*, p. 101.

Table A-4. *Cultivated Acreage, by Province*
(thousands of hectares)

Province	1957			1979		
	Arable acreage	Sown acreage	Double cropping index[a]	Arable acreage	Sown acreage	Double cropping index[a]
Northwest						
Heilongjiang	7,287	n.a.	n.a.	8,698	8,524	98
Jilin	4,719	4,609	98	4,060	4,060	100
Liaoning	4,751	n.a.	n.a.	3,778	3,967	105
Northwest						
Xinjiang	2,015	n.a.	n.a.	3,316	3,018	91
Gansu	3,959	n.a.	n.a.	3,543	3,472	98
Qinghai	500	n.a.	n.a.	577	508	88
Ningxia	n.a.	n.a.	n.a.	899	908	101
Shaanxi	4,467	n.a.	n.a.	3,845	5,114	133
North						
Beijing	n.a.	n.a.	n.a.	426	677	159
Tianjin	n.a.	n.a.	n.a.	468	688	147
Hebei	9,002	n.a.	n.a.	6,650	9,243	139
Nei Monggol	5,543	5,117	92	5,364	4,881	91
Shanxi	4,541	n.a.	n.a.	3,906	4,297	110
Shandong	9,333	n.a.	n.a.	7,255	10,665	147
Henan	8,973	n.a.	n.a.	7,136	10,918	153
East/Central						
Shanghai	n.a.	n.a.	n.a.	355	771	217
Jiangsu	6,200	n.a.	n.a.	4,640	8,491	183
Anhui	5,867	n.a.	n.a.	4,447	8,005	180
Zhejiang	2,252	n.a.	n.a.	1,829	4,517	247
Jiangxi	2,813	5,439	193	2,533	5,700	225
Hubei	4,287	7,320	171	3,757	7,777	207
Hunan	3,827	n.a.	n.a.	3,444	8,334	242
Southeast						
Fujian	1,479	n.a.	n.a.	1,297	2,645	204
Guangdong	3,827	7,642	200	3,224	6,995	217
Guangxi	2,531	n.a.	n.a.	2,630	5,102	194
Southwest						
Sichuan	7,687	13,058	170	6,617	11,844	179
Yunnan	2,841	3,886	137	2,785	4,122	148
Guizhou	2,033	3,130	154	1,894	3,011	159
Xizang	n.a.	n.a.	n.a.	229	222	97
National[b]	111,830	157,244	141	99,649	148,477	149

Note: Data on arable land, particularly for 1979, are believed to be underreported.

n.a. Not available.

a. Sown ÷ arable × 100.

b. The provincial figures do not add up to the national total because of rounding errors and the omission of certain figures (only for 1957).

Sources: The 1979 data are derived from Ministry of Agriculture, *Zhongguo nongye nianjian, 1980*, p. 100. The 1957 data are from Committee on the Economy of China, *Provincial Agricultural Statistics for Communist China* (Ithaca: Social Science Research Council, 1969); and Chen, *Chinese Economic Statistics*.

Table A-5. *Grain Yields, by Province*
(tons per hectare of unhusked grain)

Province	1957		1979	
	Sown area	Arable area (estimated)	Sown area	Arable area
Northeast				
Heilongjiang	1.242	1.22	1.98	1.98
Jilin	1.262	1.26	2.51	2.51
Liaoning	1.650	1.73	3.59	4.19
Northwest				
Xinjiang	1.976[a]	1.80	1.73	1.90
Gansu	1.337	1.31	1.55	1.65
Qinghai	1.654	1.46	1.95	1.95
Ningxia	n.a.	n.a.	1.38	1.49
Shaanxi	1.128	1.50	2.12	2.93
North				
Beijing	n.a.	n.a.	3.09	5.23
Tianjin	n.a.	n.a.	2.37	3.65
Hebei	0.914	1.27	2.30	3.56
Nei Monggol	0.668	.61	1.26	1.26
Shanxi	n.a.	n.a.	2.23	2.49
Shandong	0.920[b]	1.35	2.83	4.83
Henan	1.011[b]	1.55	2.36	3.89
East/Central				
Shanghai	n.a.	n.a.	5.06	12.26
Jiangsu	1.868	3.42	3.93	7.89
Anhui	1.300	2.34	2.56	4.40
Zhejiang	2.859	7.06	4.68	10.46
Jiangxi	1.870	3.61	3.38	6.25
Hubei	2.048	3.50	3.37	6.38
Hunan	1.703	4.12	3.89	7.58
Southeast				
Fujian	2.933[c]	5.98	3.53	7.05
Guangdong	1.596	10.50(?)	3.11	6.98
Guangxi	1.443	6.85	2.87	5.64
Southwest				
Sichuan	2.115	3.60	3.12	5.93
Yunnan	1.890	2.60	2.15	3.19
Guizhou	2.138	3.29	2.45	3.77
Xizang	n.a.	n.a.	2.05	2.06
National	1.531	2.150	2.783	4.275

n.a. Not available.   a. Data are for 1956.   b. Data are for 1958.   c. Data are for 1955.
Sources: The 1979 figures are derived from data in Ministry of Agriculture, *Zhongguo nongye nianjian, 1980,* p. 101. The 1957 sown area yields, for the most part, are from Chen, *Chinese Economic Statistics.* The arable yields were derived from the 1957 sown area yields by multiplying by the double cropping index (see Table A-4). Except where the 1957 double cropping index was available, the 1979 index was used. Some error is introduced by this assumption and by the fact that the double cropping index refers to more than just grain crops.

Appendix B

~~~~~~

Estimating the Marginal
Product of Labor

BECAUSE DATA on a large cross-section of Chinese farms is not available outside of China, the marginal product of labor in Chinese agriculture must be estimated indirectly. Furthermore, many of the indirect kinds of evidence typically used to indicate the existence of "surplus" labor are not available in the Chinese case. Urban wages, for example, are not set by market forces, and hence no conclusions can be drawn from the constancy over time of those wages. The analysis here, therefore, starts with a general production function

$$Q_t = f(K_t, L_t, L_{dt}, C_t, T)$$

where Q_t = output in time t, K_t = capital in time t, L_t = labor in time t, L_{dt} = land in time t, C_t = current inputs in time t, and T = time trend.

Differentiating with respect to t and assuming constant returns to scale, produces an equation for the sources of growth:

$$\frac{dQ}{dt} = \frac{\delta F}{\delta T} + \left(\frac{\delta F}{\delta L} \cdot \frac{dL}{dt} \right) + \left(\frac{\delta F}{\delta K} \frac{dK}{dt} \right) + \left(\frac{\delta F}{\delta C} \cdot \frac{dC}{dt} \right) + \left(\frac{\delta F}{\delta L_d} \cdot \frac{dL_d}{dt} \right).$$

Solving for $\delta F/\delta L$, the marginal product of labor, produces the equation

$$\frac{\delta F}{\delta L} = \frac{1}{dL/dt} \left[\frac{dQ}{dt} - \left(\frac{\delta F}{\delta K} \frac{dK}{dt} \right) - \frac{\delta F}{\delta T} - \left(\frac{\delta F}{\delta K} \frac{dK}{dt} \right) \right.$$
$$\left. - \left(\frac{\delta F}{\delta C} \frac{dC}{dt} \right) - \left(\frac{\delta F}{\delta L_d} \cdot \frac{dL_d}{dt} \right) \right].$$

Table B-1. *Data Used to Calculate the Marginal Product of Labor*

Item	1957	1976
Gross value of agricultural output (billions of 1970 yuan)[a]	77.38	133.98
Agricultural value added (billions of 1970 yuan)[a]	46.07	73.23
Farm labor force (millions of persons)[b]	231.5	328.8
Labor days per farm worker[c]	161	262
Distributed income per capita (yuan)	49	65
Payment per labor day (yuan)	0.68	0.56

Sources:

a. Tables 3-1 and 3-2.

b. Thomas G. Rawski, *Economic Growth and Employment in China* (New York: Oxford University Press, 1979), p. 39 (Version B).

c. The 1957 figure is from the 1957 survey of 228 agricultural cooperatives. The number of labor days per capita in 1957 and 1976 can be derived from data on distributed income per capita per year and per day. If family size and the number of workers per family were unchanged, then labor days per worker would have grown by the same percentage as labor days per capita.

It is possible to estimate dQ/dt and dL/dt, but what about the other variables? The highest possible figure for $\delta F/\delta L$ would be obtained by assuming that the marginal product or the growth over time of the other variables was zero. Then, using 1957 and 1976 data given in Table B-1,

$$\frac{\delta F}{\delta L} = \frac{dQ/dt}{dL/dt} = \frac{(133.98 - 77.38) \times 10^9}{[(262)(328.8 - 231.5) \times 10^6] + [(262 - 161)(231.5) \times 10^6]}$$

$$= \frac{56.6 \times 10^9}{48,874.1 \times 10^6} = 1.158 \text{ yuan per labor day.}$$

But, since the contribution of the other inputs was not zero, this figure is obviously much too high, even though it only implies an annual output per farm worker of 303.7 yuan (less than half the average wage of an urban worker).

A somewhat more realistic calculation can be obtained by assuming that the net contributions of land and capital were zero and that there was no "residual" or time trend in productivity. Land actually declined, so this assumption would imply some contribution by capital and "technical progress." Actually, much rural capital was created by rural labor, and little else but current output is produced by past as well as current labor inputs in that case. Still, if this assumption is allowed for the moment, the following equation results:

$$\frac{\delta F}{\delta L} = \frac{1}{dL/dt}\left[\frac{dQ}{dt} - \left(\frac{\delta F}{\delta C} \times \frac{dC}{dt}\right)\right].$$

The figure in the brackets is the change in agricultural value added, assuming that the price of current inputs equals their marginal product. This assumption implies that commune cadres maximized the returns to current inputs, which is not entirely realistic, but perhaps does not add too much error. Then,

$$\frac{\delta F}{\delta L} = \frac{(73.23 - 46.07) \times 10^9}{48,874.1 \times 10^6} = 0.556 \text{ yuan per labor day.}$$

This figure could either overstate or understate the marginal product of labor. On the one hand, the denominator includes labor used for capital construction rather than farm production in the current year. On the other hand, the numerator includes returns to capital, much of which was created by labor inputs in previous years.

A crude check on this figure can be obtained by assuming that the elasticity of output with respect to labor inputs was similar in China to that in, say, the Republic of Korea, for which we do have econometric estimates. Using the labor elasticity estimates of Jamison and Lau for Korea,[1] the following equation is derived:

$$\frac{\delta F}{\delta L} \cdot \frac{L}{Q} = \text{Elasticity} = 0.36$$

$$\frac{\delta F}{\delta L} = 0.36 \times \frac{Q}{L} = 0.36 \times \frac{133.98 \times 10^9}{262 \times 328.8 \times 10^6}$$

$$= 0.560 \text{ yuan per labor day}$$

where Q is the gross value of agricultural output in 1976, and labor is the total number of labor days.

Given that the data used are as crude as the assumptions made, the near identity of the two estimates of labor productivity owes something to luck. Still, there is some reason to think that 0.56 yuan may not be too bad an estimate of the marginal product of labor (on average) in Chinese agriculture in the 1960s and 1970s. If the estimate is in error, it is probably in the direction of an overestimate because technical progress was excluded. If the marginal product of labor were this high, then the "high assumptions" used to calculate total factor productivity would be correct, and total factor productivity growth might be negative.

1. Dean T. Jamison and Lawrence J. Lau, *Farmer Education and Farm Efficiency* (Baltimore, Md.: Johns Hopkins University Press, 1982).

Appendix C

~~~~~~

Additional Data and Derivations

THE DATA FOR GROSS VALUE of output used in the regression equations that explain differences in provincial per capita output are from Table 6-3. Data on per capita sown acreage adjusted for quality and on the share of subsidiary output, cash crop, and animal husbandry in total gross value output are in Tables C-1 and C-2.

Table C-1. *Acreage Data Used in Regressions, by Province*

Province[a]	Per capita sown acreage (mu per commune member)	1957 grain yield per unit area (as index of national average yield)	1979 grain yield (as index of national average yield)	Sown acreage adjusted for quality	
				Using 1957 yield index	Using 1979 yield index
Northeast					
Heilongjiang	6.90	0.81	0.71	5.59	4.90
Jilin	4.12	0.82	0.90	3.38	3.71
Liaoning	2.67	1.08	1.29	2.88	3.44
Northwest					
Xinjiang	6.48	1.07	0.62	6.93	4.02
Gansu	3.23	0.87	0.56	2.81	1.81
Qinghai	2.85	1.08	0.70	3.08	1.99
Shaanxi	3.20	0.78	0.76	2.50	2.43
North					
Beijing	2.71	n.a.	1.11	n.a.	3.01
Tianjin	2.87	n.a.	0.85	n.a.	2.44
Hebei	3.08	n.a.	0.82	n.a.	2.53
Nei Monggol	5.58	0.53	0.45	2.96	2.51
Shanxi	3.17	n.a.	0.80	n.a.	2.54
Shandong	2.45	0.73	1.02	1.79	2.50
Henan	2.50	0.66	0.85	1.65	2.13
East/Central					
Shanghai	2.70	n.a.	1.82	n.a.	4.92
Jiangsu	2.53	1.15	1.41	2.91	3.57
Anhui	2.82	1.02	0.92	2.88	2.60
Zhejiang	2.04	1.87	1.68	3.81	3.43
Jiangxi	3.06	1.22	1.21	3.73	3.70
Hubei	2.98	1.34	1.21	3.99	3.61
Hunan	2.71	1.11	1.40	3.01	3.79
Southeast					
Fujian	1.86	1.39	1.27	2.59	2.37
Guangdong	2.21	1.04	1.12	2.30	2.47
Guangxi	2.49	0.94	1.03	2.34	2.56
Southwest					
Sichuan	2.06	1.38	1.12	2.84	2.31
Yunnan	2.24	1.23	0.77	2.76	1.72
Guizhou	1.88	1.40	0.88	2.63	1.65

Note: 15 mu = 1 hectare.

n.a. Not available.

a. Excluding Xizang and Ningxia.

Source: 1979, Ministry of Agriculture, *Zhongguo nongye nianjian, 1980*. 1957, N. R. Chen, *Chinese Economic Statistics* (Chicago: Aldine, 1967); and Table A-5.

Table C   *Components of Gross Value of Agricultural Output,*
by Province, 1979
(percentage of total gross value of agricultural output)

Province[a]	Animal husbandry	Subsidiary output	Agricultural crops	Share of crop area in cash crops
Northeast				
Heilongjiang	12.5	9.0	74.4	4.8
Jilin	12.2	14.4	70.9	5.8
Liaoning	13.2	15.0	66.2	8.1
Northwest				
Xinjiang	22.3	6.9	69.0	14.1
Gansu	18.1	11.5	68.2	5.9
Qinghai	47.3	7.8	43.8	14.5
Shaanxi	11.4	11.5	73.8	8.1
North				
Beijing	17.8	27.4	53.6	5.4
Tianjin	8.4	55.5	34.9	5.8
Hebei	10.0	26.6	60.9	10.9
Nei Monggol	29.3	10.0	57.1	10.8
Shanxi	9.9	25.4	62.1	10.1
Shandong	10.7	13.7	71.8	13.5
Henan	10.7	16.7	70.9	13.0
East/Central				
Shanghai	16.4	36.1	43.7	19.4
Jiangsu	12.9	21.5	63.5	11.4
Anhui	12.7	8.9	76.6	11.4
Zhejiang	16.3	16.4	60.9	7.3
Jiangxi	10.7	13.0	71.4	8.2
Hubei	12.7	11.6	70.7	12.8
Hunan	15.1	11.2	69.5	7.7
Southeast				
Fujian	10.3	16.5	62.7	7.7
Guangdong	12.7	13.0	62.5	13.1
Guangxi	11.6	11.4	71.3	11.2
Southwest				
Sichuan	20.0	7.3	70.6	8.3
Yunnan	17.0	12.7	63.6	6.2
Guizhou	17.5	14.8	63.9	9.9

a. Excluding Xizang and Ningxia.
Sources: Ministry of Agriculture, *Zhongguo nongye nianjian, 1980*, pp. 100 and 130.

References

~~~~~~

The word "processed" describes works that are reproduced from typescript by mimeograph, xerography, or similar means. Such works may not be cataloged or commonly available through libraries, or may be subject to restricted circulation. *"FBIS, China"* refers to the *Daily Report: China*, published by the U.S. government, which contains current news and commentary monitored by the Foreign Broadcast Information Service. *"BBC"* refers to the *Summary of World Broadcasts, Part III: The Far East*, published by the British Broadcasting Corporation.

Agren, H. "Patterns of Tradition and Modernization in Contemporary Chinese Medicine." In A. Kleinman and others, eds., *Medicine in Chinese Cultures*. Washington, D.C.: National Institutes of Health, 1975.

Aird, J. S. "Population Studies and Population Policy in China." *Population and Development Review*, vol. 8 (June 1982), pp. 267–97.

Alitto, G. S. *The Last Confucian*. Berkeley: University of California Press, 1979.

American Herbal Pharmacology Delegation. *Herbal Pharmacology in the PRC*. Washington, D.C.: National Academy of Sciences, 1975.

American Plant Studies Delegation. *Plant Studies in the People's Republic of China*. Washington, D.C.: National Academy of Sciences, 1975.

American Rural Small-scale Industry Delegation. *Rural Small-Scale Industry in the People's Republic of China*. Berkeley: University of California Press, 1977.

Andors, P. "The Four Modernizations and Chinese Policy on Women." *Bulletin of Concerned Asian Scholars*, vol. 13, no. 2, part 1 (1981), pp. 47–50.

Andreano, R. L. "The Recent History of Parasitic Disease in China: The Case of Schistosomiasis, Some Public Health and Economic Aspects." *International Journal of Health Services*, vol. 6, no. 1 (1976), pp. 53–61.

Area Handbook for the PRC. Washington, D.C.: Government Printing Office, 1972.

Ban, S. H., P. Y. Moon, and D. H. Perkins. *Rural Development: Studies in the Modernization of the Republic of Korea, 1945–1975*. Cambridge, Mass.: Council on East Asian Studies, 1980.

Banister, J., and S. H. Preston. "Mortality in China." *Population and Development Review*, vol. 7 (March 1981), p. 107.

Barnett, A. Doak. *China's Economy in Global Perspective*. Washington, D.C.: Brookings, 1981.

Bastid, M. "Chinese Educational Policies in the 1980s and Economic Development." *China Quarterly*, no. 98 (June 1984), pp. 194–95 and 200.

Beijing Ribao (October 14, 1979), p. 1 (in *FBIS, China*, October 25, 1979, p. R2).

Beijing, Xinhua (October 27, 1982) (in *FBIS, China*, October 28, 1982, p. K2).

Bernstein, T. P. *Up to the Mountains and Down to the Villages*. New Haven, Conn.: Yale University Press, 1977.

Bonavia, D. *The Chinese*. New York: Lippincott and Crowell, 1980.

Borthwick, S. *Education and Social Change in China: The Beginnings of the Modern Era*. Stanford, Calif.: Hoover Institution Press, 1983.

Bray, F. "Agriculture." In J. Needham, *Science and Civilization in China*. Vol. 6. *Biology and Biological Technology*, part 2. Cambridge: Cambridge University Press, 1984.

Broaded, C. Montgomery. "Higher Education Policy Changes and Stratification in China." *China Quarterly*, vol. 93 (March 1983), pp. 136–37.

Buck, D. D. "Cities and Education in Modern China." *Comparative Education*, vol. 11 (March 1975), pp. 74–75.

Buck, John Lossing. *Land Utilization in China*. Nanking: University of Nanking, 1937.

Buck, P. *American Science and Modern China*. Cambridge: Cambridge University Press, 1980.

Burki, Shahid Javed. *A Study of Chinese Communes, 1965*. Cambridge, Mass.: Harvard East Asian Monographs, 1969.

Butterfield, F. *China: Alive in the Bitter Sea*. New York: Times Books, 1982.

Buxbaum, D. C., ed. *Chinese Family Law and Social Change*. Seattle: University of Washington Press, 1978.

Cairns, J. "The Cancer Problem." *Scientific American* (November 1975), pp. 64–78.

Central Intelligence Agency. *People's Republic of China: Chemical Fertilizer Supplies, 1949–74*. Washington, D.C.: August 1975.

Chambers, D. I. "The 1975–76 Debate over Higher Education Policy in the PRC." *Comparative Education*, vol. 13, no. 1 (March 1977), pp. 3–14.

Chan, A., R. Madsen, and J. Unger. *Chen Village*. Berkeley: University of California Press, 1984.

Chang, Chung-li. *The Chinese Gentry*. Seattle, Wash.: University of Washington Press, 1955.

Chang, John K. *Industrial Development in Pre-Communist China*. Chicago: Aldine, 1969.

Chang, K. C., ed. *Food in Chinese Culture*. New Haven, Conn.: Yale University Press, 1977.

Chang, P. H. *Power and Policy in China*. 2nd edition. University Park: Pennsylvania State University Press, 1978.

Chaudhri, D. P. *Education, Innovations, and Agricultural Development*. London: Croom and Helm, 1979.

Chen, N. R. *Chinese Economic Statistics*. Chicago: Aldine, 1967.

Chen Pi-Chao. *Population and Health Policy in the PRC*. Occasional Monograph Series no. 9. Washington, D.C.: Smithsonian Institution, 1976.

Cheng Tsun, and others. "Medical Education and Practice in the PRC." *Annals of Internal Medicine*, vol. 83 (1975), p. 717.

China Daily, Beijing (November 14, 1982), p. 4 (in *FBIS, China*, November 16, 1982, pp. K14–K15).

————. "State to Increase Pay of Twelve Million Teachers" (November 22, 1981), p. 1 (in *FBIS, China*, November 23, 1981, p. K11).

"Chinese Report Surge of Some Cancer Types among Local Groups." *New York Times* (September 24, 1979).

"Circulatory Ills Leading Cause of Death." *Korea Newsreview* (October 8, 1983), p. 23.

"Cleaning up Third World Diseases." *Economist* (September 10, 1983), pp. 92–93.

Committee on the Economy of China. *Provincial Agricultural Statistics for Communist China*. Ithaca, N.Y., Social Science Research Council, 1969.

Connor, W. D. "Education and National Development in the European Socialist States: A Model for the Third World." *Comparative Studies in History and Society*, vol. 17 (1975), p. 335.

Croizier, R. C. *Traditional Medicine in Modern China*. Cambridge, Mass.: Harvard University Press, 1968.

Croll, E. *The Family Rice Bowl*. London: Zed Press, 1983.

Dawson, R. *Confucius*. New York: Hill and Wang, 1981.

De Francis, J. "Mao Tse-tung and Writing Reform." In J. A. Fogel and W. T. Rowe, eds., *Perspectives on a Changing China*. Boulder, Colo.: Westview Press, 1979.

Diamond, E. Grey. "Medical Education and Care in the PRC." *Journal of the American Medical Association*, vol. 218, no. 10 (1971), pp. 1552–57.

Domes, J. "New Policies in the Communes: Notes on Rural Social Structures in China, 1976–1981." *Journal of Asian Studies*, vol. 41 (February 1982), p. 264.

Dong Furen. "Relationship between Accumulation and Consumption." In Xu Dixin and others, *China's Search for Economic Growth: The Chinese Economy since 1949*. Beijing: China Statistical Publishers, 1983.

Donnithorne, A. *China's Economic System*. New York: Praeger, 1967.

Dore, R. P. *Education in Tokugawa Japan*. Berkeley: University of California Press, 1965.

Dorris, C. E. "Peasant Mobilization in North China and the Origin of Yenan Communism." *China Quarterly*, no. 68 (December 1976), pp. 697–719.

Ecklund, George. *Taxation in Communist China*. Chicago: Aldine, 1966.

Eckstein, Alexander. *The National Income of Communist China*. Glencoe, Ill.: Free Press, 1961.

Egawa, H. "Chinese Statistics: How Reliable?" *China Newsletter*, no. 33 (1982), pp. 12–15.

Erisman, Alva Lewis. "Potential Costs of and Benefits from Diverting River Flow for Irrigation in the North China Plain." Ph.D. dissertation, University of Maryland, 1967.

Fairbank, J. K. "Introduction: The Old Order." In J. K. Fairbank, ed., *The Cambridge History of China*. Vol. 4, *Late Ching, 1800–1911*, Part I. Cambridge: Cambridge University Press, 1978.

————. "The State That Mao Built." *World Politics*, vol. 19 (July 1967), p. 676.

Fairbank, J. K., and Kwang-Ching Liu. *The Cambridge History of China*. Volume 11, Part 2. Cambridge: Cambridge University Press, 1980.

Feachem, Richard G., David J. Bradley, Hemda Garelick, and D. Duncan Mara. *Sanitation and Disease: Health Aspects of Excreta and Wastewater Management*. World Bank Studies in Water Supply and Sanitation, no. 3. Chichester: John Wiley and Sons, 1983.

Feiliao zhichi. Shanghai: Shanghai People's Press, 1974.

Food and Agriculture Organization (FAO). *FAO Production Yearbook*. Rome, annual.

Freedman. M. *The Study of Chinese Society*. Stanford, Calif.: Stanford University Press, 1979.

Frolic, B. Michael. *Mao's People*. Cambridge, Mass.: Harvard University Press, 1980.

"Further Sum-up, Perfect and Stabilize the Agricultural Production Responsibility System." *Sichuan Ribao* (July 8, 1982) (in *FBIS, China*, July 14, 1982, p. Q1).

Gardner, J., and W. Idema. "China's Educational Revolution." In S. R. Schram, ed., *Authority, Participation, and Cultural Change in China*. Cambridge: Cambridge University Press, 1975.

Garfield, R., and J. Warren Salmon. "Struggles over Health Care in the PRC." *Journal of Contemporary Asia*, vol. 11, no. 1 (1981), pp. 91–103.

Gibson, E. J., and H. Levin. *The Psychology of Reading*. Cambridge, Mass.: M.I.T. Press, 1975.

Goldman, N. "Far Eastern Patterns of Mortality." *Population Studies*, vol. 34, no. 1 (March 1980), pp. 5–17.

Gonzales, N. L. "The Organization of Work in China's Communes." *Science*, vol. 218 (September 3, 1982), pp. 898–903.

Goody, J. *Cooking, Cuisine, and Class*. Cambridge: Cambridge University Press, 1982.

Gray, J. "The High Tide of Socialism in the Chinese Countryside." In J. Chen and N. Tarling, eds., *Studies in the Social History of China and Southeast Asia*. Cambridge: Cambridge University Press, 1970.

Greenblatt, S. L. "Campaigns and the Manufacture of Deviance in Chinese Society." In A. Auerbacher Wilson and others, eds., *Deviance and Social Control in Chinese Society*. New York: Praeger, 1977.

Griffin, Keith, and Ashwani Saith. *Growth and Equality in Rural China*. Singapore: ILO Asian Employment Programme, 1981.

Guangming ribao (December 7, 1978).

Hama, K. "China's Agricultural Production Responsibility System." *China Newsletter*, no. 40 (1982), pp. 2–11.

Harlan, J. R. "Plant Breeding and Genetics." In L. A. Orleans, ed., *Science in Contemporary China*. Stanford, Calif.: Stanford University Press, 1980.

Harvey, R. G. "Polycyclic Hydrocarbons and Cancer." *American Scientist* (July–August 1982), pp. 386–91.

Hinton, William. *Fanshen*. New York: Random House, 1966.

Ho Ping-ti. *The Ladder of Success in Imperial China*. New York: Columbia University Press, 1962.

Hofheinz, R. "The Ecology of Chinese Communist Success: Rural Influence Patterns, 1923–45." In A. Doak Barnett, ed., *Chinese Communist Politics in Action*. Seattle: University of Washington Press, 1969.

Hook, B., ed. *The Cambridge Encyclopedia of China*. Cambridge: Cambridge University Press, 1982.

Howe, C. *China's Economy*. New York: Basic Books, 1978.

Hsiao Kung-Chuan. *Rural China*. Seattle: University of Washington Press, 1960.

Hu Teh-wei. *An Economic Analysis of the Cooperative Medical Services in the PRC*. NIH no. 75–672. Washington, D.C.: Department of Health, Education, and Welfare, 1973.

Huang Kun-Yen. "Infectious and Parasitic Diseases." In J. R. Quinn, ed., *Medicine and Public Health in the PRC*. Washington, D.C.: Department of Health, Education, and Welfare, 1973.

"Hypertension in China." *Science News*, vol. 118 (November 29, 1980), p. 344.

Inkeles, A., and D. H. Smith. *Becoming Modern*. Cambridge, Mass.: Harvard University Press, 1974.

Ishikawa, Shigeru. *National Income and Capital Formation in Mainland China*. Tokyo: Institute of Asian Economic Affairs, 1965.

Jamison, Dean T., and Lawrence J. Lau. *Farmer Education and Farm Efficiency*. Baltimore, Md.: Johns Hopkins University Press, 1982.

Johnson, G. "Reponsibility Reaps Reward." *Far Eastern Economic Review* (October 6, 1983), p. 55.

Kaplan, H. S., and P. J. Tsuchitani, eds. *Cancer in China*. New York: Alan R. Liss, 1978.

Kataoka, T. "Communist Power in a War of National Liberation: The Case of China." *World Politics*, vol. 24, no. 3 (April 1972), pp. 420–27.

Keyfitz, N. "The Population of China." *Scientific American* (February 1984), pp. 38–47.

King, H. "Selected Epidemiologic Aspects of Major Diseases and Causes of Death among Chinese in the U.S. and Asia." In A. Kleinman and others, *Medicine in Chinese Cultures*. Washington, D.C.: National Institutes of Health, 1975.

Kleinman, A. *Patients and Healers in the Context of Culture*. Berkeley: University of California Press, 1980.

Kuan-I Chen. "China's Changing Agricultural System." *Current History*, vol. 82, no. 485 (September 1983), pp. 259–62.

Kuhn, P. A. "Local Self-government under the Republic: Problems of Control, Autonomy, and Mobilization." In F. Wakeman, Jr. and C. Grant, eds., *Conflict and Control in Late Imperial China*. Berkeley: University of California Press, 1975.

————. *Rebellion and Its Enemies in Late Imperial China*. Cambridge, Mass.: Harvard University Press, 1970.

Kuo, Leslie Tse-chiu. *The Technical Transformation of Agriculture in Communist China*. New York: Praeger, 1972.

Langome, J. "Acupuncture." *Discovery* (August 1984), pp. 70–73.

Lardy, Nicholas. *Agriculture in China's Modern Economic Development*. Cambridge: Cambridge University Press, 1983.

————. "Centralization and Decentralization in China's Fiscal Management." *The Chinese Quarterly* (March 1975), pp. 25–60.

————. "Comparative Advantage, International Trade, and Distribution of Income in Chinese Agriculture." Yale University, 1982. Processed.

————. *Economic Growth and Distribution in China*. New York: Cambridge University Press, 1978.

Leichter, H. M. *A Comparative Approach to Policy Analysis: Health Care Policy in Four Nations*. Cambridge: Cambridge University Press, 1979.

"Leprosy Declines in China but Remains Feared." *New York Times* (May 31, 1983), p. C-2.

Li Bingkun. "Rural Commune Family Sideline Occupations in China." *Zhongguo jingji nianjian* (1982), p. v–20.

Li Chengrui. *Zhonghua renmin gongheguo nongye shui shrgao*. Beijing: Finance and Economics Press, 1962.

Lindbeck, J. M. H., ed. *China: Management of a Revolutionary Society*. Seattle: University of Washington Press, 1971.

Lippit, V. *Land Reform and Economic Development in China*. White Plains, N.Y.: International Arts and Science Press, 1974.

Liu, Alan P. L. *Communications and National Integration in Communist China*. Berkeley: University of California Press, 1975.

Liu Xumao. "A Brief Introduction to Several Important Kinds of Production Responsibility Systems Currently in Use in Our Country." *Jingji Guanli*, no. 9 (September 15, 1981), pp. ix–12–14.

Lock, M. M. *East Asian Medicine in Urban Japan*. Berkeley: University of California Press, 1980.

Lofstedt, J. I. *Chinese Educational Policy*. Stockholm: Almqvist and Wiksell International, 1980.

Lu Gwei-Djen and J. Needham. *Celestial Lancets: A History and Rationale of Acupuncture and Moxa*. Cambridge: Cambridge University Press, 1981.

MacFarquhar, Roderick. *The Hundred Flowers*. London: Stevens, 1960.

————. *The Origins of the Cultural Revolution. Volume 2. The Great Leap Forward, 1958–60*. New York: Columbia University Press, 1983.

Machlup, F. *Education and Economic Growth*. New York: New York University Press, 1975.

Maddox, P. G. "Value Change in China." *Problems of Communism*, vol. 30 (November–December 1981), p. 75.

Maloney, J. M. "Recent Developments in China's Population Planning." *Pacific Affairs* (Spring 1981), pp. 100–15.

Mauger, P. "Changing Policy and Practice in Chinese Rural Education." *China Quarterly*, no. 93 (March 1983), pp. 139–46.

Mechanic, D., and A. Kleinman. "Financing of Medical Care in Rural Health in the PRC." Report of a Visit by the Rural Health Systems Delegation, June 1978. NIH no. 81–2124, U.S. Department of Health and Human Services, Washington, D.C., November 1980, pp. 17–22.

————. *The Organization, Delivery, and Financing of Rural Health Care in the PRC*. Center pub. 10–70. Madison, Wis.: Center for Medical Sociology and Health Services, 1978.

Meskill, J. M. *A Chinese Pioneer Family*. Princeton, N.J.: Princeton University Press, 1979.

Miller, J. A., and G. McQuerter. "The Great Struggle against Carcinoma." *Science News*, vol. 113, no. 8 (1978), pp. 124–25.

Ministry of Agriculture, *Zhongguo nongye nianjian, 1980*.

Ministry of Agriculture, People's Commune Management Office. "The Situation Nationwide with Respect to Poor Countries, 1977–1979." *Xinhua yuebao*, no. 2 (February 1980), pp. 117–20.

Ministry of Health, Statistics and Finance Bureau. *China Encyclopedia, 1980*. Beijing, 1980.

Miyazaki, I. *China's Examination Hell*. New Haven, Conn.: Yale University Press, 1981.

Montaperto, R. N. "Introduction: China's Schools in Flux." *Chinese Education*, vol. 11, no. 4 (Winter 1978–79), pp. 6–12.

Mosher, S. W. "Birth Control: A View from a Chinese Village." *Asian Survey*, vol. 22 (April 1982), pp. 356–68.

Mote, F. W. "China's Past in the Study of China Today—Some Comments on the Recent Work of R. Solomon." *Journal of Asian Studies*, vol. 32 (November 1972), pp. 107–20.

————. *Intellectual Foundations of China*. New York: Knopf, 1971.

"Nationwide Fertility Survey Conducted." *Beijing, Xinhua* (March 28, 1983) (in *FBIS, China*, April 1, 1983, p. K21).

Nee, V. "Post-Mao Changes in a South China Production Brigade." *Bulletin of Concerned Asian Scholars*, vol. 13, no. 2 (April–June 1981), pp. 32–40.

Needham, J. *Clerks and Craftsmen in China and the West*. Cambridge: Cambridge University Press, 1970.

———. *Science in Traditional China*. Cambridge, Mass.: Harvard University Press, 1981.

New China News Agency. Releases of December 31, 1971 and December 26, 1972.

———. (February 9, 1979) (in *FBIS, China*, February 12, 1979).

———. (April 20, 1980); *BBC* (May 23, 1980).

Nickum, James E. *Hydraulic Engineering and Water Resources in the People's Republic of China*. Stanford, Calif.: Stanford University Press, 1977.

Nunn, S. S. "Research Institutes in the PRC." *U.S.-China Business Review*, vol. 3 (March–April 1976), pp. 39–50.

O'Leary, G., and A. Watson. "The Role of the People's Commune in Rural Development in China." *Pacific Affairs*, vol. 55, no. 4 (Winter 1982–83), pp. 607–11.

Orleans, L. *Professional Manpower and Education in Communist China*. Washington, D.C.: National Science Foundation, 1961.

Parish, William L. "Egalitarianism in Chinese Society." *Problems of Communism* (January/February 1981), pp. 37–53.

Parish, William L., and M. K. Whyte. *Village and Family in Contemporary China*. Chicago: University of Chicago Press, 1978.

"Peasants' Income Goes Up." *Beijing Review* (June 21, 1982), p. 7.

Peking Review (November 9, 1973), p. 10.

Pepper, S. "China's Schools Turning an Old Leaf." *Asian Wall Street Journal Weekly* (September 21, 1981), p. 11.

———. *Civil War in China: The Political Struggle, 1945–49*. Berkeley: University of California Press, 1978.

———. "Education and Revolution: The Chinese Model Revisited." *Asian Survey*, vol. 18, no. 9 (1978), pp. 852–74 and 883.

Perkins, Dwight H. *Agricultural Development in China, 1368–1968*. Chicago: Aldine, 1969.

———. "An American View of the Prospects for the Chinese Economy" (in Chinese), compiled by *jingji yanjiu, guowai jingjixuezhe lun Zhongguo ji fazhanguo zhong guojia jingji* (Beijing: Finance and Economics Press, 1981).

———, ed. *China's Modern Economy in Historical Perspective*. Stanford, Calif.: Stanford University Press, 1975.

———. *Market Control and Planning in Communist China*. Cambridge, Mass.: Harvard University Press, 1966.

"Pesticides: The Human Body Burden." *Science News* (September 24, 1983), p. 199.

Piazza, A. *Trends in Food and Nutrient Availability in China, 1958–81*. World Bank Staff Working Paper, no. 607. Washington, D.C.: World Bank, September 1983.

Population Census Office. *Zhongguo disanci renkou puchade zhuyao shuzu*. Beijing: China Statistics Publishers, 1982.

Price, R. F. "Community and School and Education in the PRC." *Comparative Education*, vol. 12, no. 2 (June 1976), pp. 168–69.

———. *Education in Communist China*. New York, Praeger, 1970.

Printz, P., and P. Steinle. *Commune: Life in Rural China*. New York: Dodd, Mead and Co., 1973.

Prybyla, J. *The Chinese Economy*. Columbia: University of South Carolina Press, 1979.

Pye, L. W. "Mass Participation in Communist China: Its Limitations and the Continuity of Culture." In Lindbeck, ed., *China: Management of a Revolutionary Society*. Seattle: University of Washington Press, 1971.

Pye, V. I., and R. Patrick. "Groundwater Contamination in the U.S." *Science* (August 19, 1983), p. 715.

"Quarterly Chronicle and Documentation (April–June 1983)." *China Quarterly*, no. 95 (September 1983), p. 588.

Rada, E. L. "Food Policy in China." *Asian Survey*, vol. 23 (April 1983), p. 531.

Rawski, E. S. *Education and Popular Literacy in Ching China*. Ann Arbor: University of Michigan Press, 1979.

Rawski, Thomas G. *Economic Growth and Employment in China*. New York: Oxford University Press, 1979.

Renmin Ribao, Beijing. "On Improving Secondary Education" (November 12, 1981) (in *FBIS, China*, November 18, 1981, p. K4).

———. (November 17, 1981), p. 3 (in *FBIS, China*, November 20, 1981, p. K7).

———. (February 5, 1982) (in *FBIS, China*, February 16, 1982, p. K11–K14).

———. "Wan Li's Speech of November 5" (December 23, 1982) (in *FBIS, China*, January 4, 1983, pp. K2–K20).

———. "Editorial on Rural Responsibility System" (January 22, 1983) (in *FBIS, China*, January 22, 1983, pp. K6–K9).

———. "Wan Li Discusses the Role of Ecological Economics" (April 6, 1984) (in *FBIS, China*, April 18, 1984, pp. K7–K13).

"Restructuring Middle Education Is a Major Task." *Peking Daily* (October 14, 1979); *FE/6256/BII/4* (October 27, 1979).

Rogers, E. M. "Barefoot Doctors." In *Rural Health in the PRC*. NIH no. 81–424. Washington, D.C.: Department of Health and Human Services, November 1980.

Roll, C. Robert. "The Distribution of Rural Income in China: A Comparison of the 1930s and the 1950s." Ph.D. dissertation, Harvard University, Cambridge, Mass. 1974.

Rosen, S. "Chinese Education in Transition." *Current History*, vol. 82, no. 485 (September 1983), p. 257.

———. "Obstacles to Educational Reform in China." *Modern China*, vol. 8 (January 1982), p. 34.

Rudra, A. "Organization of Agriculture for Rural Development: The Indian Case." *Cambridge Journal of Economics*, vol. 2 (December 1978), p. 383.

"Rural School Enrollment Decline Reported." *Beijing Domestic Service* (November 16, 1982) (in *FBIS, China*, November 17, 1982, pp. K9–K10).

Saith, A. "Economic Incentives for the One Child Family in Rural China." *China Quarterly*, no. 87 (September 1981), pp. 493–500.

Scherer, J. L., ed. *China: Facts and Figures Annual.* Vol. 4. Gulf Breeze, Fla.: Academic International Press, 1981.

Schran, Peter. *The Development of Chinese Agriculture, 1950–59.* Champaign: University of Illinois Press, 1969.

Schultz, T. W. *Economic Crises in World Agriculture.* Ann Arbor: University of Michigan Press, 1965.

————. "The Value of the Ability to Deal with Disequilibria." *Journal of Economic Literature*, vol. 13 (March 1975), pp. 827–46.

Schurmann, F. *Ideology and Organization in Communist China.* Berkeley: University of California Press, 1968.

Shanghai World Economy Guide (October 18, 1981); *BBC FE/6894/BII/10* (December 1, 1981).

Shirk, S. "Educational Reform and Political Backlash: Recent Changes in Chinese Educational Policy." *Comparative Educational Review*, vol. 23, no. 2 (June 1979), pp. 185–91.

Shue, V. *Peasant China in Transition.* Berkeley: University of California Press, 1980.

Sidel, R., and V. W. Sidel. *The Health of China.* Boston: Beacon Press, 1982.

Sidel, V. W. "Health Services in the PRC." In J. Z. Bowers and E. F. Purcell, eds., *Medicine and Society in China.* New York: J. Macy Foundation, 1974.

Sigurdson, Jon. *Rural Industrialization in China.* Cambridge, Mass.: Harvard Council on East Asian Studies, 1977.

————. "Technology and Science: Some Issues in China's Modernization." In "Chinese Economy Post-Mao." Papers for the Joint Economic Committee, vol. 1. Washington, D.C., November 9, 1978.

Skinner, G. William. "Marketing and Social Structure in Rural China, Part 3." *Journal of Asian Studies*, vol. 24 (May 1965), pp. 382–85 and 397–98.

Smil, V. "Environmental Degradation in China." *Asian Survey*, vol. 20 (August 1980), p. 781.

————. *The Bad Earth.* Armonk, N.Y.: M. E. Sharpe, 1984.

State Statistical Bureau. *Beijing (Peking) Review* (October 28, 1977, pp. 29–30; April 13, 1973, p. 10; July 27, 1979, p. 29; February 4, 1980, p. 7.

————. "Communique on Fulfillment of China's 1978 National Economic Plan," June 27, 1979.

————. "Communique on Fulfillment of China's 1982 National Economic Plan," April 29, 1983.

————. *The Present Conditions of the Statistical Work in China.* Beijing, 1981.

————. Release (April 29, 1981).

————. "Report on the Results of the 1980 National Economic Plan," April 29, 1981.

————. *Statistical Yearbook of China, 1981* and *1983*. Hong Kong: Economic Information Agency, 1982, and 1984.

————. *Ten Great Years*. 1960.

————. *Zhongguo tongji zhaiyao, 1983*. Beijing: China Statistical Publishers, 1983.

Stavis, Benedict. *Making Green Revolution*. Ithaca, N.Y.: Cornell University Press, 1974.

————. *The Politics of Agricultural Mechanization in China*. Ithaca, N.Y.: Cornell University Press, 1978.

Stone, Bruce. "A Review of Chinese Agricultural Statistics, 1949–1978." In Anthony M. Tang and Bruce Stone, *Food Production in the People's Republic of China*. Washington, D.C.: International Food Policy Research Institute, 1980.

"Studies by Chinese Finds Much Stomach Cancer." *New York Times* (April 1, 1980).

Sun, Marjorie. "China Faces Environmental Challenge." *Science*, vol. 221 (September 23, 1983), pp. 1271–72.

"Talks on Rural Work." *Dazhong Ribao* (June 28, 1982) (in *FBIS, China*, July 9, 1982, p. O5).

Tang, Anthony M., "Food and Agriculture in China: Trends and Projections." In Anthony M. Tang and Bruce Stone, *Food Production in the People's Republic of China*. Washington, D.C.: International Food Policy Research Institute, 1980.

————. "Trend, Policy Cycle, and Weather Disturbance in Chinese Agriculture." *American Journal of Agricultural Economics*, vol. 62, no. 2 (1980), pp. 334–48.

Tannahill, R. *Food in History*. New York: Stein and Day, 1973.

"Team Leader on New Contract System." *China Reconstructs* (November 1981), pp. 50–51.

Thaxton, R. *China Turned Right Side Up*. New Haven, Conn.: Yale University Press, 1983.

Tien, H. Yuan. "Age at Marriage in the PRC." *China Quarterly*, no. 93 (March 1983), pp. 90–107.

Tongji yanjiu, no. 8 (August 23, 1958), pp. 8–9, 12.

Trowell, H. C., and D. P. Burkitt, eds. *Western Diseases: Their Emergence and Prevention*. Cambridge, Mass.: Harvard University Press, 1981.

Tsou, T., M. Blecher, and M. Meisner. "The Responsibility System in Agriculture." *Modern China*, vol. 8, no. 1 (January 1982), pp. 41–103.

Tuan, Francis C., and Crook, Frederick W. *Planning and Statistical Systems in Chinese Agriculture*. Washington, D.C.: U.S. Department of Agriculture, 1983.

"Two Views on China's Urbanization." *Beijing Review* (March 17, 1980), p. 7.

Unger, J. "Bending the School Ladder: The Failure of Chinese Educational Reform in the 1960s." *Comparative Educational Review*, vol. 24, no. 2. Part I (June 1980), p. 221.

————. *Education under Mao*. New York: Columbia University Press, 1982.

United Nations. *Statistical Yearbook, 1978* (New York, 1978).

Veith, I., trans. *The Yellow Emperor's Classic of Internal Medicine.* Berkeley: University of California Press, 1972.

Vermeer, E. B. "Income Differentials in Rural China." *The China Quarterly*, vol. 89 (March 1982), pp. 1–33.

Wakeman, F. W. "The Price of Autonomy: Intellectuals in Ming and Ching Politics." *Daedalus*, vol. 101 (Spring 1972), pp. 43–45.

Walker, Kenneth. *Planning in Chinese Agriculture.* Chicago: Aldine, 1965.

Wang Bingqian. "Report on the Final State Accounts for 1979, the Draft State Budget for 1980, and Financial Estimates for 1981," August 30, 1980.

———. "Report on the Final State Accounts for 1980 and Implementation of the Financial Estimates for 1981," December 1, 1981.

———. "Report on the Final State Accounts for 1982," June 7, 1983.

Welch, F. "Education in Production." *Journal of Political Economy*, vol. 78, no. 1 (January/February 1970), pp. 46–47.

Welch, H. *Buddhism under Mao.* Cambridge, Mass.: Harvard University Press, 1972.

———. "The Fate of the Religion." In R. Terrill, ed., *The China Difference.* New York: Harper and Row, 1979.

Whyte, M. K. *Small Groups and Political Rituals in China.* Berkeley: University of California Press, 1971.

Whyte, M. K., and W. L. Parish. *Urban Life in Contemporary China.* Chicago: University of Chicago Press, 1984.

Whyte, R. O. *Rural Nutrition in China.* London: Oxford University Press, 1972.

Wiens, Thomas. "Declining Factor Productivity? A Counterview." 1979. Processed.

Wilenski, P. *The Delivery of Health Services in the PRC.* Ottawa: International Development Research Center, 1976.

Wingerson, L. "Painkilling Needles Make the Body Soothe Itself." *New Scientist* (November 27, 1980), p. 370.

Womack, B. "Modernization and Democratic Reform in China." *Journal of Asian Studies*, vol. 43, no. 3 (May 1984), pp. 428, 433–43.

Wong, Christine. "Two Steps Forward, One Step Back? Recent Policy Changes in Rural Industrialization." Paper presented to Social Science Research Council workshop. February 1980. Processed.

Wong, John. *Land Reform in the People's Republic of China.* New York: Praeger, 1973.

World Bank. *China: Socialist Economic Development.* Vol. 3. Washington, D.C., 1983.

World Health Organization. *Primary Health Care: The Chinese Experience.* Geneva, 1983.

———. "Report on a Technical Visit to the PRC." Western Pacific Advisory Committee on Medical Research, Regional Office for Western Pacific (July 1979).

Worth, R. M. "Health in Rural China: From Village to Commune." *American Journal of Hygiene*, vol. 77 (May 1963), pp. 228–39.

———. "The Impact of New Health Programs on Disease Control and Illness Patterns in China. In A. Kleinman and others, eds., *Medicine in Chinese Cultures*. Washington, D.C.: National Institutes of Health, 1975.

Wortzel, L. M. "Incentive Mechanisms and Remuneration in China: Policies of the Eleventh Central Committee." *Asian Survey*, vol. 21, no. 9 (September 1981), pp. 961–76.

Xinhua, Beijing. "Specialized Households Are Boon to Rural Economy" (September 26, 1983) (in *FBIS, China*, September 28, 1983, pp. K2–K4).

Xinhua, Beijing (December 12, 1979) (in *FBIS, China*, December 14, 1979, pp. L2–L3).

Xu Dixin and others. *China's Search for Economic Growth: The Chinese Economy since 1949*. Beijing: New World Press, 1982.

Yang, C. K. *Chinese Communist Society: The Family and the Village*. Cambridge, Mass.: M.I.T. Press, 1959.

Yang Fangxun. "Persist in the Principle of 'Giving Simultaneous Consideration to the Profits of the State, the Collectives and the Individuals' and Stabilize the Prices of Agricultural Products." *Jingji yanjiu* (April 1982), p. 28.

Yang Jianbai and Li Xuezeng. "The Relations between Agriculture, Light Industry, and Heavy Industry in China." *Social Sciences in China*, no. 2 (June 1980), pp. 182–212.

Yip Ka-che. "Warlordism and Educational Finances, 1916–27." In J. A. Fogel and W. T. Rowe, *Perspectives on a Changing China*. Boulder, Colo.: Westview Press, 1979.

Zachariah, M. " 'Massliners' vs. 'Capitalist Roaders' in China's Education Ring: Round Four to Capitalist Roaders." *Comparative Education Review*, vol. 23, no. 1 (February 1979), p. 102.

Zhang Yulin. "Readjustment and Reform in Agriculture." In Lin Wei and A. Chao, eds., *China's Economic Reforms* (Philadelphia: University of Pennsylvania Press, 1982).

Zhang Zehou and Chen Yuguang. "On the Relationship between the Population Structure and National Economic Development in China." *Social Sciences in China*, vol. 2, no. 4 (December 1981), p. 73.

Zhongguo baike nianjian, 1981. Beijing, 1981.

Zhongguo jingji nianjian, 1981. [Economic Yearbook of China, 1981]. Beijing: Jingji guanli, 1981.

Zhongguo jingji nianjian, 1982. [Economic Yearbook of China, 1982]. Beijing: Jingji guanli, 1982.

Zhonghua renmin gongheguo fagui huibian (January–June 1958), p. 263.

Zweig, D. "Opposition to Change in Rural China." *Asian Survey*, vol. 23, no. 7 (July 1983), pp. 883–84.

Index

The full range of World Bank publications, both free and for sale, is described in the *Catalog of Publications*; the continuing research program is outlined in *Abstracts of Current Studies*. Both booklets are updated annually; the most recent edition of each is available without charge from the Publications Distribution Unit, Department B, The World Bank, 1818 H Street, N.W., Washington, D.C. 20433, U.S.A.

DWIGHT PERKINS is director of the Harvard Institute for International Development and H. H. Burbank Professor of Political Economy at Harvard University.
SHAHID YUSUF is a economist in the East Asia and Pacific Department of the World Bank.